Renewing Class Analysis

A selection of previous *Sociological Review* Monographs

Life and Work History Anaylses†
ed. Shirley Dex

The Sociology of Monsters†
ed. John Law

Sport, Leisure and Social Relations†
eds John Horne, David Jary and Alan Tomlinson

Gender and Bureaucracy*
eds Mike Savage and Anne Witz

The Sociology of Death: theory, culture, practice*
ed. David Clark

The Cultures of Computing*
ed. Susan Leigh Star

Theorizing Museums*
ed. Sharon Macdonald and Gordon Fyfe

Consumption Matters*
eds Stephen Edgell, Kevin Hetherington and Alan Warde

Ideas of Difference*
eds Kevin Hetherington and Rolland Munro

The Laws of the Markets*
ed. Michael Callon

Actor Network Theory and After*
eds John Law and John Hassard

Whose Europe?*
eds Dennis Smith and Sue Wright

† Available from The Sociological Review Office, Keele University, Keele, Staffs ST5 5BG.
* Available from Marston Book Services, PO Box 270, Abingdon, Oxen OX14 4YW.

The Sociological Review Monographs

Since 1958 *The Sociological Review* has established a tradition of publishing Monographs on issues of general sociological interest. The Monograph is an edited book length collection of research papers which is published and distributed in association with Blackwell Publishers. We are keen to receive innovative collections of work in sociology and related disciplines with a particular emphasis on exploring empirical materials and theoretical frameworks which are currently under-developed. If you wish to discuss ideas for a Monograph then please contact the Monographs Editor, Martin Parker, at *The Sociological Review*, Keele University, Newcastle-under-Lyme, North Staffordshire, ST5 5BG. Email m.parker@mngt.keele.ac.uk

Renewing Class Analysis

Edited by Rosemary Crompton, Fiona Devine, Mike Savage and John Scott

Blackwell Publishers/The Sociological Review

First published in 2000

Blackwell Publishers
108 Cowley Road, Oxford OX4 1JF, UK

and
350 Main Street
Malden, MA 02148, USA

British Library Cataloguing in Publication Data

A CIP catalogue record for this book is available from the British Library

Library of Congress Cataloging-in-Publication Data applied for

ISBN 0 631 22187 5

Printed and bound by Page Brothers, Norwich

This book is printed on acid-free paper.

Contents

Introduction: the state of class analysis

Rosemary Crompton and John Scott

'Class' is frequently under discussion both in academic contexts and in more popular debates in the mass media.[1] The social background of individuals and the question of whether they can rise above (or fall below) their class of origin seems to be an endless source of fascination for the British. The relative significance of 'class' in different nation states has a similar attraction. The United States, for example, is widely regarded as much less 'class-bound' than 'class-obsessed' and 'class-ridden' Britain (see Devine, 1997). The idea that the United States is a peculiarly 'open' society goes back to early discussions of the significance of the frontier in American life and was a central theme in Sombart's (1913) discussion of the failure of socialism to take root in the United States.

While the 'death' of class continues to be announced, at fairly regular intervals, by leading sociologists (eg, Nisbet, 1959; Clark and Lipset, 1991; Pakulski and Waters, 1996a), even more books are being produced that claim to document the continuing salience of class.[2] Part of the problem, it may be suggested, lies in questions of definition – popular debates about individual social mobility, for example, have as much to do with status or prestige as they do with 'class' as defined in economic terms. This is clear from Ross's (1956) delineation of class attitudes in terms of accent, vocabulary, and style of dress, and the recent media debate about whether the Labour Deputy Prime Minister John Prescott had abandoned his working class origins in favour of a 'middle class' life style. For 'class' is a word with many different meanings, and in some writers it has become so stretched as to encompass virtually any aspect of structured social inequality (see Millet, 1970; Delphy, 1977).

The word 'class' has been used to describe broad and diffuse groupings within a national population that are seen as forming a set of layers or strata in a hierarchy, as in the terms 'upper', 'middle' and 'lower' class. More specifically, but still at an aggregate level, it has been used in various sociological class schemes based on occupational groupings. It has been used as a term to describe a collective historical actor, as in the notion of the 'revolutionary proletariat', or the 'aristocracy' of the English seventeenth century and the 'ascendant bourgeoisie' of the eighteenth and nineteenth. 'Class' has also been used to describe status groupings or prestige rankings, or particular types of consumption categories, such as in the National Readership Survey and various market research categorizations.

No doubt we all have our preferences about how the word class ought to be used, and it is tempting to prescribe a particular usage (Scott, 1996). It has to be recognized that some of the debates in this area are, in fact, pseudo-debates (Crompton, 1998: 27) in which the protagonists talk past one another, rather than to each other, because they employ different concepts of class. However, no attempt to legislate usage in the present climate would be successful. Indeed, very little would be gained from any attempt to exclude particular usages. The power and excitement of sociological research comes from the confrontation between rival, but genuinely held, positions. In this introductory chapter, therefore, we recognize the plurality and diversity of meaning and definition that, however frustrating they may seem at times, provides an essential backdrop to the current debates.

The chapters in this book all seek, in their different ways, to move forward the debates and discussions on class analysis. An understanding of where these ideas are coming from is necessary – if not essential – in order to comprehend the new ways forward that are proposed. We must, therefore, review the state of past debates, particularly those in Britain, if we are to set the scene for current discussions.

Conflicts over class analysis

Sociological research on class in Britain in the post-war period has been dominated by two issues, both of which derive from the political debates of the period. These are the issues of 'openness' and 'embourgeoisement'. The questions of openness and of the possibility of a 'meritocracy' were central to debates over educational policy and stimulated a spate of investigations into social mobility between classes. The key study in this area was that of David Glass (1954). The question of embourgeoisement – of workers becoming 'middle class' – pointed to changes in the shape of the class structure and to consequent changes in political outlook and action. Changing class identities and forms of class consciousness were seen as underpinning the electoral fortunes of the Labour Party. Key contributions to this debate were the works of David Lockwood and John Goldthorpe (Lockwood, 1958; Goldthorpe and Lockwood, 1963). It is no exaggeration to say that these works and the three volumes emanating from the 'Affluent Worker' project (Goldthorpe *et al.*, 1969a,b,c) had a decisive influence on British sociology until at least the middle of the 1980s.

In this research, class was closely linked to occupation. Indeed, the occupational structure and the class structure were often referred to as if they were synonymous with each other. There are a number of problems with this assumption, as has been documented in much of the critical literature. For example, the occupational structure does not give any direct indication of the wealth or property holdings that many have seen as central to the formation of the higher classes (Westergaard, 1995; Scott, 1991, 1994b). Similarly, many adult persons, most notably students, the retired, and many married women, do not have a paid occupation and there are, therefore, problems in allocating them to a class situation. Perhaps most fundamentally, the occupational structure bears the imprint of other major stratifying factors, most particularly those of gender, race and age, that are difficult to disentangle from those of class. These and other criticisms have been summarized in Crompton (1998: 56–8). Such criticisms of the use of occupational class schemes were predated by arguments rooted in particular theoretical positions to the effect that existing schemes – such as, for example, the Registrar General's Social Class classification – did not, in fact, measure 'class' in a theoretically sophisticated way (see Rex, 1961; Goldthorpe, 1980).

From the 1970s onwards, two major cross-national projects, both of which had developed their own, improved, occupation and employment-based class schemes, were established. The International Class Project, directed by Erik Wright, was explicitly Marxist in its inspiration, and Wright devised class schemes that classified jobs according to a Marxist analysis of relations of domination and exploitation in employment (Wright, 1997). The Comparative Analysis of Social Mobility in Industrial Societies (CASMIN) project used a scheme that was initially derived from the Hope-Goldthorpe occupational classification that originated in the Nuffield Social Mobility project (Goldthorpe, 1987; Erikson and Goldthorpe, 1992).[3] Of particular relevance to British debates on class is the fact that a major Economic and Social Research Council (ESRC) survey, the Essex Class Project, began its existence as part of the International Class Project, using Wright's class scheme, but also coded its data using Goldthorpe's scheme. The resulting book that reported on the project (Marshall *et al.*, 1988) incorporated a 'beauty contest' between the two class schemes and that of the Registrar General, using project data to adjudicate between them. The Goldthorpe scheme was declared the winner, and the principal author has subsequently become closely associated with the Nuffield research programme.

Somewhat separately from these studies, occupational class has also been widely used in research on inequalities in health. Indeed, this tradition of research goes right back to the creation of the Registrar General's scheme, which was devised within the General Register Office as an instrument for exploring medical statistics and social differences in material conditions of life. The major investigation of these issues in the post-war period was the Black Report (1980), which documented the long-term persistence of class inequalities in disease and mortality. Studies have shown that, despite the overall improvements in the population at large, class differences persist over a range of health indicators, such as life expectancy, rates of infant mortality and susceptibility to diseases such as bronchitis. Indeed, these have widened, with unskilled manual workers retaining a permanent place at the bottom of the health hierarchy (McPherson and Coleman, 1988). The Government's Chief Medical officer of Health's report (Acheson, 1998) is the most recent contribution to this research.[4]

Much of the sociological discussion of class in Britain, then, has come to be dominated by the 'employment-aggregate' approach in which occupations are allocated to various classes. The initial concerns with the changing shape and openness of the class structure and its impact on life chances has progressively narrowed down to a concern with occupational classification. One outcome of the developments that we have sketched above is that a considerable amount of energy has been devoted to establishing the superiority (or otherwise) of the various occupation and employment-based classifications. The creators of other systems of occupational classification, most notably the Cambridge Scale (Prandy, 1991), have also joined these debates. As a result, debates have become increasingly focused on methodological questions, rather than on substantive issues of class inequality and class action.

This drift away from major substantive issues and towards ever more esoteric methodological questions is highlighted in a recent debate over the significance of social mobility – rates of which, as we have seen, have been used as an indication of societal 'openness'. Saunders (1990) has argued that the changes in the occupational structure that have produced an increase in absolute rates of social mobility are more important than the persistence of class-associated differences in relative mobility rates which the Nuffield group considered more important, but this substantive debate has been all but obliterated in recent exchanges, which have been primarily focused upon methodological issues (Goldthorpe and Breen, 1999).

These two features of sociological debates on class – increasing technical complexity and an apparent insistence that nothing, really, has changed – drew the dominant empirical tradition of class analysis in Britain further and further away from the major concerns of other British sociologists.[5] It is fair to say that this impasse in relation to class analysis in British sociology (and elsewhere) was one of the major factors contributing to the widespread diagnosis of the 'death of class'. The failure of conventional class analysis to say much about what was actually happening in the world simply seemed to underline the irrelevance of class in contemporary society.

The last three decades have seen massive changes in employment relations and occupational structures. These changes include an increasing feminization of the labour force, together with a movement of women into higher-level occupations (Crompton, 1997); an increase in long-term unemployment; changes in the size of particular occupational groups, in particular the decline of manual occupations and the growth of service sector employment; the increasing flexibility of work relations through deskilling and reskilling; the casualization of employment relations; increasing job insecurity and instability at all levels; and the increasing globalization of capital and labour markets, with consequent implications for divisions of labour. Recent work by those in the mainstream of class analysis shows an apparent indifference to these major developments in class and occupational structuring. It has become increasingly clear that the Nuffield version of employment aggregate class analysis is not concerned with the actual nature or processes of labour market structuring, but solely with the outcomes of these processes[6] (see Goldthorpe and Marshall, 1992; Marshall *et al.*, 1996; and the commentaries by Pahl, 1989; Scott, 1994a; Morris and Scott, 1996; and Crompton, 1996).

This highlights the point that the employment aggregate approach is, in fact, rather a narrow one. It relates to only one particular strand within class analysis as a whole. In the employment aggregate and related approaches, classes are represented by occupational groupings, but the term class has also been used, less visibly, in studies of neighbourhoods and communities, of identities, social movements, and status groupings, as well as in exploring actual or potential political actors. An extensive body of work has explored the processes of struggle and jockeying for power, property, and influence contributing to the emergence of these kinds of groupings. Thus one of the avenues out of the impasse described above has been a renewed focus on other approaches to class analysis, and, in particular, the study of class processes. For example, the changing middle classes have been extensively investigated in the work of Savage and his colleagues (Savage *et al.*, 1992; Butler and Savage, 1995). Occupation has still been utilized as one non-exclusive basis for the identification of classes or class fractions, but the emphasis of these investigations has been on the changing nature of middle class occupational assets and the implications of these changes, rather than the stability of middle class occupational inheritance.

However, it is important to realize that criticisms of the employment aggregate approach have not been limited to its apparent indifference to the changing occupational structure.[7] There are also many difficulties in respect of other features associated with discussions of class – most notably the questions of class identity and action (Pahl, 1989). In the theories of Marx, Weber, and those influenced by their ideas, the economic relations of class had been seen as shaping attitudes and behaviour more generally. Marx's account of social change, for example, saw this as emerging from the class conflict that expressed economically conditioned class interests. However, the occupational aggregates produced by the conventional class schemes were, Pahl argued, not capable of helping to account for the links in the chain between class structure, class consciousness, and class action. That is, they could not help to show the manner in which class interests are generated and articulated. However, it can be suggested that a re-focus onto the study of class processes can bring about the closer investigation of interests and identities. This requires an investigation of changes in the structures that shape and perpetuate classes as well as the actions and struggles of the individuals and groups affected by these structures.

Such concerns – which we have discussed in relation to British debates – highlight global processes. The changes in occupational and employment relations that we have summarised are part of a global shift in work and property relations that has repercussions for many areas of sociological analysis (Sayer and Walker, 1992; Castells, 1996), The collapse of state socialism and the opening up of the economies of Russia and eastern Europe to capitalist markets, have also served to fuel arguments about the death of class

(Eyal *et al.*, 1998). Capitalism triumphant has been widely interpreted as marking the final death knell for Marxist theory. The demise of Marxism is often linked with the demise of other grand narratives of history in which class consciousness or action plays a crucial role. This kind of assertion conveniently fails to note that the capitalist class would seem, despite recent upheavals, to be both remarkably well organized and able to protect its interests (Scott, 1997). According to many commentators, increasing individuation in personal lives and in employment makes ever more remote the possibility of collective consciousness and action. What oppositional fervour remains, it is argued, is directed at 'classless' objectives such as the preservation of the environment (Beck, 1992). More generally, it is argued that 'work', in the form of employment, and thus of class, has lost the capacity that it once had to shape the lives and identities of individuals (Offe, 1985). Indeed, some have argued that consumption, or 'multiple mosaics of status communities' now provide the focus for identity that once came from paid employment (Pakulski and Waters, 1996b; Turner, 1988). What responses, therefore, have been made to these and many other criticisms of the failure of 'class analysis'?

Responding to the crisis

With considerable over-simplification, two broad (yet arguably complementary) responses may be identified. The first is to develop and argue for new and improved approaches to class and stratification to replace the previous approaches, which are seen to have failed or to be inadequate. The second is to suggest that the apparent failure of class analysis is more a matter of misplaced emphases and misunderstandings, and that the answer is to recognize the limitations of some approaches whilst reviving others that have fallen into abeyance. In making the case for new approaches to class analysis, many have been influenced by post-modern arguments to the effect that the unifying meta-narrative of class theory has proved inadequate and that new insights are therefore required in order to reflect the contemporary diversity of culture and identity (Bradley, 1996; Anthias, 1998). In contrast, others have argued that new approaches to class are best constructed out of the elements that have already been identified by the class theorists of the past, notably by Weber and Marx (Scott, 1996; Gubbay, 1997).

In respect of the first strategy, Bradley has developed a sophisticated framework that identifies the different structures or dynamics that constitute the social categories of class, gender, race, and age. These dynamics operate together and interdependently to perpetuate inequalities and social hierarchies. Bradley's most recent work (1998) explores the autonomization of cultural lifestyles and uses the concept of hybridity to examine the complex interdependencies that result. Her work may be seen as a useful reaction to the tendencies to over-generalization that have prevailed in some approaches to class analysis in the 1970s and 80s. The work influenced, directly or indirectly, by structural Marxism, in particular, had an undeniable tendency towards economic reductionism. That is, it tended to suggest that the systematic inequalities associated with gender and race, for example, were in fact systematically related to, and largely a product of, class processes (see eg, Crompton and Gubbay, 1977).

Bradley (1996) does not seek to develop a comprehensive framework that would abandon the modernist project of class analysis and encompass all of the dimensions of inequality that she discusses in her book. Her aim is rather to '... rework modernist analysis ... benefiting from the critical insights of post-modern and post-structuralist thought' (1996: 214). Nevertheless, it might be suggested that such an approach is not 'new', but rather, repeats and updates earlier arguments concerning the multidimensional character of stratification systems that were, in fact, being developed at the height of the 'modernist' era of social theorizing (see Lenski, 1954). Indeed, it is doubtful whether even the most committed of structural Marxists ever argued that all stratifying phenomena could be reduced to a single variable.

Scott (1996) takes the second strategy sketched above. He argues for a reworking of a Weberian approach to class analysis that would retain the familiar Weberian distinction between 'class' and 'status', together with the third dimension of command or authority.[8] Scott proposes a Weberian research programme that attempts to map the formation of classes as demographically constituted groupings, while recognizing that class relations are always gendered, racialised, and aged. Unlike Bradley, Scott still holds to the view that a comprehensive framework for the analysis of stratification may be developed by analytically separating class from the other social divisions with which it is combined in concrete situations.

It should be noted that the authors of this chapter would not be in agreement on this issue. While Scott argues for the development of a comprehensive framework of concepts and methodologies for the analysis of 'class', Crompton suggests that, as there are insuperable obstacles to achieving this end, a genuinely pluralistic approach is to be preferred. That is, that the complexities of class and stratification processes cannot be encompassed by a single approach or methodology. Thus any attempt to construct an over-arching model (or claims that a single approach is 'the best' or 'most fruitful'), are bound to be found wanting in some respects (Crompton, 1993, 1998). Nevertheless, despite their differences, both Crompton and Scott share an emphasis upon the necessity for class analysis to take on board the extensive changes that have been taking place in the spheres of production, distribution, and consumption in class societies and to recognize the interdependence of class, gender, ethnicity, and age. All of the authors discussed here share a commitment to the view that the way ahead lies in a recognition of both the limitations and potentialities of existing approaches to class analysis

We have argued above that the employment aggregate approach has generated a rather static vision of class analysis. However, class processes of change, transformation and regeneration, may also be researched using the whole range of social science methodologies. To uncover the links in the chain between structure, consciousness, and action requires a focus on what Esping-Andersen (1993) has described as 'institutional filters' that mediate structures of power, ownership, and control. These are welfare states, educational systems, and other mechanisms of government policy. Varying cultural and social resources are also mobilized by differentially advantaged groups, and their contribution to both the structuring of social classes and the perpetuation of inequalities is also an important avenue of sociological enquiry (Devine, 1998). At a more fundamental level, although capitalist societies remain capitalist, the changes brought about by globalization and other generic trends in capitalist societies, such as the improvement in the position of women, must be recognized and incorporated into a broadened and enriched framework of class analysis.

The contributions

The chapters in this book suggest new and improved approaches to class analysis in general, as well as drawing upon established sociological approaches to address the task of exploring processes of change. Many contributions are from authors who are not usually associated with the mainstream tradition of class analysis, but who, nevertheless, share an interest in the processes whereby classes are generated.

The first two papers develop specific critiques of existing approaches to class analysis and suggest alternative formulations. Sørensen suggests a new theoretical approach to the analysis of labour market structuring, while Gershuny develops a new measure, moving beyond occupation taken on its own, for the analysis of life-chances. The subsequent chapters all focus on process and change, and two broad dimensions of change may be identified. The chapters by Ingham, Pahl, Wacquant and MacDonald are all concerned with the consequences of the changes in the institutional filters of class wrought by nearly two decades of international neo-liberalism. These have lead to growing social and economic polarization, the negative consequences of which are increasingly being recognized by governments. The chapters by Edwards and Crompton deal with broader social trends that, arguably, lie beyond overt party political manipulations and their outcomes. Edwards investigates the changes taking place in the arena of paid employment, while Crompton examines one aspect of what may eventually prove to be one of the most significant social changes of the twentieth century – the transformation of the social and political status of women, together with associated changes in the gender division of labour.

In Chapter 2, Sørensen proposes a move beyond narrowly defined Marxist and Weberian theoretical approaches while, nevertheless, retaining their structural concerns and realist methodology. Like Marx, Sørensen wishes to define classes in relation to exploitation, but in place of the discredited labour theory of value he suggests that class be seen in terms of the control of or property rights over income producing assets. Thus rent, seen as a 'wealth transfer at the expense of others' is argued to be the proper basis for a sound class concept. From this standpoint, exploitation classes are structural locations that provide rights to rent producing assets (pp. 23). Besides material property, certain types of employment relationships generate job properties that also produce rents, and Sørensen proceeds to develop an analysis of different classes in relation to the kinds of compromises and struggles that are generated by these monopoly and composite rents. In doing so, he gives a novel twist to the argument that class must be seen in terms of market situation and employment relations. It is these rent-based relations of exploitation, Sørensen argues, that generate the variations in life-conditions that have been studied by empirical sociologists.

Gershuny, in Chapter 3, is also concerned with the determination of life chances and with using a human capital model. Unlike Sørensen, however, Gershuny concentrates on the development of an empirical measure. Unlike Goldthorpe's categorical occupational class scheme, Gershuny's 'Interim Essex Scale' (IES) is a continuous measure that incorporates individual resources such as education, household circumstances, sex and age, as well as occupation. Such a measure, argues Gershuny, captures the essentially recursive nature of the interplay between structure and agency that is responsible for the determination of 'life chances'. There is, of course, a tension between prediction and explanation. Including more and more variables into a single measure in order to increase predictive power reduces the analytical capacity of the measure and, therefore, its explanatory power. Gershuny is careful to emphasize, however, that particular measures of life chances will vary, depending on which particular facet of the complex bundle of chances is being investigated. Thus he does not argue that the IES is a better measure than the Goldthorpe class scheme, but rather that it is a more suitable technique for the investigation of the impact of biographies on life chances – such as, for example, the changing effect of career breaks on women's earning capacities. Thus Gershuny shares a commitment, emphasized above, to the view that the 'way ahead' in the complex field of class analysis is to recognize the strengths of the range of different measures and approaches available, rather than to continue to argue for the one best way.

The four chapters in the next section of the book all focus on a process of structural shift that has increasingly preoccupied class analysts – social and economic polarization. Ingham's paper (Chapter 4) helps to build an analytical bridge between the concerns of Sørensen and Gershuny and the work of the other contributors to the book. Beginning from a critique of classical class theories, he moves on to a substantive account of what he sees as the major factor contributing to social polarization. This is the increasing dominance of money capital in contemporary capitalism. Ingham argues that the classical theorists identified classes in relation to productive activity alone, failing to appreciate the significance of both money as a social relation and, following from this, of finance capital more generally in structuring class inequalities. The dynamics of money capital are relevant not only to the formation of a capitalist class, as recognized by some writers (Hilferding, 1910; Scott, 1997. See also Ingham, 1984), but also to the existence of poverty and the polarization between rich and poor. This points to the need to explore capital markets, as well as labour markets, and at the new forms of money that circulate through them. Globalization of these financial markets has had a major impact on labour markets and employment relations and on the social distribution of credit. The operation of these markets creates patterns of financial exclusion as integral elements in the wider pattern of social exclusion. Ingham demonstrates that recent attempts to evade or circumvent the negative impact of lack of access to money capital by the very poorest are characterized by weaknesses that make success unlikely.

Pahl (Chapter 5) also focuses on the inequalities that result from differential access to financial resources. She discusses household access to new forms of money – in particular, to credit cards and electronic bank transfers – which are described as marking 'a revolution in the ways in which ordinary people receive, hold and spend their money'. Pahl's research shows that credit worthiness is class stratified, and lends further confirmation to the 'Matthew effect': 'For to everyone that hath, shall be given ... but from him that hath not, shall be taken away'. Her stress on the gendering of lending raises critical issues that have not hitherto been considered in class analysis, and one of the key implications of this is that researchers must also begin to examine the racialization of lending as a critical element in the perpetuation of ethnic disadvantage.

Chapters 6 and 7 explore further the institutional changes that have increased the extent of social and economic polarization in recent decades. In Chapter 6, Wacquant explores four different 'logics of polarization': the macrosocial, the economic, the political, and the spatial – tracing their consequences for the increasing immiseration of the very poorest that make up the group often described as the underclass. However, he makes it clear, as did Ingham, that the question of polarization must be seen as involving two poles and must not be seen in relation to the poor alone (Scott, 1994b). Despite the similar experience of increasing inequality since the late 70s (and in the British case, of the application of neo-liberal policies), Wacquant argues that a direct parallel cannot be drawn between the US and the European experiences. He assesses the different strategies that have been proposed in order to arrest social polarization and its negative effects, arguing that the solution to the deteriorating life chances of those at the bottom of the class structure lies in establishing a form of basic income that redistributes resources away from the privileged. MacDonald and Marsh, in Chapter 7, investigate the plight of the poorest in a very specific British locale – Teeside – emphasizing the combination of structural factors that have created the world of unemployment and casualized under-employment inhabited by so many young people. Reiterating the influential argument of Wilson (1987) about the ghetto poor in the United States, they emphasize that an important facet of the 'failure' of the many policies aimed at combating youth unemployment has been their attempts to transform young people themselves, who in fact show little evidence of any lack of commitment to employment, rather than the circumstances in which the young people find themselves.

This study highlights the importance of considering the spatial aspects of class inequalities and social polarization. The localization of disadvantage in areas such as Teeside is matched by the localization of advantage in privileged enclaves from which others are excluded. For the most privileged, this localization is linked to the forces of globalization, as the advantages of the very wealthy depend, to a great extent, on global flows of money capital and the use of localized tax havens within these circuits.

The final section of the book includes two papers that analyse the processes of occupational and labour market restructuring that are leading to substantial changes in class structures and class relations. Both of these chapters rest on an awareness of the limitations of the employment aggregate approach, the version of class analysis that relies on the statistical analysis of occupational groupings and which has been extensively discussed in the first section of this chapter. In Chapter 8, Edwards examines a range of case studies that have shown the emergence of new occupations and changes in the employment situation of significant established occupational groupings. As Edwards argues, '... we need to know the processes occurring in society which generate distinct occupational groups that the sociologist can then observe as having shared market and work situations'.[9] In particular, evidence for the demise of the bureaucratic career among managers is discussed and evaluated.

In Chapter 9, Crompton addresses one aspect of the consequences of the changing division of labour between the sexes – the increasing numbers of women gaining higher-level qualifications and entering the service sector of 'middle class' occupations. The increasing entry of women into such 'career' jobs, she argues, has sharpened the tensions that are associated with the gender division between paid and unpaid work that were emphasized by the first generation of 'second-wave' feminists in the 1960s and 70s. She demonstrates that there are sustained differences in the management of the employment-family interface, as well as in family formation, between women in 'professional' as compared to 'managerial' jobs – differences that are also apparent amongst men in the same occupations studied (doctors and bank managers). This evidence of systematic variation in family/household and employment strategies between different major occupational groups is likely to be carried forward into the socialization and education of children. Thus, it is becoming increasingly problematic to draw a sharp distinction between 'gender' and 'class' processes in labour market structuring, or to put the same point in a slightly different fashion, the interdependence of social and material production is becoming ever more apparent. Indeed, it may be argued that major changes in occupational and labour market structuring in the relatively near future will derive as much from tensions and pressures relating to the work of caring as they do from conflicts over productive activity.

Discussion and conclusions

We must leave the last word to our editorial colleagues in their final chapter. Nevertheless, even at this stage we may suggest how our brief survey of the present state of class analysis points to a fruitful way forwards for future research, as well as enabling us to avoid past mistakes.

The first general precept is to recognize that class and stratification are multi-dimensional (not to say multi-purpose) concepts. It follows that it is important to steer clear of any tendency to suggest that any particular dimension (or approach) constitutes the only – let alone the best – way of understanding concrete relations of social stratification and social inequality. It must immediately be emphasized that this is not to suggest that 'anything goes'. Nor is it to suggest that debates should be stifled in any way. Rather, we have suggested that an excessive focus on the outcomes of class structuring as measured by employment aggregates – what Sørensen would describe as the empirical investigation of 'life conditions' or life chances – has, unfortunately, resulted in a relative lack of attention being given to the exploration and documentation of class processes.

Second, we would wish to move class analysis decisively beyond the hiatus of 'post-modern' and 'postructuralist' critiques in sociology. This is not to deny that analyses of the discourses of class, for example, have not produced any insights. It is, rather, to insist that lived experiences and understandings are a consequence of sustained and enforceable patterns of human behaviour (social relations and social institutions) relating to the processes of production, distribution and consumption and which structure access to these processes. These processes are class processes, and they produce classes.

Third (and notwithstanding our comments above in relation to postmodernism and postructuralism), we would wish to argue for a genuine pluralism in the area of class and stratification theory and research. Class processes operate across a number of different societal levels (Scott, 1997), as would be expected in any set of concepts that are attempting, however inadequately or imperfectly, to link social structures to individual action, as well as to identify sources of social change. Thus, within the complex whole that is class analysis, we might expect to find different topics requiring different methodologies, as well as variations in theoretical perspective (Crompton 1998). It is to this approach that this volume, as well as the series of seminars that generated it, is dedicated.

Notes

1 The papers in this book derive from a series of seminars funded by the ESRC (R451264 57996) under the title 'Investigating Social Stratification'. Seminars were held at Essex (Jan. 1998), Manchester (April 1998 and 1999), Leicester (Sept.1998) and Oxford (Jan. 1999).

2 From among the many that have appeared in recent years, we may cite those of Scase (1992), Edgell (1993), Devine (1997), Cannadine (1998), McKibbin (1998), and Milner (1999), as well as the compilation produced by Lee and Turner (1996).

3 The Goldthorpe/CASMIN approach has in fact been a pragmatic one, and the scheme has been freely modified in response to comparative research needs – eg the later identification of agricultural workers as a separate category.

4 A member of the Essex Class Project (David Rose), together with David Lockwood, have been involved in the construction of a new occupational class scheme, based on that of Goldthorpe, that will replace the existing Registrar General's scheme in medical and social policy research (Rose and O'Reilly 1998).

5 Another important factor influencing this deepening rift was the apparent failure of the employment aggregate tradition properly to address feminist criticisms. This topic is discussed in Chapter 8.

6 Here a contrast may be drawn with the Marxist variant of the employment-aggregate approach (Wright 1997), in which Marxist theory is employed in identifying and describing contemporary processes of occupational structuring.

7 The rather limited exception of the attention paid to changes over time in the proportions in particular occupational categories, which is accommodated via log-linear modeling.

8 For Weber, all three dimensions of stratification were aspects of the social distribution of power, a point that has been misunderstood by those who see Weber as talking about class, status, and power (Runciman 1968, Bendix and Lipset 1953). Even more misleading is the conventional misinterpretation of Weber's three dimensions as class, status, and party.

9 Though presented as a comment on Goldthorpe, it should be noted that Goldthorpe no longer employs the concept of 'market situation' and would claim that his class scheme is grounded in the concept of 'employment relations', as if these were somehow distinct from labour market relations.

Bibliography

Acheson, D., (1998), *Independent Inquiry into Inequalities in Health Report*, London: HMSO.

Anthias, F., (1998), 'Rethinking social divisions: some notes towards a theoretical framework', *Sociological Review*, 46, 3.

Beck, U., (1992). *Risk Society*, London: Sage.

Bendix, R. and Lipset, S.M. (eds), (1953), *Class, Status and Power*, New York: Free Press.

Bradley, H., (1996), *Fractured Identities*, Cambridge: Polity.

Bradley, H., (1998), *Gender and Power in the Work Place*, London: Macmillan.

Butler, T. and Savage, M. (eds), (1995), *Social Change and the Middle Classes*, London: UCL Press.

Cannadine, D., (1999) *Class in Britain*, London: Weidenfeld and Nicholson.

Castells, M., (1996), *The Network Society*, Oxford: Basil Blackwell.

Clark, T. and Lipset, S.M., (1991), 'Are social classes dying?', *International Sociology*, Vol. 6, No. 4: 397–410.

Crompton, R., (1993, 2nd ed. 1998), *Class and Stratification*, Cambridge: Polity.

Crompton, R., (1996), 'The fragmentation of class analysis', *British Journal of Sociology*, 47.

Crompton, R., (1997), *Women and Work in Modern Britain*, Oxford: Oxford University Press.

Crompton, R. and Gubbay, J., (1977), *Economy and Class Structure*, London: Macmillan.

Delphy, C., (1977), *The Main Enemy*, London: Women's Research and Resources Centre.

Devine, F., (1997), *Social Class in Britain and America*, Edinburgh: Edinburgh University Press.

Devine, F., (1998), 'Class analysis and the stability of class relations', *Sociology*, Vol. 32, No. 1: 23–42.

Edgell, S., (1993), *Class*, London: Routledge.

Erikson, R. and Goldthorpe, J.H., (1992), *The Constant Flux*, Oxford: Clarendon Press.

Esping-Andersen, G. (ed.), (1993), *Changing Classes: Stratification and Mobility in Post-Industrial Societies*, London: Sage.

Eyal, G., Szelényi, I. and Townsley, E., (1998), *Making Capitalism Without Capitalists: The New Ruling Elites in Eastern Europe*, London: Verso.

Glass, D.V. (ed.), (1954), *Social Mobility in Britain*, London: Routledge.
Goldthorpe, J.H. and Marshall, G., (1992), 'The promising future of class analysis', *Sociology*, 26, 3: 381–400.
Goldthorpe, J.H., (1980; 1987), *Social Mobility and Class Structure in Modern Britain*, Oxford: Clarendon Press.
Goldthorpe, J.H. and Breen, R. (1999), 'Class mobility and merit: the experience of two British cohorts', Paper to ESRC Conference *Investigating Social Stratification*, Nuffield College, Oxford.
Goldthorpe, J.H. and Lockwood, D., (1963), 'Affluence and the British class structure', *Sociological Review*, Vol. 11, No. 2.
Goldthorpe J.H., Lockwood, D., Bechhofer, F. and Platt, J., (1969a), *The Affluent Worker: Industrial Attitudes and Behaviour*, Cambridge: Cambridge University Press.
Goldthorpe J.H., Lockwood, D., Bechhofer, F. and Platt, J., (1969b) *The Affluent Worker: Political Attitudes and Behaviour*, Cambridge: Cambridge University Press.
Goldthorpe J.H., Lockwood, D., Bechhofer, F. and Platt, J., (1969c) *The Affluent Worker in the Class Structure*, Cambridge: Cambridge University Press.
Gubbay, J., (1997) 'A Marxist critique of Weberian class analysis', *Sociology*, 31 1: 143–52.
Hilferding, R., (1910), *Finance Capital*, London: Routledge and Kegan Paul, 1981.
Ingham, G.K., (1984), *Capitalism Divided?*, London: Macmillan.
Lenski, G., (1954), 'Status crystallisation: a non-vertical dimension of social status', *American Sociological Review*.
Lockwood, D., (1958; 1989), *The Black-Coated Worker*, London: Allen and Unwin, Oxford: OUP.
Marshall, G., Newby, H., Rose, D., Vogler, C., (1988), *Social Class in Modern Britain*, London: Unwin Hyman.
Marshall, G., Roberts, R. and Burgoyne, C., (1996), 'Social Class and Underclass in Britain and the United States', *British Journal of Sociology*.
Millet, K., (1970), *Sexual Politics*, New York: Doubleday.
Milner, A., (1999), *Class*, London: Sage.
Ross, A.S.C. *et al.*, (1956), *Noblesse Oblige*, London: Hamish Hamilton.
McKibbin, R., (1998), *Class Cultures*, Oxford: Basil Blackwell.
McPherson, •. and Coleman, •., (1988), •••.
Nichols, W.A.T., (1979), 'Social class: official, sociological and Marxist', in Levitas, R. and Guy, W. (eds), *Interpreting Official Statistics*, London: Routledge, 1996.
Nisbet, R.A., (1959), 'The decline and fall of social class', *Pacific Sociological Review*, 2.
Offe, C., (1985), '"Work" – a central sociological category?', in Offe (ed.) *Disorganized Capitalism*, Cambridge: Polity.
Pahl, R.E., (1989), 'Is the Emperor Naked?', *International Journal of Urban and Regional Research*, Vol. 13, No. 4: 711–20.
Pakulski, J. and Waters, M., (1996a), *The Death of Class*, London: Sage.
Pakulski, J. and Waters, M., (1996b), 'The reshaping and dissolution of social class in advanced society', *Theory and Society*, 25: 667–691.
Prandy, K., (1991), 'The revised Cambridge scale of occupations', *Sociology*, 24, 4: 629–56.
Rex, J. A., (1961), *Key Problems of Sociological Theory*, London: Routledge and Kegan Paul.
Runciman, W.G., (1968). 'Class, Status and Power', in Scott, J. (ed.), *Class*, London: Routledge, 1996.
Saunders, P., (1990), *Social class and stratification*, London: Routledge.
Savage, M., Barlow, J., Dickens, A. and Fielding, T., (1992), *Property, Bureaucracy, and Culture*, London: Routledge.
Sayer, A. and Walker, R., (1992), *The New Social Economy: Reworking the Division of Labour*, Oxford: Basil Blackwell.
Scase, D., (1992), *Class*, Buckingham: Open University Press.
Scott, J., (1991), *Who Rules Britain?*, Cambridge: Polity Press.
Scott, J., (1994a), 'Class analysis: back to the future', *Sociology*, Vol. 28, No. 4: 933–942.
Scott, J., (1994b), *Poverty and Wealth*, Harlow: Longman.

Scott, J., (1996), *Stratification and Power*, Cambridge: Polity.
Scott, J., (1997), *Corporate Business and Capitalist Classes*, Oxford: Oxford University Press.
Scott, J. and Morris, L., (1996), 'The attenuation of class analysis', *British Journal of Sociology*.
Sombart, W., (1913), *Why Is There No Socialism In The United States?*, London: Macmillan, 1976.
Turner, B.S., (1988), *Status*, Buckingham: Open University Press.
Westergaard, J.H. and Resler, H., (1976), *Class In A Capitalist Society*, London: Heinemann.
Wilson, W.J., (1987), *The Truly Disadvantaged*, Chicago: Chicago University Press.
Wright, E.O., (1997), *Class Counts*, Cambridge: Cambridge University Press.

Employment relations and class structure

Aage B. Sørensen

Introduction

Most sociologists acknowledge that the concept of class is among our most important concepts, providing the most influential formulation of the central idea of sociology – that is, the idea of a social structure shaping individual action as well as creating social change, that is, history.

Class certainly is one of the most discussed and revised concepts in sociology. The discussions are usually preceded by a description of the origins of the concept and its main varieties. The standard account is that class originated with Karl Marx and obtained its first major revision by Max Weber, claimed to be the bourgeois antidote to Marxist determinism and Marx's single-minded preoccupation with economic class (see, for example, Ritzer, 1994, for this version of history). From then on, the standard account see two branches of class analysis, called Neo-Marxist and Neo-Weberians, since almost everything written on the concept of class between the turn of the century and the early nineteen seventies is ignored. The Neo-Marxists think that Marx was right, that classes originate in production in a process of exploitation based on domination and property. The Neo-Weberians think less about where classes come from. Presumably they originate in the market and determine life chances that are protected by processes of closure or usurped by those denied those chances. For the Neo-Weberians, the main concern is for class formation by the way of processes of closure, social mobility and what is called structuration by Giddens (1973).

Why is Marx not good enough? The standard account points out that he never defined class explicitly, that he used the term in different meanings, and that all of his predictions about the transformation of capitalist society based on class conflict as the engine turned out to be wrong. So class analysis has much to do remedying Marx's mistakes and failures. It is not at all clear why Weber is seen as the main source of better wisdom on class analysis and why he is believed to be the remedy for the defects of Marx. Weber was not very interested in class analysis, he wrote very little about it, and he did not use the concept. He was translated into English and he is not considered a functionalist. Perhaps these are the reasons for Weber's popularity in class analysis.

In this chapter, I will first argue that the main contrast is not between a Neo-Marxist and a Neo-Weberian concept of class. A more useful distinction is between class as conflict groups where conflict originates in *exploitation*, and class as a determinant of individual actions and mentalities where these consequences originate in the *life-conditions* created in different classes. The exploitation-based concept of class originates with Marx. The concept of class as life conditions has dominated empirical class analysis in both European and American sociology.

I go on to suggest that both class concepts have properties that reflect the wealth, or rights to the returns on assets, of incumbents of class positions. This proposal sees class as based in property rights, as did Marx, but the concept of property used here is broader than legal property rights definition usually employed. It is a concept of economic property rights defined as the ability to receive the return on an asset, directly, or indirectly through exchange (Barzel, 1997). Some of these rights may be supported by the state, and they are then legal rights, but people also obtain advantages from rights that are not legally enforceable. Property rights define a person's wealth and I suggest that the *class as life-conditions* reflects a person's total wealth and the variability of this wealth over time. Part of a person's wealth may be in assets that generate returns or payments that are *rents*. Rents are returns on assets that are in fixed supply because single owners of the asset to the market control their supply so that the supply will not respond to an increase in price. I propose to define *exploitation class* as structural locations that provide rights to rent producing assets. Exploitation classes defined by the presence and absence of rent producing assets have antagonistic interests because rents create advantages to owners of rent producing assets, obtained at the expense of non-owners. Class locations defined by class as life-conditions do not necessarily have antagonistic interests, because rent producing assets may not be part of a person's total wealth.

A main task for any proposal for a class concept is to show that it can resolve the 'problem of the middle classes' (Wright, 1986), that is, that the proposed concept provides insights into the class situation of the large majority of the population who is employed, but do not seem to be a homogenous proletariat as predicted by Marx. The utility of the present proposal is in this paper tested by showing its usefulness in the conceptualization of class categories within the labour market. I will argue that class within labour markets are created by employment contracts that provide more or less wealth to the employee. The amount of wealth obtained from employment adds to the amount of personal wealth possessed by the person in the form of human and physical capital, and the total amount of wealth and its variability in turn create the consequences attributed to the life-condition concept of class for the majority of the population having no substantial physical assets.

While research on social mobility, educational attainment and the like has focused on class as living-conditions (eg, Goldthorpe, 1987), class analysis focusing on labour market structures has sought to identify exploitation classes within the labour market. This will also be my main concern. The last part of the paper concentrates on the analysis of the wealth created by employment contracts that generates returns that are economic rents. There are two main types of employment rents to consider, monopoly rents created by unions and professional associations, and composite rents created by asset specificity. Monopoly rents in the labour market reflect restrictions on the quantity or quality of labour supplied and accrued to employees. Monopoly rents often depend on and support rents created outside the labour markets as rents on skills caused by restrictions on access to training opportunities. Composite rents are shared among employers and employees and the main issue to consider is the partitioning of the rents. Employers' strategies to increase their share of the composite rents produce the incentive and supervisory schemes that have occupied so much of the literature on labour markets. My first task is to identify the two main types of classes and their basis in property right arrangements.

Exploitation and life-condition class concepts

The conventional account of class analysis taught to sociologists[1] first contrasts Marx and Weber and then identifies the main camps by their neo-successors. This account misses about 50–70 years of writings about class, both by important European class analysts, such as Geiger (1932) and Halbwachs (1912, 1925), and by American scholars with a keen interest in empirical research on how class affects the lives of individuals and communities, such as Warner *et al.* (1949), Hollingshead (1949), Hollingshead and Redlich (1958) and the Lynds (1929). Empirically oriented scholars on both side of the Atlantic used class in a sense that is not easily accommodated by the Weberian class concept and they are clearly not employing Marxist concepts. Classes are seen as sources of differences among people in mentalities (eg, Halbwachs, 1925, Geiger, 1932); in lifestyles (eg, Hollingshead, 1949; Lynd and Lynd 1929; Warner *et al.*, 1949); and life chances (Halbwachs, 1912; Hollingshead and Redlich, 1958). These investigations use class in a sense that covers the idea of class as life chances, what Weber called economic class, and the idea of class as lifestyles, or social class, for Weber associated with 'stand'.[2]

Weber's distinctions are more confusing than illuminating and never inspired empirical research. It is not at all clear that separating life styles and life chances is possible and useful in empirical research. The idea that class only refers to market situations ignores that people obtain wealth and resources from other sources than the market. For example, they obtain wealth from the organizations that employ them through non-market allocations, as we shall see below. The idea that life styles only relate to prestige or honor is also misleading. Life styles reflect consumption patterns, and consumption patterns reflect wealth, or permanent income.

The class concepts employed by the older and empirically oriented American and European class analysis saw class-effects being produced by a combination of wealth and socialization or inoculation mechanisms, though the exact mechanisms never were precisely identified. Class shapes values, preferences, tastes and action orientations, and provides the resources for realizing the actions these preferences make desirable. Research on classes in this tradition is research on differences in *life-conditions* in different structural locations in society. It is an inherently geographical conception of social class. Different locations in social space provide for differences in life conditions and therefore differences in life styles and cultures, just as different locations in physical space provide for differences in life conditions described and analysed by anthropologists and geographers. There is an enormous amount of evidence showing that these locations matter a great deal for almost everything. In fact, it has been claimed that social class or socioeconomic status – the two most often used labels for these class locations – form the main independent variable for sociology.

This conception of class as life-condition contrasts clearly to Marx's conception of class as the engine of social change because of the antagonism and struggle created in social structure by relationships of exploitation. These properties obtain, not because classes shape the life courses and life forms of people, but because classes generate antagonistic interests. Interests are in conflict because classes are defined by relationships of exploitation where one class obtains an advantage at the expense of another. These antagonistic interests and the conflict they create change society and class analysis can therefore produce a theory of history. Classes may, of course, also shape people in the manner described by the concept of class as life conditions. In the extreme Marxist version of class analysis, class determines everything. However, the emphasis in what has become seen as Marxist class analysis is on antagonistic interests, exploitation, conflict and struggle, not on life styles, preferences, tastes and values of incumbents of social classes.

The contrast between the life-condition concept of class and the *exploitation* concept of class is clear. The two concepts serve different theoretical purposes. Class as life-condition explains differences in individual behaviour and orientation, class as exploitation explains differences in interest and collective action. This is a much clearer contrast than the contrast between the Weberian and the Marxist class concept.

There are problems with both traditions of class analysis. The class as exploitation concept proposes a theory of inequality and exploitation based on an economic theory that nobody believes in, the labour theory of value. So, while the Marxist concept does propose a mechanism for producing class conflict, this theory is not to be believed. The class as life condition concept proposes essentially no theory of the mechanism by which class outcomes are produced. Except for some vague general notions of socialization processes and consciousness development, nobody has cared to explicate, in an empirically usable way, how class outcomes are produced.

I propose to remedy these defects by suggesting that class be seen as based on the control of, or property rights to, income producing assets, where these rights are understood in a broader sense than legal property rights. These rights define a person's wealth.

Class and wealth

Marx thought that classes were based on rights to the payments on wealth and Weber thought property to be very important for the emergence of economic classes. Dahrendorf (1959) is usually seen as the start of the many revisions of the original class concepts that were to culminate in the neo-class analysis of the nineteen seventies. He rejects that property could be the basis for class formation, using a concept of property rights as legal property rights, that is state supported rights. He bases the argument on the existence of inequality in state socialist society where private property of the means of production presumably does not exist, and on the emergence of the modern corporation with separation of legal ownership and control. Dahrendorf proposes to instead define class by authority. Authority also is key for the class scheme of Wright (1979), again because property does not seem to differentiate class locations within the 'propertyless' employed part of the population.

For Marx exploitation is a question of economic advantage and right to the returns on wealth is indeed essential for the distribution of these returns. That legal ownership rights are required to identify class categories defined by relationships of exploitation is an unnecessary strong requirement. Rights to the advantage provided by assets or resources need not be legal rights to be effective. Following Barzel (1997) economic property rights are properly seen as reflecting an individual's ability to consume a good or asset directly or consume through exchange. Such economic rights may be enforceable by law and are then stronger, but need not be supported by the state. Property rights are not absolute and constant, and they can be changed through individual action to protect and enhance the rights. Such action incurs transaction costs that are the costs of transfer, protection and transfer of rights. When transaction costs are positive, rights are not perfectly delineated. Some of the attributes of the asset are costly to measure and not fully known to actual or potential owners. These attributes are subject to capture by others who then obtain rights to the benefits from these attributes.

For example, in the modern corporation stockholders do not own all of the assets of the organization, but share it with other parties inside and outside the organization that have rights to gains from various attributes of the assets. Managers obtain some gains because stockholders cannot fully control their use of assets because of lack of information. Other employees may obtain advantages, to be discussed below, for example by retaining control over their effort. That ownership is divided does not mean that the concept of property as the basis for exploitation should be abandoned, as Dahrendorf (1959) proposes. Exploitation has to do with obtaining advantages and therefore clearly involve rights. Also, the absence of individual legal property rights to productive asset in socialist society, does not mean that individuals do not gain from controlling the use of an asset (Barzel 1997) in such society. Only their property rights are more restricted and it may be more difficult to identify those who obtain the gains.

The broader concept of property rights proposed by Barzel (1997) implies that individuals usually have some property rights to assets, even slaves do, under some circumstances (Barzel, 1997: 105). The rights are never complete unless there are no transaction costs, but are usually shared with other actors. This means that all individuals will have some wealth, if nothing else their ability to execute a task that can be exchanged for a wage. They have an interest in maximizing their wealth and will try to capture rights to attributes of assets that increase their wealth. Using a formulation proposed by Coleman (1990), we may define this wealth as:

$$r_j = \sum_i c_{ij} v_i \qquad (1)$$

where r_j is the wealth of actor j, c_{ij} is the control of actor j over asset or resource i, and v_i the value of asset j. The value of an asset may be expressed by the income returns it generates. The amount of control thus determines how much of this return is obtained by actor j. Value of an asset is defined as $v_i = \sum x_{ji} c_j$, where x_{ji} is the interest of actor j in asset i. Assets are valuable if wealthy actors have a high interest in them. In employment relations, as I will show below, actors have control initially over the wealth provided by their own labour. In employment, they exchange control over that labour with the employer for a wage and other benefits. However, they usually do not exchange all attributes of their labour and can use the control they maintain over certain attributes to increase their return on their labour. For example, if employees exchange their labour for hourly pay, they may keep control over their effort. Effort is a cost, and by varying effort they can vary the amount of benefit they receive from the employment contract, or the return on their wealth.

The individual's total wealth, as defined by her control of assets, will determine her socioeconomic welfare and thus her class location in terms of class as life-condition. It will be argued below that the consequences of these conditions are not only dependent on the total wealth, but also on the over-time variability in the returns on that wealth (which define the variation in the value of the wealth). Part of the total wealth may generate benefits obtained at the expense of someone else, who would be better off with a different distribution of control or property rights to the various attributes of the assets. This *rent* generating part defines class as exploitation. These ideas are further developed next.

Wealth, rents and exploitation

The issue for the formulation of a theory of exploitation is to define a process by which some holder of an economic property right obtains an advantage at the expense of persons without these rights. The presence and absence of property rights then create antagonistic interests that may create collective action and conflict. The stipulation that it is an advantage obtained at the expense of others is very important.

Inequality in assets by itself does not create antagonistic interests. In other words, using the definition of wealth given above, the interests of person j in assets i, x_{ji}, need not be in conflict with those of other actors. Coleman (1990) shows that in a perfect market, with no transaction costs, actors will exchange control over assets or attributes of assets to reach an equilibrium that maximizes the wealth of everyone and where nobody suffers at the expense of someone else.[3] However, this assumes that there are no transaction costs so that all attributes of assets and goods can be exchanged. When this occurs, people obtain the highest possible returns on their assets and interests are not antagonistic. People will differ in wealth, but the wealth differences will not generate conflict since nobody can be made better off. In a perfect market, the inequality in wealth creates different living conditions, but do not reflect exploitation.

If there are transaction costs, some may acquire wealth at the expense of others who would be better off with a different distribution of control prevented by the transaction costs. Such wealth transfer represents the acquisition of the right to an economic *rent*. When this occurs, interests are in conflict or antagonistic. Those who obtain the rent have an advantage at the expense of nonowners. The property relations that create rents are a source of inequality that creates conflict.

Marx's concept of class sees exploitation as the transfer of surplus value from owners to non-owners of productive assets. Surplus value is defined by the labour theory of value. Should the labour theory of value provide a valid concept of value, exploitation would take place even under perfect competition that Marx saw as characteristic of the most advanced stage of capitalism. However, if the labour theory of value is abandoned, as it should be, the concept of surplus value becomes a metaphysical quantity with no empirical reference. The concept of rent suggests an alternative concept of exploitation consistent with modern economics and with the idea that exploitation provides an advantage that is a wealth transfer at the expense of others (see Sørensen, 1996, for an elaboration).

Rents are payments to assets in fixed supply that depend on the ability of the owner of the asset to control the supply. The classic example is the tenancy contract associated with Feudalism. Part of the benefit from the land goes to payment for the labour of the peasant and another part to payment for capital expenditures on the land by the landlord. The rent benefit obtained from a tenancy arrangement is the remainder, the payment not needed to employ the peasant and keep the land fertile. It is an unearned advantage going to the landlord because of his rights to the returns on the property.[4] The peasant would be better off by a change in the distribution of property rights that would allow him to keep the advantage now obtained by the landlord.

The association of rents with land is not required. Alfred Marshall ([1920], 1949) devoted much attention to the concept of rents and generalized its applicability to benefits received from any productive resource or asset. He showed that rents also may appear as payments for the use of capital and labour in restricted supply; as payments for the use of unique combinations of capitals and labours, such as those created by certain technologies; and, as payments for unusual and rare individual abilities that cannot be developed by training alone (musical talents, artistic creativity, athletic ability, etc.). Rent thus may be obtained from any productive asset. The salient property is that a component of the payment obtained from the asset, or its return, is obtained independently of the past efforts and savings of the person who has property rights to the relevant attribute of the asset for the rent.

In a competitive economy, others ordinarily discover when there is an excess profit available from owning a particular resource and then increase the use or the supply of the resource. This reduces the excess profit and eventually makes it disappear. Marshall ([1920], 1949) calls such temporary rents *quasi-rents*.

Rents defined in this manner satisfy the requirements of structural theory of inequality. Rents are created by social relationships of control of rent-producing assets (with the obvious exceptions of rents on natural abilities, to be treated later). Rents generate antagonistic interests because the advantage provided by a rent represents a disadvantage to others. Rent is the proper basis for a sound class concept, (see Sørensen, 1997, for an elaboration). Positively privileged exploitation classes are positions in social structure that allow individuals to gain control or economic property rights over assets or attributes of assets that generate rents, negatively privileged exploitation classes are defined by the absence of these rights. Changing the property relations that generate rents will change the distribution of wealth and hence the class structure.

I will show below that only certain types of employment relationships are likely to generate job properties that produce rents, those employment relations that are in some degree closed to outsiders. There are two types of rents of special interest here. One is what is usually called *monopoly rents* where an actor, or a set of actors, controls the supply of an asset, thereby increasing the returns on the asset over what it would have generated in the absence of the monopoly. The immediate example for the discussion of class categories in employment systems is the control over the supply of labour by unions. Another important source of monopoly rents in the labour market is the restricting of free access to training opportunities by schools, universities and by those controlling access to apprenticeships.

The other type of rent of special interest for my discussion is what Marshall ([1920], 1949) calls *composite* rents. These are rents generated by the unique combination of two productive assets that are more productive in joint use than separately. In more recent literature, composite rents are the rents or quasi-rents generated by asset specificity (Williamson, 1985). They are of special interest in the analysis of the emergence of rents in the employment relations that generate internal labour markets.

Finally, Marshall argues that rents can also be obtained on natural abilities, a type of monopoly rent created by nature or culture. When created by nature they result from genetic endowments. To the restrictions by nature may also be added restrictions by difficult-to-learn cultural tastes and competencies called cultural capital (Bourdieu, 1977). Since these culturally or genetically abilities are properties of persons and not of positions defined by social relations, they do not generate class categories in the labour market. They have social consequences, as noted below, and can be an important component of an individual's personal wealth and thus of class as life-conditions.

Wealth and living conditions

There is an abundance of research that shows that socioeconomic status or class as life-conditions indeed is a powerful determinant of all kinds of outcomes. There is much less knowledge and understanding of how these outcomes come about. We have, of course, a rich literature on socialization that demonstrates that class is associated with important socialization differences, we know about important value differences among different classes, and we also know about a host of life style differences associated with different classes. However, this moves only the question one level back. What is it about the life-conditions of different classes, or different socioeconomic levels, that accounts for these differences?

I propose that the answer is lifetime wealth and the expected variation in returns on that wealth for incumbents of different classes. There is abundant evidence that social class accounts for more outcomes, the more homogeneous class categories are with respect to a variety of resources, or their wealth. Socioeconomic status in the meaning of 'goodness' (Goldthorpe and Hope, 1974) seems to reflect people's beliefs about the life-conditions associated with different occupations, and this is measured by the wealth of incumbents. There is no fundamental difference between what is measured by class schema, such as Goldthorpe's schema (Goldthorpe, 1987) and by socioeconomic status, except that the discrete class schema may capture non-vertical variation ignored by socioeconomic status measures.

It is important to consider not the cross-sectional distribution of income, but the long-term wealth profile that determines what economists call permanent income and consumption patterns. A person who obtains a higher education will orient his life style not to the level of income in her youth, but to the long-term expected living conditions corresponding to the wealth associated with her human capital.

Further, the variation in the returns on the wealth is important, particularly for the socialization patterns that emerge in different classes. An older literature found strong differences between social classes in what was called ability to defer gratification (eg, Schneider and Lysgaard, 1953). This literature was largely dismissed in the seventies because it was seen as reflecting an attempt to 'blame the victim' – see Ryan (1971). More recently, psychologists and economists have suggested a different formulation of the same phenomena (see Ainslie, 1992). People discount future rewards, often at very high rates. In particular, there are strong differences among social classes or different socioeconomic levels in time orientation, with persons at low socioeconomic levels having a much shorter time horizon than others. Those with high discount rates invest less in their health and education, and in the health and education of their children.

These differences among classes in time orientation or deferred gratification patterns reflect the level of uncertainty in living conditions or the variability of returns. Such uncertainty is not the fault of the 'victim', but is a rational reaction to the expected high uncertainty of returns.[5] Banks also charge a higher interest rate with uncertain investments and banks presumably are acting rationally. The impact of uncertainty on people's investments in themselves and their children should be greater the lower the overall level of resources.

The idea that wealth and wealth variation is of paramount importance for the consequences of the living conditions of different classes is particularly useful here. Persons' total wealth has two main components. One part is personal, human and physical, wealth, mostly acquired outside of the labour market in and from families and schools, but some acquired from on-the-job training. The other component is wealth acquired from employment relations when these relationships provide access to rent-producing assets, to be discussed below.

The personal part of wealth that exists independent of a person's employment relationships has several components. For my discussion, the amount of human capital obtained through investments in training and health is particularly important. There may also be skills and abilities that command rents. Finally, the amount of wealth obviously depends on the endowments of physical capital provided by the family of origin and augmented by the person through entrepreneurship and investment independently of his involvement with the labour market. This component of personal wealth is obviously of major importance for a full analysis of the class structure. However, I shall concentrate here on the wealth that relates to a person's employment.

The duration of employment relationships is crucially important for the variability of returns and therefore for the consequences of differences in wealth because the shorter the employment relationships, the more variable will be the returns on a person's wealth. The duration of the employment relation also is important for the amount of wealth obtained in the relationship – the shorter the expected employment relationship, the less rent the relationship is likely to provide.

Employment relations and wealth

The employment relationship defines two positions: The employer and the employee. The employer may be a person or a corporate actor – the distinction makes little difference for the discussion that follows. It is possible to conceive of employment relationships involving corporate actors as employees. However, I shall only consider employment relationships involving natural persons. These persons have abilities, skills and levels of efforts that determine how well and how fast they can complete tasks. Tasks vary in complexity. Persons vary in their ability to complete tasks at a certain level of complexity. Those who can do better have more skills and/or ability than those they outperform. Skills refer to the amount of human capital acquired through training and therefore at a cost. Ability refers to the component of the competence to handle tasks at a certain level of complexity that is independent of training, or a 'free gift of nature' (or culture) to use Marshall's formulation ([1920], 1946). Persons also vary in the amount of effort they exert. This is a matter of motivation and perhaps overall level of energy. Together skills, ability and effort determine the productivity supplied by the employee. This personal productivity and the production technique determine the output from the person per period.

The theoretical power, as well as the empirical inadequacy, of neoclassical labour economics derives from the application of standard price theory to these processes. This assumes that labour is a commodity like any other good. In fact, it assumes that it is a good with all attributes well known and transferable in exchange, a property that often does not hold even for ordinary goods (Barzel, 1997).[6] Sellers and buyers of ordinary goods engage in a multitude of single transactions in markets characterized by a large number of sellers and buyers and perfect information. They are assumed to have perfect information and are therefore able to enforce their control over all attributes of the commodity.

The exchanges established in markets for commodities are exchanges of money for single specific goods with well-known properties. If purchase of labour by firms should be of this nature, transactions presumably establish payments for the execution of single tasks. One should imagine many workers, who bid for payments for performing tasks, while a number of firms are offering payments for the performance of tasks. When an agreement is reached, the task is performed and payment received. Next, the worker will look for another task (not necessarily with the same firm) while the firm will offer another task to the labour market. This scenario will assign prices for tasks that constitute wages for workers. Firms will be in competitive equilibrium when these prices equal the increase in the value of the product resulting from the performance of the tasks, or the marginal product. Employment contracts then are like sale contracts, where a payment is exchanged for a completed task.

Empirically, such scenarios are rare in labour markets, though there are situations that approximate them, for example the daily auctions for work that exist or have existed for dock workers. There is a huge literature in the economics and sociology of labour markets that attempts to provide more realistic scenarios for the description and understanding of labour markets. The approach here is to suggest that variation in the wealth created by employment relationships the major source of differentiation in the labour market.

For theoretical purposes, employment contracts for single tasks are of considerable interest. They establish a base line for determining the returns on the amount of wealth a person possesses when employment relations do not generate wealth and therefore forms a measure of the amount of personal wealth that is independent of the employment of the person. This base line is the market wage, determined by the productivity of the employee, and reflecting the effort, skills and abilities of the employee (where the latter are a source of rent). Since the exchange of labour for pay is for a short duration to complete a single task, there is the potential for high variability in the returns obtained in these 'spot-market' exchanges.

Most employment contracts are not like sales contracts. They are rental contracts. The employer rents the asset labour, or the productivity of the employee, from the owner, the employee, for a period of time. Employment relationships are then for a set of tasks to be performed in a period. The relationships define positions in a firm, which are jobs of some duration.[7]

Jobs emerge when tasks are less well defined and/or interconnected with other tasks. Firms then prefer to be able to direct the activities of workers. New tasks then can be dealt with as they emerge without new contracting, and activities can be coordinated in the execution of specific tasks. These advantages can be obtained employing workers over a period of time and establishing an employment contract for a job. In this contract, the employer, in return for a schedule of payments, is granted authority over the activities of the worker for the period (Simon, 1957).

The payment for the rental is established in an (often implicit) employment contract. The employment contract is usually incomplete, that is, it will not include provisions for all conceivable contingencies. This incompleteness is the origin of the transaction cost literature. The incompleteness allows the owner of the asset rented, the employee, to retain control of some part of what is being rented, for example the amount of effort. It also implies that there will arise a governance issue, that is the creation of an authority relationship to direct the worker and supervise her performance.

Since an employee typically will retain control of the part of his asset, labour, that is being rented, there is divided ownership of the asset. The concern of the employer is to get the highest output for the pay and other benefits offered, and also to minimize costs in the form of waste of raw materials, damage to equipment and the like. The concern of the employee is to maximize his benefit which is the pay, and other benefits, in relation to the cost of labour to him – the main costs being the disutility of effort, exposure to health hazards, and the alienation produced by supervision. With respect to the latter, it should be noted that Simon (1957) points out that the alienation costs of being subjected to authority under market competition should be compensated by a higher wage. This is, of course, the very opposite prediction of the Neo-Marxist idea of the effect of authority on wage differences (Wright, 1979).

The existence of an employment relationship for a job of some duration, or for a series of jobs, means that there is a joint advantage to the two parties of continuing the relationships. The advantage derives from the specific knowledge, skill and experience an employee possesses with the execution of the particular job she holds, and from the knowledge the firm has of the employee and her competencies. Both types of skills and knowledge are obtained at some costs and therefore represent investments the two parties have made in each other. When these investments are less useable elsewhere, both parties increase their returns by maintaining a long-term relationship.

The joint advantage of a continuing relationship is a composite rent as defined by Marshall ([1920], 1949), or a rent generated by asset specificity. In other words, there is a wealth available in the jointly controlled asset, the labour that is being rented by the employer from its owner, the employee. As pointed out by Marshall, the division of this joint advantage is a matter of 'higgling and bargaining' ([1920], 1949: 520). Since the advantage is a rent, the two parties have antagonistic interests. They each have strategies to increase their part of the composite rent.

The main strategies available to employees are to adjust effort, avoid exposure to health hazards, and take advantage of access to facilities, perks and tools made available by the employment. In managerial jobs, employees may themselves influence compensation schemes and gain access to fringe benefits and perks.

The employer has three main remedies at his disposal: (1) replace the employee with another producing more for the same pay; (2) direct the activities of the worker through supervision; and, (3) organize the job so that there are incentives for effort. Of course, the employer can alternatively reduce the composite rent joint advantage by redesigning jobs, to reduce the importance of job specific investments in the employee.

The three main strategies available to the employer all have costs. Supervision incurs pay to the supervisor and incentives usually add to the wage bill. These strategies will be discussed more fully below. Replacing the worker may seem the least costly and most effective strategy. The remedy, of course, destroys whatever returns are obtained from the composite rents generated in the employment and thus eliminates the joint advantage of the employment relationship. If dismissals are used frequently and in an arbitrary manner, we obtain a spot market relationship and this should only be efficient when there are no composite rents.[8] It follows that the expected duration of the employment relationship is an indicator of how much composite rent is available in the employment relationship. I shall refer to this property as the degree of closure of the employment relationship.

It is useful to consider a continuum defined by whether the employer or the employee typically has the initiative in terminating the contract. At one end of this continuum, the employer will dismiss the worker whenever a better worker is available for the job (one willing to work for a lower pay or more productive at the given pay). The employment relationship can then be said to be completely *open* to outsiders, and we have a competitive labour market. At the other end of the continuum, the worker will only be dismissed in exceptional circumstances, for example when the firm disappears. The employment relationship then is *closed* to outsiders.

The degree of closure is an indicator of the amount of wealth potentially available to the employee from the employment relationship. The amount of wealth obtained depends on the division of the composite rents with the employer, and therefore on the amount of supervision and on the effectiveness of incentives constructed by the employer.

The degree of closure is relevant for the amount of wealth obtained in employment in other ways. First, collective action by unions may obtain monopoly rents by restricting labour supply. The formation of the collective action is facilitated by closed employment relationships because this will ensure some stability of membership in the union. Also, the ability of restricting labour supply is facilitated by closed employment and well-defined jobs because potential employees will typically queue for closed jobs, as described below. Finally, closed-jobs make it easier to realize monopoly rents on restrictions of training opportunities, for example in apprenticeship systems.

Second, closed employment enhances the individual's ability to increase her wealth by getting access to better jobs. An important career implication of closed positions is that workers only need to move to another job when a better job is available. This creates a growth pattern similar to the one predicted by human capital theory, with attainment peaking in middle age (Sørensen, 1977). Thus, closed jobs not only increase the opportunity for wealth acquisition in the current job. Closed employment also increases the individual's ability for taking advantage of opportunities in acquiring more wealth over the career.

I will now discuss in more detail how the wealth of a person depends on the employment contract she obtains. The discussion is organized around the expected duration of the employment relationships. I shall first comment further on the scenario contracting for specific tasks and open jobs. Next, I will discuss the scenario where the employment is for a longer, indefinite duration for a set of tasks, that is, for a job. Finally, I consider the scenario created by contracts for a sequence of jobs, or a career.

Employment contracts for single tasks

When employment contracts are established for single tasks in a competitive labour market, there are no stable rents created by employment relationships. Friction in the labour market may create quasi-rents, presumably of short duration. The wealth of individuals is given by their personal wealth acquired outside of the labour market. Part of the personal wealth may be rents, but they will be rents on abilities, endowments and skills not connected to employment relationships.

In such a labour market structure, it does not matter to the employer whether the employee works hard or shirks. The market will adjust the pay to the level of effort and the employer can be indifferent to who is hired and how hard the employee works. Supervision, and the creation of incentives, is therefore not a problem for employees.

It is tempting to see such labour markets as the labour markets of the poor. However, this is not a correct inference. Persons have no wealth from employment relations, but may, of course, have considerable wealth from their human capital and abilities. Artisans and craft workers are often in markets for single tasks, so are many professionals, such as doctors, lawyers and accountants. They sell a service, the completion of a specific task, in an open market. When the task is completed, the association between the two parties of the transaction may cease. These high skilled groups may be self-employed or employed. When they are employed, their relationship with the firm is a peculiar one, quite different from the 'normal' employment relationship. These high skilled groups have a very high degree of autonomy, even when they are not self-employed, consistent with the contracts for single tasks.

The usual employment relationship for jobs and careers involve the rental of the asset labour from the employee by the firms. When employed, the high skilled and autonomous professional and craft groups are better seen as renting their tools of production from the firm. These firms are usually partnerships formed to establish office facilities, client lists, and certain equipment. Partners contribute part of their revenue to the firm as payment for the rental. Partners are very concerned about having partners that make the best of their rentals. Performance is difficult to evaluate both because of the complexity of tasks executed and because of the autonomy. The result is that promotion to partner takes place only after quite long probationary periods in up-or-out systems.

Skills are obtained by training and education. Training has costs in the form of direct outlays to tuition and fees, and in the form of earnings foregone while in training. These costs represent investments in human capital. In a competitive labour market, competition will equalize returns on these investments. Above-average returns on certain skills, or levels and types of education, will result in an increase in the number of people acquiring these skills. Life-time earnings will be the same for all even though there may be cross-sectional inequalities by level of skills. In a perfectly competitive market personal wealth will tend to become equal, except for inequalities produced by unequal socioeconomic endowments from the family of origin and whatever rents people obtain on their abilities and skills.

Banks are reluctant to finance human capital investments, because of their riskiness, and will therefore charge a higher interest rate than for other investments, if they will support such investments at all. Inequalities in socioeconomic endowments therefore create unequal training costs, favouring those with the means to finance their human capital investments from their own endowments and creating rents to those with such endowments from their families of origin.

Rents relevant for people's earnings are not derived from employment relationships in such labour markets, but are part of people's personal wealth. They obtain from restrictions of supply by nature or culture, as rents on abilities, or from restrictions by social organization, as rents on skills when training opportunities for these skills are limited directly or indirectly (through influence on admission policies) by professions, guilds or unions.

Abilities create rents in two ways. Abilities may directly affect pay because they are unusual and in demand. This would be the case for unusual talents in the arts, sports and the like. Ability may also have an indirect effect by reducing training costs. In both cases unusual abilities command a rent that is not eliminated by the market. However, such rents are not attached to positions defined by employment relationships. No reorganization of society will re-organize the distribution of innate and unique talents. A class of concert pianists or Larry Birds is not likely to emerge. However, a social organization of rent receivers may come about from an organization of those who obtain rents on their skills.

Suppose training opportunities for certain skills are in limited supply because of restricted admissions to schools and apprenticeships. Then cumulated lifetime earnings as returns on human capital will not be equal in competitive labour markets. Those possessing the skills for which training opportunities are restricted, will obtain an advantage that is a rent. It will be a higher return on the skill than would be necessary to bring about training for the skill. There are numerous examples of situations where this seems to occur. The training needed to enter a profession is usually not available to everyone who wishes and is able to undertake that training. Similarly, the apprenticeship training that provides access to crafts and other skilled occupations is usually only available to candidates meeting certain criteria. These criteria may have very little to do with candidates' qualifications for the training. The candidate's father, for example, needs to be a member of the union controlling the training programme. The stability of monopoly rents on skills usually depends on the effective enforcement of restrictions on the employment of skills, eliminating employment of skills not acquired by the proper training institutions. These rents therefore need the support of some agency to persist. For professions and some crafts, this agency is typically the state, using licencing to ration access to employment of the skills. For other groups, access to employment of the skills depends on the existence of employment relationships of some stability, to be considered below.

Rents on skills thus generate classes, but they are created outside the labour market.[9] The relevance of skill classes, for labour market processes, depends on the existence of employment contracts other than the employment for single tasks. These employment relationships are considered next.

Employment relations for closed jobs

There are two types of closed employment relations to consider: (1) closed single jobs and (2) closed employment relations for careers. The second type represents a particular solution to the incentive problems caused by closed employment relationships. Closed careers are jobs organized into sequences of jobs in an internal labour market for incentive reasons. These job structures will be considered in the next section. Here the focus is on closed single jobs that create flat careers in terms of job titles and occupational status, though not necessarily in terms of earnings, as shown below. These job structures are typical of many semi-skilled and skilled blue-collar occupations, and also of lower white-collar work. The firms using closed employment relationships form a primary sector of the labour markets, while those firms establishing open employment relationships forming the secondary or competitive sector, to use a distinction often employed in the labour market literature.

There are several sources of the rents that create closed employment relationships and closed jobs. Jobs may be closed by collective or union action without a basis in the technological and organizational factors that create composite rents. This would, for example, occur if a farm workers' union succeeded in controlling the labour supply to unskilled work in the fields and in this way creating pure monopoly rents. A pure monopoly rent is to the advantage of the employees only. The employer therefore has a direct interest in destroying such rents by eliminating the restrictions of labour supply imposed by the union. The relative political strength of the two parties determines the outcome. If destruction of the union is not possible, or not advantageous, the issue becomes one of determining the distribution of the rent.

In many cases the destruction of union power is not advantageous or feasible because the effect of union action on the creation of rents is confounded with the effect of technical and organizational forces that create composite rents reflecting a mutual advantage. The 'higgling and bargaining' process identified by Marshall ([1920], 1949) then applies. The bargaining is about obtaining the greatest share of the mutual advantage. There are basically three strategies for the employer to pursue all meant to obtain the most output at the lowest possible labour cost: (1) hire the worker likely to be the most productive in the long run; (2) adjust the pay of the worker to the productivity of the worker; and (3) set the pay and other job rewards so as to obtain the maximum productivity from the worker. The employee has symmetrical interests in obtaining the highest level of job rewards available at the lowest costs. Here the main cost usually considered is effort. Other costs, such as alienation, isolation, and exposure to health hazards presumably are relevant too, though these costs usually are ignored in the literature on these matters.

An alternative to 'higgling and bargaining' is of course to destroy the composite rents. This will involve a cost to the employer, but the long term advantage of not having to share any advantage with the employee, may outweigh that cost. Such destruction usually involves changes in technology and/or work organization. It is an important Neo-Marxist idea that the way capitalism increases exploitation is by deskilling of work (Braverman, 1974). A general trend toward deskilling has never been established, despite many attempts, nor does it make theoretical sense that employers inevitably stand to gain by reducing the general level of skills required. However, reducing composite rents due to specific on-the-job training would be a plausible strategy and it is quite likely that deskilling could be documented with respect to the specific skills that create composite rents (see Sørensen, 1996), though nobody has tried to document this.

The first of the three strategies for increasing the employer's share of the composite rent is to hire the person expected to be the most productive for the job. This can be seen as an issue of matching people to closed jobs.

Matching people to jobs

When the match of a person to a job is expected to be of longer duration, the problem for the firm is one of predicting future productivity. The actual performance will not be known before the worker is on the job and has completed job and firm specific training. Therefore, observable characteristics of the worker believed to be correlated with future performance, and/or are believed to be relevant for the cost of providing the job and firm specific training, will be used to rank candidates for the job, in a 'labour queue' (Thurow, 1975). It is commonly accepted in the large literature on screening that this implies a reliance on easily observable characteristics, in particular educational credentials, but also characteristics such as race, ethnicity and gender thought to be providing information about expected performance. Closed jobs create rent seeking as zero-sum competition for positional goods (Hirsch, 1976) in what I have called vacancy competition (Sørensen, 1983).

Matching based on rankings means that more of whatever is considered a relevant characteristic is better when the primary concern is to predict future performance or trainability for the tasks of the job (Thurow, 1975). It is commonly argued that workers will queue for the vacant positions and employers pick the highest ranked in the queue. This poses the problem of why workers will queue to begin with. Efficiency wage theory (Akerlof and Yellen, 1986) suggests that some firms offer above market wages for vacant jobs in order to ensure a superior work force thus creating queues of candidates for vacant positions.[10] This is a restatement of the basic argument here that closed jobs provide a composite rent that will make the employee better off than under market competition.

Queuing creates interdependence among people. The particular worker's characteristics in relation to characteristics of other workers in the queue matters. Consider education. It will not be the absolute level of education that matters for access to jobs and the wage rate, but the educational qualification relative to those of other workers. There are strong cohort differences in the distribution of educational attainments. Queuing suggests that educational attainments should be measured in a manner standardizing for the overall attainment of the cohort because the same level in terms of years of schooling will provide a different rank for different cohorts. This simple idea is rarely implemented (for exceptions see Lieberson, 1978, Sørensen, 1979), even though the conventional metric of years of schooling assumes the validity of the labour market scenario of human capital theory.

Queuing for vacancies in closed primary jobs suggests an explanation for the persistence of discrimination, high youth unemployment, the continued increase in schooling, and a number of other labour market phenomena. It nevertheless is not an idea that has interested sociologists doing quantitative research on career outcomes a great deal.

Hiring the most promising from a queue of candidates does not ensure an adequate performance once in the job. A strategy to reduce the worker's share of the composite rent is to adjust pay to performance. Another is to adjust performance to pay. The latter involves two strategies. One is supervision and direction of the activities of the employee. As noted this requires outlays to the wage of a supervisor, may create alienation, and impose other costs. Though supervision is probably inevitable in most closed employment relationships, I will concentrate here on the strategies that do not involve supervision.

Performance reflects partly a person's effort, partly his willingness to take on new and unfamiliar tasks including training for these tasks. For simplicity I shall below discuss the main ideas about strategies to affect performance as strategies for eliciting effort.

There is a large literature that proposes theories for payments schemes designed to elicit superior performance (see Sørensen, 1994, for a review). Much of this literature sees the issue as an instance of the principal-agent problem. In other words, the problem is one for the employer of creating an employment contract that will elicit desired performance in the employee. There are three types of payment schemes of particular interest here: Efficiency wages, so-called rank-order tournament schemes, and payment by output. Efficiency-wage theory will be discussed below and rank order tournament schemes are characteristic of employment contracts for careers. Here I will briefly note the main issue in adjusting pay to performance as measured either by output, in terms of actual amount produced in a period, or to performance measured by input, but using a ranking of effort.

Adjusting pay to performance

A straightforward and well-known strategy to increase the employers' share of the composite rent is to make wages directly dependent on output in the form of piece rates. Workers get paid for what they produce. It may seem possible that a properly designed piece rate system could bring about the situation of the competitive labour market: Employers need not worry about performance or whom they hire, only about setting the piece rates so that they minimize labour costs. Should this arrangement be feasible all the advantage goes to the employer and workers obtain no rent.

Piece rate systems often do not work in the manner just described. The effort of an individual worker constitutes an externality to other workers because it provides information to the employer about how much effort can be obtained. The result is the establishment of production norms so richly documented in the industrial sociology literature on piece rate systems.

There are other problems with piece rates. Uncertainty in production such as failures of machines and shortages of raw material becomes costs charged to the worker alone. A wage floor is often adopted to mitigate this, but then the pure piece rate system has disappeared. Workers' incentive is to maximize quantity of production over quality of production and they may disregard tool and machine maintenance that may lower output. Co-operation among workers may be difficult to obtain under piece rate systems.

Piece rate systems depend on measurability of output. Measurability may not be achievable, because of the nature of the output, or because of interdependence of production. The performance evaluation that is to be linked to the wage then has to be done by evaluating inputs. This may also be found desirable when output measurement produces wrong incentives or when uncertainty in production is a major problem. Instead of measuring how much is done, the employer will try to measure how hard a person tries. The result is a variety of rating systems used to establish merit pay and promotion schemes, many apparently quite ineffective. The most important and effective system is the promotion system discussed in the next section. Before it is considered, I will discuss the possibility of linking performance to pay, rather than pay to performance, however measured.

Adjusting performance to pay

The rent provided by the employment relationships for closed-jobs by the very definition of rent provides the employee with an above market wage. *Efficiency wage theory* suggests that this above the competitive wage by itself will be an incentive for effort. The increase in effort increases productivity and the rent share to the worker is reduced, if not eliminated. There are several different explanations for the incentive effect of above market wages. The most common explanation for this relationship is that the worker will not be able to find alternative employment at the same pay, with this higher wage, should he be dismissed for shirking. Thus, fear of unemployment creates the relationship between wage and effort. Indeed, the efficiency wage theory is usually introduced as a way to explain the persistence of unemployment and wage rigidity that always has been a puzzle for standard theory (Solow, 1979; Akerlof and Yellen, 1986).

There is evidently something of a paradox here. Closed jobs are jobs with high job security. The employer reduces the worker's rent share by threatening to dismiss the worker for shirking. Acting on this threat, by dismissing the worker, reduces the rent advantage to the employer. The gain to the employer is greatest if the threat is not acted upon, but that evidently makes the threat less believable to the worker, and the incentive effect will disappear. Some non-linear relationship between degree of closure and the elimination of the rent advantage to the worker is evidently assumed for this version of efficiency wage theory to go through.

This version of efficiency wage theory has the implication that the rate of entering re-employment should depend on the duration of unemployment spells in a particular manner. The rate of re-employment should first decline as the worker is less and less likely to obtain a job where he can recapture the employment rent. When the worker eventually lowers his aspirations, the rate of re-employment should start to increase. This corresponds to the pattern found empirically (Sørensen, 1990) for unemployment spells originating in industries with mostly closed jobs. Another implication of the threat mechanism is that productivity should vary with the rate of unemployment, over time and across industries with closed employment relationships. Evidence for such a pattern has been reported by Rebitzer (1987).

There is a different explanation for efficiency wages suggested by Akerlof (1982) using reference group theory – workers compare their situation to the one of similar workers elsewhere and react accordingly. If the workers feel well treated in these comparisons, they return their appreciation for the 'fair' wage in higher effort and the rent share they obtain is reduced. There is, surprisingly, no quantitative evidence available on these mechanisms in the sociology of labour markets, despite the apparent plausibility of the arguments to sociologists.

The supervisory and rating mechanisms for adjusting pay to performance, and the threat and reference group mechanisms of adjusting performance to pay, reduce the worker's share of the composite rents generated in closed employment relationships. The rent share may even be eliminated if workers' pay is made to reflect their productivity. There will be variation across employers in the degree of success, and there will be variation over time created by changes in managerial styles and in technology. The emergence of stable exploitation class categories in the labour market will depend on the extent to which this variation over time and across firms prevents the formation of collective action.

The most stable source of positional advantage and hence of class interests probably are rents on skills preserved by closed employment relationships. The rents generated by restrictions on training opportunities for skilled and craft occupations will not be eliminated by supervision or incentive schemes. These are the positions that form the traditional basis for unions and other collective movements. Strangely, these are not the positions that have received attention in the use of class analysis in the sociology of labour markets (see Berg and Kalleberg, 1987) for a review. Here the attention has been on employment positions identified by authority over others (supervisors and managers), or by the absence of being subjected to authority – the semi-autonomous employees in Wright's first class scheme (1979). Authority, I argued earlier, does not identify rents as sources of positional advantages and class interests. Wright's concept of semi-autonomous employees can be considered as groups that obtain efficiency wages, and hence composite rents. However, they are usually not considered in the empirical research and later abandoned by Wright (1985) as a class category.

Employment contracts for careers

The incentive problem created by closed employment relationships has an important solution that deserves to be treated separately because of its importance in research on class locations in the labour market. The solution is the establishment of employment contracts for sequences of jobs that form promotion ladders in internal labour markets.

It is an old idea among sociologists that promotion schemes can be important for generating effort (Weber, 1968; Stinchcombe, 1974). The effort generating mechanism is captured in the idea of a rank-order tournament (eg, Lazear and Rosen, 1981). A set of candidates competes for a promotion and the candidate ranked highest will achieve the promotion. The ranking is in terms of actual or expected performance. In these tournaments, the effort of an actor, A, acts as incentive to actor B in the contest for career outcomes. If A works hard, B must also work hard to maintain his or her chance for a promotion.

There is a fair amount of theory about what determines the incentive effect of tournaments (see, for example, Lazear, 1995). Two main determinants are the size of the prize, ie, the value of the promotion to the contestant, and the probability of success – the more evenly matched the contestants, the more effort is generated. For the employer, the size of the prize is a cost and therefore reduces the benefit of the promotion. It is here important that relative status is probably a more salient prize than salary gain (Frank, 1985) and the promotion tournament therefore is often organized as a contest about positions with different job titles and perks. Less attention has been focused on when such tournaments become ineffective. This can happen when the incentive effect produced by the interdependency of outcomes in tournaments is overcome by collective manipulation of effort. To see this, it is useful to consider the structure of competition in a tournament as a prisoner's dilemma game. Actors A and B face the following pay-off matrix depending on whether they show high effort (HE) or low effort (LE):

		B	
		HE	LE
A	HE	(2, 2)	(4, 1)
	LE	(1, 4)	(3, 3)

Here the entries are satisfaction units that are functions both of the costs of effort and the chance of promotion. The lower the cost and the higher the probability promotion, the higher the satisfaction. Actor, A, reasons that if he shows effort and B does not, his satisfaction will be four. B reasons the same, and they will end up in the HE, HE situation both displaying high effort with lower probability of promotion. This is the reason tournaments can work. However, if both A and B can agree to show low effort, they will achieve a higher satisfaction (3, 3) since the probability of promotion will be the same as in the HE, HE cell and the cost of effort is lower. The agreement is obviously very vulnerable to defection. So, such agreements to be effective demands effective sanctioning. This implies that stable groups of candidates are more likely to set up such collective manipulations of efforts. However, the stability of the group of candidates depends itself on the rate of promotion. The higher the rate, the lower the stability. Higher rates of promotion lower the incentive value of the promotion. Firms therefore need to find an optimum with not too high rates and not too low rates to elicit the most effort, and therefore gain the largest share of the composite rent embodied in the employment relationship.

The rent share is obviously dependent on the costs of providing the wage increases that accompany promotions. The job ladders create an upward-sloping career trajectory. If the promotion incentive is effective, the productivity will be higher, but there is no reason to believe it will increase (other than as a result of on-the-job training and experience). Hence the rent share accruing to the employee will be increasing. Firms can capture more of the overall rent by paying younger workers less than their productivity would justify elsewhere, in effect paying negative rents. If this strategy is successful, the overall outcome may well be one where there is no advantage in life time income for the employee of entering an internal labour market. In other words, the firm will then have maximized its overall share of the composite rent. The situation is much the same as the one predicted by human capital theory in open employment systems. Here the inequality observed in the cross-section will also misinform about the overall advantage.

There is a second, and less formal, reason for why positional interests in internal labour markets are less likely to lead to collective action. Promotion schemes make individuals compete rather than cooperate. They work because the effort of one person becomes the incentive for the effort of another. Occupants of internal labour markets will not act to preserve positional advantages at a certain level in the hierarchy. This is, of course, the reason internal labour markets can be seen as social control mechanisms (Edwards, 1979). However, the conception of internal labour markets as a social control mechanism does not imply that internal labour markets establish locations for exploitation classes.

Conclusion

Two class concepts have been proposed both based on rights to returns on assets. Class as living-condition is the concept used in most empirical research focusing on class as a determinant of individual behavior and mentalities. Class as exploitation is the concept of class emphasized by Marxist analysis where classes are seen as conflict groups. Class as living-condition is based on a person's total wealth. For many outcomes such as investments in schooling and health, the variability of this wealth is of particular importance. Class as exploitation is based on a person's property rights to rent producing assets since rents provide an advantage to the holder of these rights at the expense of those not holding the rights.

The treatment of class as living-conditions has been less of a concern here. It follows from the general argument that the total wealth of people, and hence their position in terms of class as living-conditions, will be increased by closed employment relations. Further, such employment relations will also reduce the variability of returns. Therefore, we should expect that persons with substantial personal wealth from human capital and rents on skills in closed employment relationships should show the greatest tendency to invest in their own and their children's health and education. This corresponds well to what is observed. We should also expect that for a given level of personal wealth persons with more open employment relationships, or the self-employed should be less willing to provide long term investments in their offspring. This creates the non-vertical dimensions of class emphasized by, for example, Goldthorpe (1987).

My main concern has been to show how employment relations create rents and therefore may create class locations within the labour market that have antagonistic interests. Two types of rents are of interest here: Composite rents created by asset specificity and monopoly rents created by collective action by unions and professional associations.

Rent advantages to employees are costs to employers. However, in the case of composite rents employers also gain an advantage. The creation of employment relationships of some duration is an indication that such joint advantages exist. In closed employment relationships the issue for the employer is therefore to obtain as much of the joint advantage as possible. Efficiency wage theory suggests that the rent advantage by itself may act as an incentive because of the potential loss if the advantage is lost. I have shown how, in addition, supervision and a variety of incentive schemes try to increase the share to the employer. This rent, including piece-rate systems and the promotion schemes found in internal labour markets. To the extent that these strategies are successful, rents to employees are reduced or eliminated. It is therefore not possible to generally identify stable exploitation classes in the labour market based on composite rents, as proposed by in the Neo-Marxist proposals by Wright (1979, 1985) and his followers.

As an alternative to increasing the share of composite rents, employers may destroy these rents by eliminating the technical and organizational arrangements that create composite rents. Destruction of internal labour markets has been a widespread phenomenon in the last decade in a wave of downsizing suggesting that it is to the advantage of the capitalist class to produce a labour market with open employment relationships conforming to the assumptions about the labour market of neo-classical economics.

Monopoly rents in the labour market are of two kinds. There are rents obtained by restrictions of supply of the quantity of labour created by unions and other collective movements and there are rents on the quality of labour, or rents on skills for which training opportunities are rationed. The latter depend usually on closed employment relations or on licensing by the state for their maintenance. There has been a clear trend toward the reduction of union power in US labour markets suggesting that a reduction of this type of monopoly rents has also been achieved. Rents on skills may also have been reduced by the creation of more open employment relationships. There is indeed evidence for a tighter relationship between wages and productivity in the 1980s than in the 1970s (Levy and Murnane, 1992).

The elimination of employment rents should mean overall greater economic efficiency and unpredictable lives for individual workers. This increases the inequality of incomes and hence the inequality between class locations in terms of living-conditions. We should therefore expect not only an increase in inequality in overall wealth but also an increase in the inequality of the investments in human capital done by families which will perpetuate the increase in inequality into the next generation.

Notes

1 For recent examples, see Scott (1996), Goldthorpe (1987), Clement and Myles (1994), Wright (1985) and the reader by Grusky (1994).

2 Stand was translated by Gerth and Mills (1946) as status-group, adding to the terminological confusion. Parsons translated 'stand' as social class, and Weber's 'klasse' as economic class. This makes eminent sense given the traditional meaning of social class in American Sociology.

3 Coleman (1990) in fact proved the existence and properties of the general competitive equilibrium using a simpler approach than usually adopted.

4 This is the typical arrangement. As shown by Barzel (1997), matters may be more complicated dependent on the type of contact that exists between the peasant and the landlord. For example, under certain arrangements, the peasant may obtain advantages at the expense of the landlord, by depleting nutrients from the ground.

5 There is recent evidence from a population survey (Dominitz and Manski, 1997) that people's feeling of insecurity vary among population groups exactly as one would predict from the distribution of wealth and variability of wealth returns.

6 Barzel (1997) points out that goods may have properties that are not known at the time of transaction because it is too costly the ascertain them. His example is a batch of cherries in a store that vary in quality. Picking and choosing allows the customer to gain the advantage of leaving the quality of cherries to vary and therefore to gain wealth. Barzel (1997) also shows that in the exchange of ordinary goods not all attributes are exchanged. The seller may retain rights to some aspect of the goods, for example in warranty arrangements.

7 In some cases, the employment relationships will cover a series of jobs, or a career, to be discussed below.

8 Maintaining some threat of dismissal may be a device used by employers to increase effort, as discussed below.

9 It is important to note that unequal returns on skills by themselves do not suggest the creation of exploitation classes. It is the rent part that is important, not the total return as suggested by Roemer (1983) and by Wright (1985). The total return creates life-condition classes, but these classes are not of much interest to Neo-Marxists.

10 As is discussed below, concern for labour quality is only one of the reasons for the emergence of efficiency wages.

References

Ainslie, G., (1992), *Piconomics*. New York: Cambridge University Press.

Akerlof, G.A., (1981), 'Labor Contracts as Partial Gift Exchange', *Quarterly Journal of Economics*, vol. 97 No. 2: 543–69.

Akerlof, G.A. and Yellen, J.L., (1986), 'Introduction', pp. 1–21 in G.A. Akerlof and J.L. Yellen (eds) *Efficiency Wage Models of the Labor Market*, New York: Cambridge University Press.

Barzel, Y., (1997), *Economic Analysis of Property Rights*, 2nd edition, New York: Cambridge University Press.

Bourdieu, P., (1977), *Reproduction in Education, Society and Culture*, Beverly Hills, CA: Sage.

Braverman, H., (1974), *Labor and Monopoly Capital*, New York: Monthly Review Press.

Clement, W. and Myles, J., (1994), *Relations of Ruling: Class and Gender in Postindustrial Societies*, Montreal: McGill-Queen's University Press.

Coleman, J.S., (1990), *The Foundations of Social Theory*, Cambridge, MA: The Belknap Press of Harvard University Press.

Dahrendorf, R., (1959), *Class and Class Conflict in Industrial Society*, Stanford, CA: Stanford University Press.

Dominitz, J. and Manski, C.F., (1997), 'Perceptions of Economic Insecurity: Evidence from the Survey of Economic Expectations', *Public Opinion Quarterly*, 61: 261–287.

Edwards, R., (1979), *Contested Terrain*, New York: Basic Books.

Frank, R.H., (1985), *Choosing the Right Pond: Human Behaviour and the Quest for Status*, Oxford: Oxford University Press.

Geiger, T.J., (1932), *Die Soziale Schichtung Des Deutschen Volkes: Soziographischer Versuch auf Statistischer Grundlage*, Stuttgart: F. Enke.

Giddens, A., (1973), *The Class Structure of the Advanced Society*, London: Hutchinson.

Goldthorpe, J., (1987), *Social Mobility and Class Structure in Modern Britain*, 2nd Edition, Oxford: Clarendon Press.

Goldthorpe, J.H. and Hope, K., (1974), *The Social Grading of Occupations: A New Approach and Scale*, Oxford: Clarendon Press.

Gordon, M.M., (1958), *Social Class in American Sociology*, Durham, N.C.: Duke University Press.

Grusky, D. (ed.), (1994), *Social Stratification: Class, Race and Gender*, Boulder, CO: Westview.

Halbwachs, M., (1913), *Les classe ouvrière et les niveaux de vie*, Paris: F. Alcan.

Halbwachs, M., (1925), *Les cadres sociaux de la mémoire*, Paris: F. Alcan.

Hirsch, F., (1976), *The Social Limits to Growth*, Cambridge, MA: Harvard University Press.

Hollingshead, A., (1949), *Elmtown's Youth: the Impact of Social Classes on Adolescents*, New York: J. Wiley.

Hollingshead, A. and Redlich, F.C., (1958), *Social Class and Mental Illness*, New York: Wiley.

Kalleberg, A.L. and Berg, I., (1987), *Work and Industry: Structures, Markets and Processes*, New York: Plenum.

Lazear, E.P., (1995), *Personnel Economics*, Cambridge, MA: The MIT Press.

Lazear, E.P. and Rosen, S., (1981), 'Rank-Order Tournaments as Optimum Labor Contracts', *Journal of Political Economy*, vol. 89 No. 2: 841–864.

Levy, F. and Murnane, R.J., (1992), 'U.S. Earnings Levels and Earnings Inequality: A Review of Recent Trends and Proposed Explanations', *Journal of Economic Literature*, 30: 1333–81.

Lieberson, S., (1978), 'A Reconsideration of the Income Differences Found Between Migrants and Northern-born Blacks', *American Journal of Sociology*, vol. 83 (1978): 940–966.

Lynd, R.S. and Lynd, H.M., (1956), *Middletown: a Study in American Culture*, New York: Harcourt, Brace, Jovanovich.

Marshall, A., (1920), *Principles of Economics*, 8th Edition, reprinted 1949, London: Macmillan.

Rebitzer, J.B., (1987), 'Unemployment, Long-Term Employment Relations, and Productivity Growth', *Review of Economics and Statistics*, vol. 69: 627–35.

Ritzer, G., (1994), *Modern Sociological Theory*, New York: McGraw-Hill.

Roemer, J., (1982), *A General Theory of Exploitation and Class*, Cambridge, Mass: Harvard University Press.

Ryan, W., (1971), *Blaming the Victim*, New York: Orbach & Chambers.

Schneider, L. and Lysgaard, S., (1953), 'The Deferred Gratification Pattern', *American Sociological Review*, vol. 18.

Scott, J., (1996), *Stratification and Power*, Cambridge: Polity Press.

Simon, H., (1957), 'The Employment Relation', in *Models of Man*, New York: Wiley.

Solow, R.M., (1979), 'Another Possible Source of Wage Stickiness', *Journal of Macroeconomics* 1(2): 79–82.

Sørensen, A.B., (1977), 'The Structure of Inequality and the Process of Attainment', *American Sociological Review*, 42: 965–978.

Sørensen, A.B., (1979), 'A Model and a Metric for the Analysis of the Intragenerational Status Attainment Process', *American Journal of Sociology*, 85, 2: 361–384.

Sørensen, A.B., (1983), 'Processes of Allocation to Open and Closed Positions in Social Structure', *Zeitschrift für Soziologie*, 12 (July): 203–224.

Sørensen, A.B., (1990), 'Employment Sector and Unemployment Processes', pp. 96–112 in Mayer, K.U. and Tuma, N.B. (eds) *Applications of Event History Analysis to Life Course Research*, Madison, WI: University of Wisconsin Press.

Sørensen, A.B., (1994), 'Firms, Wages and Incentives', pp. 504–528 in Smelser, N.J. and Swedberg, R. (eds) *Handbook of Economic Sociology*, Princeton University Press.

Sørensen, A.B., (1996), 'The Structural Basis of Social Inequality', *American Journal of Sociology*, 101 (5, March): 1333–65.

Sørensen, A.B., (1997), 'Towards a Sounder Basis for Class Analysis', paper presented at the ECRS Conference on 'Rational Action Theory in Social Analysis: Applications and New Developments', Långholmen, Stockholm, October 16–20, 1997.

Stinchcombe, A.L., (1974), *Creating Efficient Industrial Administrations*, New York: Academic Press.

Thurow, L.C., (1975), *Generating Inequality*, New York: Basic Books.

Warner, W., Meeker, L.M. and Eells, K., (1949), *Social Class in America*, New York: Science Research Associates.

Weber, M., (1946), 'Class, Status and Power', pp. 180–95 in *From Max Weber: Essays in Sociology*, edited and translated by Gerth, H.H. and Mills, C.W., New York: Oxford University Press.

Weber, M., (1947), *The Theory of Social and Economic Organization*, translated by Henderson, A.M. and Parsons, T., New York: Oxford University Press.

Williamson, O.E., (1985), *The Economic Institutions of Capitalism*, New York: The Free Press.

Wright, E.O., (1979), *Class Structure and Income Determination*, New York: Academic Press.

Wright, E.O., (1985), *Classes*, London: New Left Books.

Wright, E.O., (1986), 'What is Middle About the Middle Class' pp. 114–40 in *Analytical Marxism*, edited by Roemer, J., New York: Cambridge University Press.

Social position from narrative data

Jonathan Gershuny

In what follows I develop a simple continuously scaled indicator of social position, an individual-level index of human capital, estimated as the potential hourly wage that this might command in the UK in the mid 1990s. I then compare the performance of this as a predictor of life chances (in the areas of finance and health) with a conventional class indicator designed for this purpose (the continuous indicator in fact performs approximately as well as the categorical class indicator), and I illustrate the usefulness of the continuously scaled indicator through a model of historical change in the impact of work-breaks on women's economic resources.

Pragmatic requirements, *not* the Boat Race

I am concerned that what follows should not be seen as part of the ongoing disputation between the categorical Oxford (Erikson and Goldthorpe, 1992) class schema and the continuous Cambridge Scale (Prandy, 1990). In fact, though it is continuously scaled, the sort of indicator I am proposing has a great deal in common with the class schema. I set out the theoretical rationale for my proposal in the next section: I do not claim that it is particularly original, its roots go back at least to the work of Blau and Duncan, and irrespective of the theoretical justification, it is developed for a number of straightforwardly pragmatic reasons connected to the new analytical possibilities that come with household panel data. What I have to argue reflects the advantages of longitudinal (particularly prospective) household level datasets over cross-sectional individual-level datasets for the understanding of the effect of social position on future prospects. To exploit these advantages effectively, I seek an indicator of social position that adequately reflects small changes in personal circumstances as well as large ones, that has even and comprehensive coverage of the whole (adult) population, and is readily and appropriately aggregable to a household level.

Panel studies give repeated, and in some cases temporally continuous, measurements of individuals' circumstances across a number of different spheres of life. These allow us to construct quite detailed accounts of the gradual process of accumulation of characteristics related to future life chances, of a sort that the discrete categories of a class schema are not designed to provide. Theories about human capital would lead us to expect that it is not simply the nature of the current job or, where there is none, the most recent previous job, that will best predict future life-chances but, rather, a more detailed long-term account of duration and trajectories in particular jobs and occupations, as well as training, and of the negative effects of dismissal and unemployment. So, for example, a recent period spent unsuccessfully seeking work that precedes the current job, indicates a relatively high probability of future misfortune, as compared with someone with the same job and no recent history of unemployment. And someone with a long period of non-employment preceded by a particular sort of job, certainly has different life-prospects to someone who currently holds that same job.

And starting from a particular job-situation at a particular point in life, individuals might have a wide range of different experiences outside the labour market, in the educational, family, recreation and health spheres, which might be expected to affect their subsequent life chances. Where more detailed information on both employment history and salient experiences in other spheres of life is available, why concentrate exclusively on the implications of just the current or immediately previous job? (However it is analytically helpful to distinguish the effects of labour market experiences from those in other spheres of life; this chapter therefore concentrates largely on the labour-market experiences together with the closely related experiences in education and those aspects of family life that impinge directly on labour market participation.)

Members of households may make collective decisions to maximize joint life-prospects by specializing in particular activities ('household work strategies': Pahl, 1984). If the individual-level indicator we develop is continuously scaled, and also interpersonally comparable, then we can straightforwardly sum the scores across the members of households to estimate the success or otherwise of such decision-making. Individuals may gain advantages from the economies of scale that arise from their membership of households – so under some circumstances it may be helpful to substitute an 'equivalized' household score for the individual score as a predictor of future welfare outcomes.

Proponents of the 'Class Programme' of sociological research (Goldthorpe and Marshall, 1992) may reasonably object that much of the above misses their point, which is a specific hypothesis, to the effect that it is the individuals' membership of the particular collectivities identified by the class scheme that causes particular outcomes over the lifecourse, and that the events and circumstances of the lifecourse that I would wish to use to construct my index of social position, are in essence no more than emanations of the original class location. I can readily accept that this hypothesis is an interesting one, and in principle a testable one. But such a test is not part of my intention in what follows. I am content to view the continuous and the categorical measures of social position, as physicists do the wave and the particle conceptualizations of light, as alternatives appropriate for the solution of different sorts of problem. I contend simply that, as ever, new instruments enable new science: household panel studies allow us to develop distinct sorts of indicators of social position, that can be used for new and different sorts of analysis.

Theoretical background

By 'social position' I mean a set of circumstances which gives an individual access to a particular range of future production and consumption activities. Social position has two aspects; on one hand it refers to a set of characteristics possessed by an individual, a set of skills and capacities and understandings; and on the other hand if refers to a set of answering characteristics of social institutions (firms, clubs, leisure services, political parties, religious institutions) – the characteristics take the form of rules of eligibility (eg, for membership or employment) or of functional requirements (possession of skills, formal qualifications, tastes etc.) which allow the individual to participate in the activities of those institutions. Neither of these two aspects is constant over time. Individuals accumulate characteristics (skills, educational certificates, tastes, habits) which may qualify them to participate in the activities of the institutions – or indeed disqualify them (as where the experience of unemployment acts as a negative signal to prospective employers). And the institutions of the society may develop new rules of eligibility, and undergo technological or organizational change that lead to new functional requirements. Thus, as a reflection of rising general educational levels and irrespective of the job content, a firm that once required a school leaving certificate to qualify applicants for employment, may now require a university degree, or conversely a new production process may reduce the skill requirements for the labour force.

This definition of social position, as covering access both to production and consumption activities, is a peculiarly general one. It derives, via Bourdieu's similarly generalized conceptualization of human capital in *Distinction* (1984), ultimately from the model of economic activity at the heart of Gary Becker's (1965) *Economic Journal* article on the theory of time. Becker reconceptualized all of what were conventionally considered to be production and consumption activities, as 'factors of production' that are input to the provision of 'final satisfactions' ('Z-goods'). Just as marketed commodities are constructed out of combinations of capital and paid labour time, so, further on down the economic line, final satisfactions are constructed out of combinations of marketed commodities and consumption (or unpaid work) time. Becker's subsequent work on human capital formation, however, concentrates exclusively on the processes of acquisition of skills related to paid labour.

Bourdieu's original contribution was to focus on the formation of skills in relation to consumption. Formal education, specific training, and on-the-job experience serve to form skills for the labour market. In Bourdieu's account, a similar trio – socialization in the household-of-origin, formal education, and adult experience – serve to form skills in (or equivalently tastes for) specific forms of consumption (and unpaid work). Individuals seek to distinguish themselves – in effect establish their distinct social position – by adopting a pattern of consumption that provides an optimal level of final satisfactions from the combination of their financial resources with their consumption skills. Now, holding non-labour income on one side, financial resources reflect skills in production. So, in its simplest form, the Bourdieu thesis is that social position can be mapped in a two-dimensional space, with production skills and consumption skills as the two axes.

In the cases both of production and of consumption skills, there is a recursive process of individual change. Possession of certain characteristics gives access, through the social institutions which control them, to participation in particular activities (ie, our work skills help us get jobs, our consumption skills motivate us to participate in particular forms of leisure). And participation in these activities, itself modifies existing characteristics (skills, of production or consumption, at the workbench or at the Opera, are improved by practice). What we do, changes who we are.

And in addition to individual, micro-level change, there is macro change at the level of the institutions. We might think of these two sorts of change as being related. rather along the lines of Coleman's (1990 p.10) boat or bathtub diagram (see Figure 1).

At the level of the institutions we have progressive adjustment of the 'rules for engagement', both as a matter of deliberate corporate strategy, and as an outcome of 'environmental' change at the micro level. At the level of the individual we have both motivated acquisition of new characteristics in response to or anticipation of institutional rules, and also the unconsidered accretion or accumulation of skills as a by-product of the activities of daily life. These processes interact to produce various familiar phenomena of social change. For example, credential inflation: firms at time *t* use a requirement for

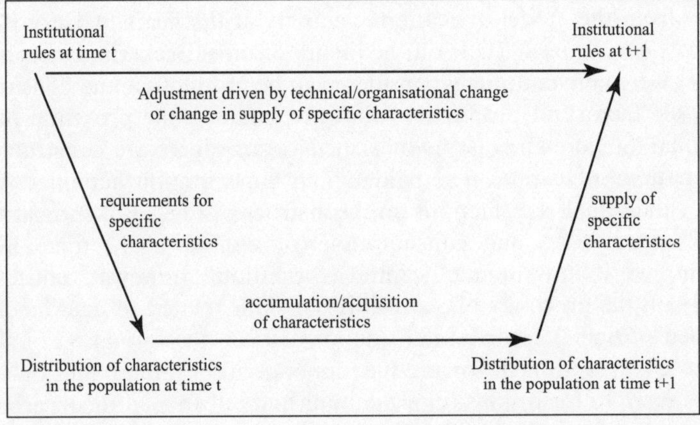

Figure 1 *Change in the social-positional salience of personal characteristics*

a given level of educational certificate as a screening device for the selection of new employees; understanding this, more individuals seek to acquire these qualifications, swelling the supply of certificated individuals, so the firms are forced to raise their requirements at time $t+1$. Or technological unemployment: individual employees become increasingly skilful in the operation of traditional machinery, but in the meantime innovative firms install new production machinery, so that the improved skills in the workforce are less 'salient' to their prospective employers' requirements. From these cases we can see clearly that the *positional advantage or disadvantage only emerges from the interaction of the two levels*; the acquisition of new production skills or qualifications ('human capital', to use the not-always appropriate metaphor we take from the economists' discussions of this issue) only provides advantages as long as their salience to production processes remain undiminished.

Exactly equivalent arguments apply also for consumption activities. We acquire consumption skills from our households-of-origin, and from the activities of daily life as well as from educational establishments; but the skills that emerge are not necessarily of constant value in giving access to subsequent consumption activities. Particular elements of 'cultural capital', to use Bourdieu's term, may become devalued, less salient to participation in social events (as for example where those skilled in formal 'ballroom' dancing were confronted – affronted – by newly developed disco clubs). 'Social capital', in the sense of personal acquaintance with members of a social élite, may decay as new socially dominant groups emerge. Just as in the case of human capital for production, new forms of consumption activity emerge and distribute advantages in new ways. We might for example observe the Coleman Bathtub process through which the computer gaming subculture emerges: initially, domestic garage-based enterprises innovate new sorts of games for a not-yet skilful group of computer gamers; as the personal skills of the gamers grow to demand new and more complex games, so the garage-firms develop more complex and sophisticated products and emerge as major public corporations.

So far, so general. There are different sorts of potential benefits ('positional advantages') that may derive from personal skills ('human capital'), relating both to consumption and to production activities. But the positional advantage emerge, not from those accumulated skilful characteristics themselves, but from their interaction with the rules of social institutions which control access to or participation in those production and consumption activities. We all accumulate new characteristics, if only as an incidental result of living our lives from day to day; and some of these new characteristics can be considered as 'skills'; but these skills only provide advantages insofar as they are salient to the requirement of the institutions providing the jobs, or the leisure or cultural activities we wish to participate in.

This is the theoretical background. But what follows just pursues one aspect of this approach. It concentrates on the lower level of Figure 1, concerning the individual's accumulation of salient skills, and avoids any further discussion of the macro-social context within which the salience of these might vary over time. It also eschews any further discussion of those particular characteristics which are salient to participation in consumption activities. The concentration on production skills in the following discussion of social position, reflects my concern, which I share with the proponents of the 'Class Programme', to explore the determinants of 'life-chances' (future income, health and psychological adjustment) as opposed to 'life-style'. F. Scott Fitzgerald proposed that what chiefly distinguishes the rich is their riches; I cannot be certain that it is principally the wealth creating production skills that determine life-chances – but it seems a good starting assumption.

An index of personal resources salient to the labour market

Economic resources and 'earnings potential'

The objective of this analysis is to explore the structuring of individual life-chances: the means employed here is the classification of social position through the possession of salient social resources, in an approach somewhat analogous to economists' conceptions of human capital. In this section I develop a new (if not especially innovative) indicator of social position, based on individuals possession of economically salient (ie job-related) resources which I will call the Interim Essex Score (the IES: 'interim' because of some current perplexities about the choice of estimation procedure discussed below).

Theoretical expectations of which characteristics are 'salient' to employment opportunities include:

- social and cultural capital from household of origin, particularly 'economic socialization'
- educational and occupational attainment
- employment and unemployment record

These sorts of characteristics (in addition to direct control of financial and similar capital) determine the accessibility of future desirable activities and circumstances. They collectively constitute the economic aspect of the individual's current social position; each of these characteristics has a distinct effect, and for many purposes we might wish to consider them separately. But in the present case, we wish to find a simple way of summarizing the net effect of these; so, straightforwardly, the disparate personal characteristics are each given a monetary value.

The value of these economically salient characteristics may be derived as well from labour market outcomes (ie, wages) as from any. A particular problem emerges at this point: everyone has the potential to earn a wage, but at any given time, some are not wage-earners. Those currently not in employment also have economically salient characteristics, so in estimating the potential value of human economic resources, we need to consider more than just current earnings.

Estimating 'earnings potential'

Earnings potential, operationalized as hourly wage that either is being earned in employment, or could be earned if that respondent were in employment, is clearly a consequence of various continuously accumulating characteristics: different quantities and combinations of education and work experience and other personal circumstances, all have particular implications for potential earnings. And there is a clear empirical procedure (though with contested details which are mentioned briefly below) for estimating their impact: simply regress longitudinal evidence on accumulated characteristics on hourly earnings at some particular point in time.

The procedure for estimating the economic value of accumulated job-related characteristics that follows makes use of a particular attribute of the panel approach to data collection: it gives in later 'waves' of data collection, information about the subsequent earnings of those non-employed in previous 'waves' of data collection. The procedure I have used here takes one or other of two different routes depending on current employment status:

- for those currently in employment: establishing the 'structural' effects of economic characteristics by relating evidence of wage levels at a particular point in time to previous labour market and other experiences.
- for those currently not in employment: using the panel evidence of structural effects on earned income (if any) in the following year as a basis for estimating potential earnings.

Econometricians will argue that this approach will produce biased results. There is a well-established econometric procedure for estimating earnings potential (Heckman, 1979) that takes explicit account of the fact that individuals with particular (by inference low) levels of human capital may decide not to seek jobs at all. However, the sociological interpretation of the problem might lead us to expect the Heckman-derived estimates to perform rather less well as indicators of future well-being. The 'selection' step of the Heckman analysis, which assumes that there is an effective 'choice' between participation and non-participation in the workforce, may underestimate the earnings potential of the currently non-employed population. The approach summarized in the previous paragraph, which assumes the presence of structural constraints preventing the participation of otherwise willing workers, will produce higher estimates (indeed, since some Heckman-type 'selection' must happen, it probably overestimates the human capital of the currently non-employed). This issue is for the moment simply side-stepped, since it is entirely tangential to the main thrust of an article arguing for the usefulness of the 'economic resources' approach to the understanding of social position. (In any case, the current 'interim' version of the estimation procedure seems to work effectively enough for the purposes of the present argument.)

The models

Table 1 lists the variables used in the estimation of earnings potential. We would expect that current occupational status (as indicated by the Hope-Goldthorpe scale) would have different affects on earnings of women and men, so we have an interaction term to represent the differential. Similarly we would expect that the age profile of earnings will be different for higher status occupations, and that the prospective earnings effects of having responsibility for a child and of being currently non-employed will both vary by sex and appropriate interaction terms are also included. We would also expect an 'inverted-U' shaped relationship between age and earnings, and that the intervals at the top end of the Hope-Goldthorpe scale should have a much larger absolute implication for potential earnings than similarly sized intervals lower down the scale, so appropriate quadratic terms have been added. And finally, we would expect the mid-life downward turn in potential earnings to come later and be smaller for higher status occupations, so a separate quadratic term for the age/HGS interaction has also been included.

The same sorts of models are used to estimate earnings potential both for those with jobs and for those outside employment. In both cases the dependent variable is the (logged) hourly wage rate in 1994 (wave 4 of the BHPS); in the former case we use as regressors the respondents' characteristics during 1994 and the three previous years, while in the latter we take just those who were unwaged in 1993, and take 1993 characteristics, together with the three previous years as the regressors.

The various regression coefficients in principle provide us with estimates of the effects of the various characteristics and combinations of characteristics on the earnings potential of the whole sample (though in the example pursued here we consider only the working-age population). It would be convenient, in terms of the theoretical discussion in Section 2, if we were able to make distinct estimates for each different category of accumulated characteristic (ie, say 'each

Table 1 Earnings potential

estimated as log hourly wage rate (1994 £)

variables in the equation:	**interaction terms in the equation:**
• sex, age	• Hope-Goldthorpe Score with sex
• current/most recent occupational status (Hope-Goldthorpe Score)	• grouped HGS with age
• employment statuses over last 4 years	• sex with child status
• highest educational qualification	• employment status with sex
• number and age of children	**quadratic terms in the equation:**
• parents' occupations	• HGS
	• age
	• grouped HGS with age

extra year in employment adds *x* to the hourly wage rate'). But it is clear from the presence of interaction terms in the equation that this sort of simple statement is not possible (for example: the level of the present or previous occupation has rather different implications for earnings potential depending on the individual's age and sex).

Instead we can use the regression coefficients together to make a single, simple estimate which is the predicted hourly wage rate, given the presence of a particular set of personal characteristics. And it is this predicted hourly wage rate that constitutes the estimate of earnings potential, which should correspond either to actual earnings for those with current jobs, or possible future earnings for those without. And furthermore, we might expect the relationship between the economic characteristics and actual wage rates to be reasonably constant over time (though it may well vary over long historical periods), so the same coefficient could be applied to the same set of characteristics in different years. This is how we calculate the Interim Essex Score.

In Section 4 we derive an IES for all working age individuals in wave 1 of the BHPS (based on wave 1 characteristics together with the BHPS retrospective evidence on previous labour market and other behaviour). We then investigate how well the wave 1 IES works as a predictor of subsequent life chances, operationalized for current purposes as income levels and subjective health statuses in BHPS waves 2 to 5. In Section 5 we derive an IES for (September of) each year in the whole adult life of all members of the BHPS sample (using the retrospective work- and life-histories in addition to the panel data), and use these to investigate in particular how periods spent in family care and out of the workforce affect wives' positional dynamics.

Estimates of individual- and household-level resources

Figure 2 shows the distribution of IES in the wave 1 sample, by age, sex and occupational status (indicated by the Hope-Goldthorpe scale). We see all the features we expected on a priori grounds: an 'inverted U' age/wage relationship, with a slightly later mid-age peak and slower subsequent decline for those in high status jobs; higher occupational status giving substantially higher wage rates; and age-for-age and status-for-status women's potential earnings less than men's except in the case of the younger non-employed (where some relatively highly qualified women leave the workforce in order to care for small children); and the non-employed with lower potential earnings than the employed.

Compare these to the actual hourly earnings in this sample (Figure 3). Two points to note. First, the pattern of actual hourly wage rates do correspond reasonably well overall to the patterns for the earnings potential. (This demonstrates *inter alia* that the procedure of applying 1994 regression coefficients to 1991 characteristics is indeed working as we intend it to). The

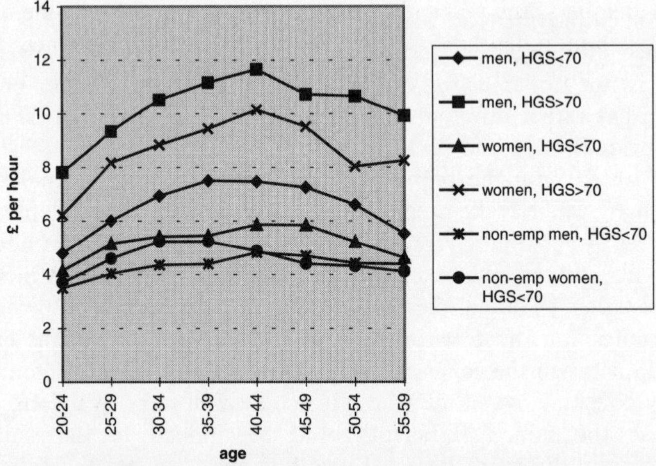

Figure 2 *Wage-earning potential in 1991*

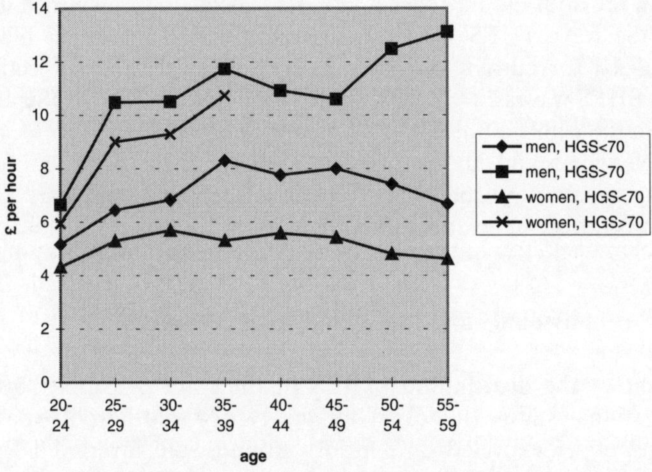

Figure 3 *Actual wage rate in 1991*

only substantial deviation between the potential and the actual wage rates for men in their 50s in high-end occupations, presumably reflecting the relatively low wages of those few well-qualified men who return to the labour force after early retirement. Second, useful in an indicator of social position, the picture covers many more people (6K vs 4.5K) – since all have an estimated potential, even if they are not currently in employment.

Of course there is much more to an individual's economic resources than his or her own future earnings potential. In particular, resources of other household members, and particularly those of co-resident family members, also make a substantial potential contribution to subsequent life-chances. Since the individual level indicator is a continuous one, it is possible to sum these across the household, to produce a total that has a perfectly straightforward interpretation, as the potential hourly wage rate (this the aggregate 'human capital') of the whole household. Households differ in size and composition, so to arrive at an appropriately scaled per capita household earnings potential (that adjusts for economies of scale in domestic production), we simply divide the total household wage rate by an appropriate equivalence scale value (here we use the McClements scale: Department of Social Security 1992).

Predicting life-chances

One of the major reasons for developing schemes of social classification is the prediction of future likely future living conditions. Predicting 'life-chances' is, for example, given as a major application for Goldthorpe's widely used class schema:

> 'Class analysis ... explores the interconnections between positions defined by employment relations in labour markets and production units in different sectors of national economies; the processes through individuals and families are distributed and redistributed among these positions over time; and the consequences thereof for their life-chances ...' (Goldthorpe and Marshall, 1992 p382)

The BHPS is of course an ideal source of evidence for exploring the role of structural characteristics in the determination of life-chances. Not only does it provide, as we saw in the preceding section, retrospective materials that allow us to estimate the extent of accumulation of structurally salient economic characteristics at wave 1 (1991); it also provides a wide range of indicators of 'outcomes' for subsequent years. This section shows the relationship between these resources, at the individual and at the household level, and three particular outcome indicators: individual labour incomes, household incomes, and subjective health status. In each case the 11 category version of the Goldthorpe class scheme (Erikson and Goldthorpe, 1993 p. 39) is used as a comparator against which to gauge the explanatory power of the 'economic resources' IES variable.

Predicting individual income

The most straightforward outcome indicator is simply the individual's monthly labour income. The (individual level) Goldthorpe class in 1991 (in combination with age and sex) does serve as a good predictor of income level (first row of Table 2). And while the proportion of variance explained does fall substantially over the four following years, it does retain a considerable explanatory power in 1995. The longitudinal importance of the class variable in explaining income is of course what we would expect from the underlying theory: occupational level persists over time, and the different employment relations represented by the various class categories are associated with different levels of material reward. In the terms of this theoretical perspective, the not-insubstantial fall in predictive power over the five year period represents the results of occupational mobility, and the determinants of this mobility at an individual level lie outside the realm of the class model itself (or to put it differently, one attribute of membership of a social class is a set of simple age/cohort/period-related probabilities of transition into each of the other classes).

Table 2 Comparison of individual earnings models explaining variance in individual income by individual characteristics

	1991	1992	1993	1994	1995
line 1: 1991 Goldthorpe Class, sex, age and age squared					
adj R**2	0.36	0.35	0.30	0.27	0.25
N	5692	5059	4850	4659	4444
line 2: 1991 IES, sex, age and age squared					
adj R**2	0.42	0.41	0.37	0.33	0.32
N	7703	6784	6473	6203	5917
line 3: 1991 IES, Goldthorpe Class cases only					
AR Square	0.38	0.36	0.32	0.29	0.27
	5690	5059	4849	4657	4442
line 4: 1991 IES plus Goldthorpe Class					
AdR Square	0.39	0.38	0.33	0.30	0.27
	5690	5058	4849	4657	4442
line 5: 1991 age, age squared and sex					
Adjusted *R*	0.19	0.17	0.16	0.15	0.14
	5692	5059	4850	4659	4444
causal inferences:					
explanation associated with either Class or IES (5–4)					
	0.19	0.19	0.17	0.15	0.13
explanation uniquely associated with Class (4–3)					
	0.01	0.02	0.01	0.01	0.00
explanation uniquely associated with IES (4–1)					
	0.03	0.03	0.03	0.03	0.02

Now consider the second row of Table 2. The 1991 IES value predicts monthly labour income in 1991 slightly better than the class variable does (though of course we would expect that a continuously scaled predictor will always show a small predictive advantage over a closely related categorical scale, simply as a result of its more even distribution and more widespread extremals), and the margin of difference in predictive power gets rather larger as the prediction period lengthens; the resources indicator performs 17% better than the class indicator in 1991, 23% better in 1993, 28% in 1995. I suspect that the reason for this relative improvement is that the class categories are acting as an imperfect proxy for the underlying personal characteristics of skills and experience which are the effective determinants of economic advantage or disadvantage; some suggestive evidence for this is found later in the Table and is discussed below.

Just as with the class variable, the absolute proportion of variance explained falls as the period lengthens, reflecting biographical changes in the individuals' personal situation and characteristics. But, in the resources model we can provide a rather more explicit modelling of these processes of biographical change. Consider for example the case of a well qualified and hitherto securely employed woman in 1991, who marries, has a child, and for this reason remains non-employed through 1993 and 1994, re-entering the labour force on a part-time basis in 1995. She has a high level of salient economic resources in 1991, which, if they had been maintained (ie, if she had kept on her 1991 career trajectory) would have yielded a high monthly income in 1995. But instead she took actions which, however positive for the early development of the child, served to deplete her own personal economic resources. Within the class discussion, we would simply assign a simple probability of moving from say class II in 1991 to class IIIa in 1995. But by contrast, through the resources argument, with its explicit recursive relationship between accumulating biographical characteristics and current activity, we can provide a much more detailed account, which moves from the age and gender, to consequent family formation behaviour, and from there to the subsequent labour market behaviour, and its consequences for human capital endowment. In short: while both the class and the resources model allow us to predict outcomes, the resources approach also allows us to explain those cases where the prior characteristics fail as predictors.

The relative advantage in predictive power is however perhaps somewhat misleading. Notice that it provides predictions for many more cases than does the individual class indicator. Simply: while not everyone has a job, which is the basis for assignment of an occupational class, everyone has an age and an educational record and a work history (which may include no jobs), and these are the bases of the resources index. Thus, in 1991 the earnings capacity index provides a prediction for 35% more cases (7703 as against 5692), and in 1995 33% more cases (5917 vs 4444). Perhaps the extra cases included in the second line of Table 2 are just easier to predict? The third line uses the IES to predict values for just those cases for which we also have class scores. The relative predictive power of the resource index is indeed somewhat reduced, to a margin of just 6% or 8%.

The fourth line of the table uses simultaneously both the IES and the class position as explanatory variables. This provides only a very small improvement of predictive power over the previous ('resource index predicting Goldthorpe cases only') line, which shows that the variance explained by the class categories is pretty much exactly the same as that predicted by the resource index. Line 5, showing the proportion of variance in monthly earnings explained by the individual's age and sex, provides the remaining information necessary to make simple causal inferences. We see that, excluding the variance explained by sex and age, the 1991 class and IES variables explain from 19% (for 1991) to 13% (for 1995) of the variance in monthly labour income. The great majority of this is common to both variables. Very little of this is uniquely attributable to class (from 1% in 1991 to 0% in 1995); a little more (3% in 1991 declining to 2% in 1995) is uniquely attributable to economic resources.

It might be asked why we should use predicted wage rates in 1991 as our index of economically-salient resources, rather than actual wage rates. In fact, and for obvious reasons, actual 1991 wage rates show higher rates of explanation of variance in labour income in 1991 than do either the class variable or the potential wage index. Nevertheless there are two clear reasons for preferring the resource index based on estimated wage-earning potential.

1. Both wages and earnings at a single historical point will reflect various particular random or other circumstances which are not connected with long term differences in earning capacity. It is this that explains the good short-term predictions from the wage rate; over time the effects of these random differences in circumstances fades, and by 1995 the actual hourly wage rate in 1991 explains about the same proportion of variance in monthly labour income as does the Goldthorpe variable, and rather less than the economic resources index. The economic resources index, by contrast, reflects the essentially non-random effects of the various accumulating advantageous or disadvantageous economic characteristics as identified in the earlier sections of this paper.
2. Wage rates are only available for those in employment, less than 75% of the working-age population; potential wage rates, by contrast, can be calculated for all.

Predicting household income and individual health

We can deal with the remaining evidence altogether more briefly. Table 3 shows the somewhat similar patterns of variance explanation at the household level where the adjusted total of accumulated human capital is used as a predictor of the (similarly adjusted) total household income. (It also takes individual age-groups and sex into account: at first sight eccentric-seeming perhaps in a household analysis, but in fact, since this is still really an individual level analysis, modelling the effect of an individual's household environment on her or his subsequent household circumstances, it allows for meaningful interactions, such as the fact that divorce rates and gender/occupational associations make it less likely that a women in a high-end Goldthorpe household in year 1 will still be in such a household in year 5 than is the case for a man.) In this table the class variable improves its performance over time relative to the resources model; but in 1995 even the 'Goldthorpe cases only' analysis (line 3) gives 'resources' a 23% margin of predictive advantage over the class model (ie, 21% of variance explained vs 17%), fallen from a 40% margin in 1991. The resources model also provides predictions for 14% more households than does the class model (eg, 6048 cases in line 1 vs 5356 in 1995).

However, unlike the previous table, the combination of the class and the resource indicators (line 4) does in this case seem to provide some additional predictive power (eg, 24% vs 21% in 1995), implying that some economically salient attributes of the household-level class indicator are not captured by the household resources. This is not entirely unexpected. The two household

Table 3 Explaining variance in household income by household characteristics

	1991	1992	1993	1994	1995
line 1: adjusted household IES age and sex					
*r***2	0.34	0.33	0.32	0.27	0.23
N	8084	7113	6559	6355	6048
line 2: Goldthorpe Class (household dominance 1)+ age and sex					
*r***2	0.22	0.23	0.21	0.19	0.17
N	7064	6247	5796	5629	5356
line 3: adj. hh. IES, age and sex (Goldthorpe cases only)					
*r***2	0.31	0.30	0.29	0.24	0.21
N	7064	6247	5796	5629	5356
line 4: Goldthorpe Class and adj. hh. IES + age and sex.					
*r***2	0.34	0.34	0.31	0.27	0.24
N	7064	6247	5796	5629	5356
line 5: dominant earner's IES, adj. hh. IES etc					
*r***2	0.33	0.33	0.30	0.25	0.23
N	7064	6247	5796	5629	5356
line 6: Goldthorpe Class, dominant earner and adj. hh.IES etc					
*r***2	0.36	0.36	0.33	0.28	0.25
N	7064	6247	5796	5629	5356

indices are in fact measuring somewhat different things: the resources are in effect a 1991 average across the household, while the class variable (in its 'dominance' incarnation) relates to the 'highest' individual occupation across the household membership in 1991. We might suspect therefore that the addition of the 1991 highest potential hourly wage in the household (the 'dominant earner's IES') as an extra predictor might have similar effect. This extra variable does indeed seem (line 5) to do most, but not all of the predictive work.

And when we estimate a rather saturated sort of model with dominant Goldthorpe class, dominant earner's potential wage and total household human capital all included (line 6), we do still see a margin of predictive advantage over the model that excludes the class variable. But despite the fact that, unlike the previous table, this shows the class variable to be doing some substantial predictive work independently of the other variables, the main point emerging from Table 3 is that the human capital type variables capture most of the same variance as the class variable. Comparing line 2 with line 5, the human capital variables add a margin of 50% of extra predictive power in 1991 43% in 1993 and 35% in 1995.

We might note, finally, that the IES also has some applications in predicting non-economic outcomes. In this case part of the theoretical argument for expecting a direct effect is weaker than in the case of the Goldthorpe class model. After all the 'employment relations' of control and supervision, which are the explicit basis of the Goldthorpe classification, are likely to be quite directly related to stress and hence in turn to general health status. However, other parts of the argument linking economic causes to health outcomes (eg, access to appropriate diet and, it must sadly be added in 1990s Britain, timely and adequate medical provision) still hold good. The overall proportions of variance explained in the two models reported in Table 4 are rather low. But in this case we would not expect any very large explanation of health status by economic factors, since other (particularly genetic inheritance and long-term lifestyle) characteristics would be expected to dominate.

I should reiterate that the point here is not a prediction tournament between the IES and the categorical class variable. The IES does explain slightly more variance that the class variable – but probably to no greater degree than is to be expected from their respective levels of measurement. It does appear that the two indicators are explaining pretty much the same aspects of variability in life chances. The point of developing the IES is however, as stated at the outset, to

Table 4 Explaining variance in subjective health status

	1991	1992	1993	1994	1995
IES	0.04	0.03	0.04	0.04	0.04
Goldthorpe	0.01	0.01	0.02	0.01	0.02

exploit more fully the continuously measured biographical narrative evidence that emerges from a longitudinal study. We now turn to an example of this.

An application to work history: the effects of work-breaks on women's economic potential

It is well established that work breaks for family care have negative effects on women's career prospects (eg, Dex, 1987; Jacobs, 1995, 1999). There is, to dramatize the point, evidence that allows us to generalize from the well known reverse-fairy-tale of Allerednic (in which the prince marries a princess and turns her into a scullery maid: Gershuny, 1998) we see that the career attainments of wives who take substantial periods out of employment to care for their families, diverge markedly from those of their husbands, and from those of wives who do not take such breaks.

But the Allerednic evidence, which relies on the Hope-Goldthorpe scores of those in the sample who are in employment, only gives us information about a particular part of the population. What about the positions of women, at various stages into their marriages who do not at present have jobs? These may perhaps be relatively well-educated, with intermittent employment but in high end jobs, who could get good jobs but choose to be outside the labour force for the present because their husbands have sufficient incomes to meet their needs. Or they could be in a much less satisfactory position, now effectively excluded from all but the most menial of jobs because of their lack of accumulated human capital.

It should be remembered that relatively high rates of women's participation in the workforce at any one point in time are still compatible with relatively low rates of continuous women's employment. Table 5 shows that the proportion of women with short work-breaks (ie, high levels of attachment to the workforce) has remained pretty much unchanged through much of this century. And even

Table 5 Wives' months in ft family care, in 15th year after marriage, by birth cohort

	<7 months	7–36	>36 months	*N*
born 1917–21	14.1	3.8	82.2	185
born 1922–26	17.5	10.1	72.4	308
born 1927–31	16.6	7.5	75.9	253
born 1932–36	9.2	9.6	81.2	261
born 1937–41	9.5	9.9	80.5	262
born 1942–46	14.5	12.2	73.3	344
born 1947–51	13.4	14.2	72.3	372
born 1952–56	14.3	17.9	67.7	279

for the most recent cohort for which we can make sensible estimates, still more than two-thirds of women have taken more than 36 months out of the workforce in full-time family care after 15 years of marriage. So there are clearly still important groups which are excluded when we concentrate on employment-related position measures – this is why we use IES.

There are certainly severe problems in using the IES in this way. The coefficients of the IES that relate the different components of education, skills and experience to earnings power have been calibrated for the 1990s: these may not apply to earlier periods. And indeed there are reasons for expecting that there will in fact have been systematic changes in these coefficients over time; the theoretical perspective set out in Section 2 would lead us to predict that employers' requirements for their workers and the determinants of women's participation in the labour force will mutually adjust over this period. But the problems here are in principle no different to those, for example of applying scores derived from empirical prestige rankings from the mid 1970s (as in the Hope-Goldthorpe Scale) to the same range of periods.

Nevertheless, though the coefficients may vary, the theoretical rationale for including the particular aspects of life and work experience – duration in occupations, degree of attachment to the labour force and so on – in the IES measure can be expected to apply with equal force throughout the period under consideration. (And there are other experimental possibilities, involving alternative simulations of economic resources, progressively adjusting the coefficients according to the theoretical expectations, or in accordance with calibrations derived from earlier data where this is available, that may be considered, though these options are not pursued in what follows.) So we might, cautiously, apply the IES to earlier periods as long as we remember that the results are no more than an indication of various aspects of individual biographies, summarized and aggregated on the basis of the impact they would have had in the 1990s.

And in doing so we arrive at a rather dramatic result. We see, in Figures 4 and 5, what looks like a historically growing polarization between wives who maintain their positions in the workplace and those who do not. In the 1952–61 birth cohort, we see that the 'no family care breaks' wives (which include up to 6 months absence from the workforce) have IES scores that are pretty well midway between those of the husbands with no work-breaks and wives with 36 months or more of work-breaks (or no post-marriage employment whatsoever). For the 1932 to 1941 birth cohort, the no-break wives are much closer to the wives with long breaks than to the no-break husbands. And by the time we get back to the 1912 to 1921 cohort, the continuously employed wives actually have lower IES scores than do the long-break wives.

Table 6 gives the size of the husbands' extra earnings potential 11 years after the first recorded marriage, for each ten-year birth cohort within the sample. For wives who take time out of the workforce, this premium has remained pretty much unchanged over the approximately 50 year period covered by the table. By contrast, the premium has halved from 31% to 18%) over the period

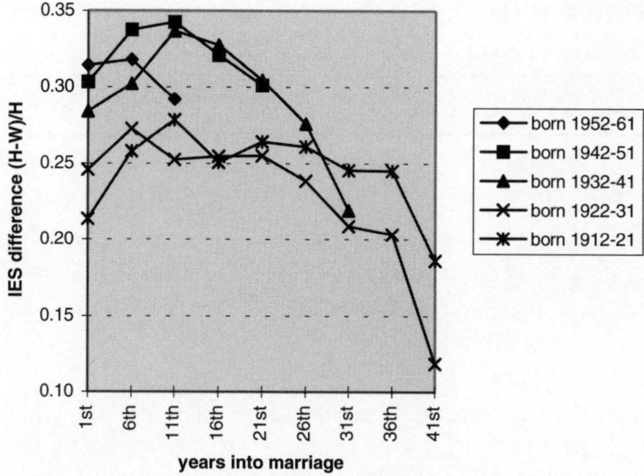

Figure 4 *Gap between husbands with no breaks and wives with 3+ years break*

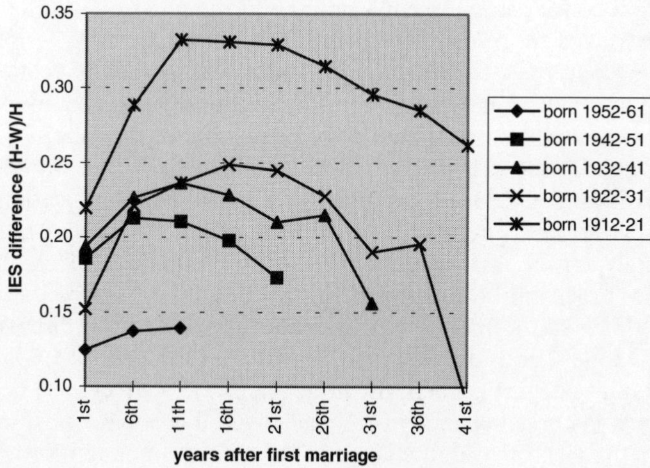

Figure 5 *Gap between husbands and wives with no work breaks*

for those wives who stay continuously in employment. Wives committed to the labour force have come progressively to look in economic terms rather more like their husbands, but still lag behind them; wives out of the workforce are in overall terms in approximately the same positions at the beginning and at the end of the period.

There is of course always the possibility that the result is driven entirely by the changing distributions of the underlying educational or family characteristics. It could be, for example, that the convergence of the no-breaks wives

Table 6 Husbands' IES Premium relatives to wives with and without work breaks, after

	no breaks	breaks >3 years
born 1912–21	31%	28%
born 1922–31	27%	25%
born 1932–41	28%	34%
born 1942–51	24%	34%
born 1952–61	16%	30%

with the no-breaks husbands reflects no more than the growth of women's education levels relative to men's, or to changes in fertility patterns (ie, smaller/later families providing a lesser inhibition of women's ability to amass human capital).

To cope with such possibilities we must turn to a more formal modelling of the pattern of association of the IES with these particular characteristics. This might, on first consideration, seem a rather odd thing to do given that the IES is itself constructed from regression coefficients including these variables. But: we are now concerned to see how the historical period is related to the processes of accumulation of the various occupation-related components of the IES – and of course historical period forms no part of the IES.

Table 7 sets out successive stages in the modelling process. Model 1 shows the relationships between educational level (with no qualifications as the default category) and number of children, with IES, for women only. Unsurprisingly, given that educational level and numbers of children form part of the procedure for estimating the IES, they emerge as strongly associated; this is not a finding, but is a necessary control for discovering any real effects. Model 2 adds dummy variables for the birth cohorts (with 1957–66 as the default category); there is little significant effect – implying no significant net historical change in women's overall economic position.

However the lack of overall change in women's economic position hides a substantial change among different groups of women. In Model 3 we add a set of interactive dummy categories, which multiply the birth-cohort indicators by an indicator of whether the respondent has taken less than 7 months out of the workforce during the first 15 years of marriage. Now we can clearly see the growth in the IES score associated with short work-breaks over successive cohorts (the default category does not fit the trend – but this reflects a sample selection bias: the relatively few born after 1957 who already have 16+ years of marriage are by definition early marriers, and early marriage is strongly correlated with low levels of human capital). As we move to the full model, a clear picture emerges: in Model 5 we see a (small but) significant overall historical decline associated with the cohort indicators, which more than compensated for by the historical increase specific to those women who have only short work-breaks. This is the polarization effect: each successive birth cohort of women with high levels of attachment to the workforce seem to do substantially better than earlier ones over time, in terms of their accumulation of accumulation of beneficial characteristics (and hence, on the basis of the discussion of the previous section, it seems reasonable to assume, life chances), relative to their husbands, while women with lower levels of attachment are doing, if anything, rather worse.

This finding of course poses more questions that answers. What are the mechanisms of this polarization? Is it, for example, that in the earlier birth cohorts, highly educated women (with rich husbands) stayed voluntarily out of the labour market, while, in the later ones, it is less well educated women (with poorer husband) achieve lower levels of continuity of attachment to the labour force (see the chapter by Crompton in this volume)? The processes at work are

Table 7 Modelling IES after 15 years of marriage

	women only					
	model 1	model 2	model 3	model 4	model 5	NOTE
WOMAN						−1.476**
higher deg	3.500**	3.520**	3.434**	3.369**	3.411**	5.116**
1st degree	3.560**	3.590**	3.546**	3.462**	3.527**	4.201**
HND, HNC etc	2.683**	2.692**	2.692**	2.625**	2.677**	2.980**
A Level	0.889**	0.917**	0.895**	0.841**	0.892**	1.451**
O Level	0.352**	0.379**	0.364**	0.296**	0.361**	0.691**
CSE	−0.206	−0.116	−0.098	0.075	−0.093	0.261
N kids,age 35	−0.186**	−0.185**	−0.129*		−0.118*	0.004
.. **2	0.090**	0.090**	0.083**		0.082**	0.043**
<6 months brk				−0.130	−0.187	−0.006
>36 months brk				−0.044	−0.079*	−0.027
born 1917–26		0.229*	0.290*	0.345**	0.328**	0.556**
born 1927–36		0.129	0.132	0.254*	0.165	0.364**
born 1937–46		0.118	0.032	0.078	0.061	0.176
born 1947–56		0.136	0.048	0.034	0.068	0.089
17–26*<6 mths			−0.384*	−0.540**	−0.462**	−0.101
27–36*<6 mths			−0.060	−0.230	−0.107	0.070
37–46*<6 mths			0.628**	0.455*	0.581**	0.530**
47–56*<6 mths			0.689**	0.562**	0.651**	0.488**
(Constant)	4.665**	4.517	4.454**	4.791**	4.622**	5.622**
Adj *R* Sq	0.382	0.382	0.391	0.309	0.393	0.563

not clear; there is a substantial programme of work here, which I do not propose to take further in this chapter. But the outcome is straightforward: a growing polarization in life-chances between those women who maintain high levels of attachment to the labour force and those women who, for whatever reason, fail to maintain this high level of attachment.

Afterword

My point for the moment is simply this: understanding life course mobility requires that we study more than just the social positions of those in employment at any particular point in time. We need indicators of social position that, like the IES, reveal the social structural characteristics of the entire population, not just the working population. The longitudinal data sources now available to us – the panel studies, the birth cohort studies, the retrospective life- and work-history studies – provide the evidence on which we can base such indicators, and hence derive more comprehensive accounts of mobility processes.

The IES is one example of a more general category of indicators of social position which reflect the way positional characteristics are accumulated. Just as our past employment experiences build up into capacities which fit us for new and better jobs, so, for example, our past activities in organizations in our local communities establish us as the sorts of people who are well fitted for future and further engagement. Or our past 'investment' in sporting or cultural activity serve to form both future capacities and tastes in these areas. And indeed, so do our past patterns of emotional relationship with family and friends structure future options for sociability and intimacy.

This is a simple and plausible model of the formation of structural characteristics, and one which is straightforward to operationalize. We seek indicators of the various potentially salient behavioural characteristics in the form of questionnaire items, and we ask these questions repeatedly, of the same respondents in interviews at successive historical time points. Then we build models of the recursive process through which activities accumulate to form characteristics, and in turn future influence patterns of participation in work and leisure activities.

References

Coleman, J., (1990), *Foundations of Social Theory*, Cambridge Mass: Belknap.
Becker, G., (1965), 'A theory of the Allocation of Time', *Economic Journal*, 75: 493–517.
Bourdieu, P. (1984), *Distinction*, London: RKP.
Prandy, K., (1990), 'The Revised Cambridge Scale of Occupations', *Sociology*, 24: 629–655.
Department of Social Security, (1992), *Households Below Average Income*, HMSO.
Dex, S., (1987), *Women's Occupational Mobility: a lifetime perspective*, Basingstoke: Macmillan.

Erikson, R. and Goldthorpe, J., (1992), *The Constant Flux: A Study of Class Mobility in Modern Societies*, Oxford: Clarendon Press.
Goldthorpe, J. and Hope, K., (1974), *The Social Grading of Occupations*, Oxford: Clarendon Press.
Heckman, J., (1979), 'Sample Selection Bias as a Specification Error', *Econometrica*, 47: 153:161.
Goldthorpe, J. and Marshall, G., (1992), 'The Promising Future of Class Analysis; a Response to Recent Critiques', *Sociology*, 26: 381–400.
Jacobs, S.C., (1995), 'Routes from Origins to Destinations: A longitudinal study of women's social, occupational and marital mobility', unpublished D Phil thesis, Oxford University.
Jacobs, S.C., (1999), 'Trends in Women's Career Patterns and in Gender Occupational Mobility in Britain', *Gender Work and Society*, 6 (1): 32–46.
Pahl, R., (1984), *Divisions of Labour*, Oxford: Blackwell.

Class inequality and the social production of money

Geoffrey Ingham

Introduction

Two rather different episodes in the financial history of the last decade – the widespread defaulting of British mortgagers in the early 1990s and, more recently, the collapse and rescue of a Wall Street hedge fund (Long Term Capital Management) in late 1998 – may be taken as examples of the relative autonomy of the capitalist credit money system's capacity to generate and reproduce inequality. However, such events, and the institutional structures which gave rise to them, are not normally examined in the mainstream sociological analysis of class or social stratification. The reason for this neglect, I would suggest, lies in sociology's unwitting and tacit endorsement of a flawed economic conception of money as a 'neutral veil' that covers and symbolises the 'real' substructure of either economic relations between commodities and/or the social relations through which they are mediated (Ingham, 1996; 1998; 1999; 2000).[1] In the division of intellectual labour that followed the *Methodenstreit* in the social sciences around the turn of the nineteenth century, sociology accepted economics' jurisdiction over money which, in orthodox circles, had come to be seen as no more than a *neutral medium of exchange*. In this view, money and the institutions that produce it are not in themselves *directly* and *independently* efficacious in social and economic processes. Moreover, this is not only true of orthodox classical and later neoclassical economics. Although Marx's critique of classical economics has provided a foundation for the modern sociological analysis of class, his conception of money was, in fact, quite close to that of Smith and Ricardo and not radically different from the one I have just outlined. Like his contemporaries, Marx saw money as a 'veil' that masked an underlying reality; but for him the underlying 'reality' was social and there were *two* 'veils'. Marx agreed that 'real' economic forces were to be found behind the monetary symbols; but for him these economic forces were to be explained as the alienated and mystified expression of the underlying 'real' social relations of capitalist production (Ingham, 1998). In short, this orthodoxy relegates money to an epiphenomenal role.

Of course, money in the broad Marxist tradition is not 'neutral' insofar as it is social 'power' (see Gannsman, 1988; Dodd, 1994); but a neutrality is implied in this theoretical position in the sense that command of money is, ultimately, the *expression* and *crystallization* of more fundamental bases for power that derive from the various forms of 'capital' (human, physical, financial, social). In this way, 'real' human and social capacities are commodified and alienated by their monetary representation the market and capitalist social relations. In contrast, I shall argue that capitalist credit money not only expresses, symbolises or mediates social relations, but itself *is* a social relation and that the production and control of money is a relatively autonomous social process that has independent effects. The power to *create* money, which derives from definite social relations and technical means, is exercised in capitalism jointly by states and the private agencies of the banking and financial systems. This is a source of social power *sui generis*, and as such has profound implications for social class and inequality. But before this argument is developed, we might briefly return to our illustrations.

The collapse and rescue of the Wall Street hedge fund, Long Term Credit Management, demonstrated how the operation of the capitalist credit system can systematically further enrich a small group of extremely wealthy individuals at almost no risk to their own private fortunes. Hedge funds trade in the purely speculative derivatives markets that play an increasingly dominant part in the global financial system (Valdez, 1997 chs 11, 12; Bernstein, 1996 ch 18; Harmes, 1998; *Financial Times*, September 25 1998; June 18, 1999). It is fundamentally important to note that these funds do not simply deploy their own members' or other people's already accumulated finance, but use their location in the institutional framework of the capitalist credit-money system to make profits. The funds are highly 'leveraged' – that is to say, they make use of enormous levels of bank credit (over $100 *billion* in this case), the interest on which, in the normal course of events, they are able to repay out of the profits from speculation.[2] Capitalist credit-money is created, as we shall see, by the *act of bank lending* within a framework of norms, practices and constraints which central banks attempt to control and regulate. Consequently, I shall argue, the form of enrichment practised by the hedge funds is 'internal' to a relatively autonomous capitalist monetary and financial system. Moreover, given the massive scale of borrowing, the LTCM's default in the wake of the East Asian and Russian crises of 1998 threatened to destabilize the US banking system. In response, the New York Federal Reserve Bank persuaded some of the country's biggest banks to organize a rescue. LTCM was saved and has resumed its profitable activities as before. To (mis)use the more familiar Marxian class terminology, the hedge fund speculators occupied a particular location in relation to the means of production of credit-money.

My second example is less exotic and comes from the other end of capitalism's class structure. By the early 1990s, the housing market situation of large numbers of mortgagers in Britain significantly worsened. First, as the result of the the attempt to curb inflation, mortgage interest rates doubled to 14% and defaults rose sharply. Second, as the housing boom was transformed into a slump, many others found themselves in possession of 'negative equity' – that is, the market price of houses fell below the size of mortgage debt. One might argue, in conventional mode, that the *market or class position* (measured in money) of a stratum of employees, which had responded to the Thatcher governments' call for a property-owning democracy, provided insufficient income to meet their commitments. But, it is *equally* the case, in the terms of the general argument I will putting forward, that the defence of the value of money, by the raising of interest rates and the rebalancing of the relations between creditors and debtors in favour of the former, was a *cause* of the defaulters' plight. Their 'monetary class location' in relation to the social relations of production of the monetary system varied *independently* of their labour market class situation.

In other words, a significant level of the inequality produced by the capitalist system can only be understood by means of an explication of the operation of the monetary and financial system itself. Money is not simply a measure and/or expression of inequality, rather, this is also generated by the institutional system that produces money itself. As I have suggested, sociology has not addressed this issue, and the reasons for the *lacuna* are to be found in classical sociology's conception of capitalism and the role played by money and finance. Although it no longer finds universal acceptance, the Marx-Weber orthodoxy continues to set the terms of the debates on 'class' (see for example Crompton 1998). In these, it is either taken for granted that the nineteenth century understanding of the fundamental structure and operation of capitalism is robust, but that secondary structural changes such as the rise of the 'middle classes' or the 'depersonalisation of property' require that it is modified. Or it is argued that 'modern society' is structurally so different from the one examined by the classical sociologists that their theories of class should be abandoned. My position is rather different in arguing that the classical theorists – both economic and sociological – misunderstood the process by which capitalist credit-money was produced and that this impaired their understanding of the dynamics of class and inequality. However, we should not be too hard on the 'founding fathers' as the nature of credit-money was imperfectly understood by the nineteenth century economists, and indeed, remains the subject of the most polemical disputes on both intellectual and political levels (Schumpeter [1954], 1994; see Smithin, 1994, especially on the seminal 19th century dispute between the Banking and Currency Schools).[3] Marx did not fully grasp the significance of credit-money and disciples such as Hilferding offered a flawed analysis of 'finance capital' which became the sociological orthodoxy on these matters (Ingham, 1998). Weber was unusually ambiguous and inconsistent on the matter. He clearly recognized the specific character of capitalist money and finance; but omitted this from his ideal type of capitalism (Weber [1927], 1981 chs. XXII and XXIV; see Ingham, 1998; 1999). Consequently, sociology has been unable to theorize this increasingly important determinant of 'life chances' in twenty first century capitalism.

In this respect, we might think of modern capitalism's monetary and financial system as having first, second, and third order effects. First, the actual process by which the capitalist form of credit-money is produced has a systematic effect in the creation of inequality. Second, the routine reproduction of the capitalist financial system necessarily maintains and exacerbates the inequality. Following Merton's usage, these may be seen as 'Matthew Effects' in which, according to the First Book of the New Testament: 'For everyone that hath shall be given, and he shall have abundance; but from him that hath not shall be taken away, even what he hath' (Merton, 1968) In neither of these effects is money 'neutral', either as a 'vehicle' for conducting efficient transactions or simply a measure or 'numeraire' of already constituted levels of inequality or class positions. Third order effects involve resistance to this generation and reinforcement of disadvantage through the development of alternative forms of money and finance. But before these effects are examined in more detail, we need to be clear about the specific characteristics of the form of capitalist credit money.

Capitalist credit-money

Somewhat paradoxically, the orthodoxy of mainstream economics finds it difficult to accord an essential place for money in its most abstract general theories (Hahn, 1987; see Ingham, 1996) This is because the fundamentals of economic theory are based on what is known as 'real' analysis which describes the ideal type operation of a 'natural' barter (ie, moneyless) economy of producer/traders (Schumpeter, 1994 [1954]: 277; Rogers, 1989). It is assumed in this model that all the essentials of economic activity can be described in terms of the relations and exchange ratios between goods and services as these are determined by individual calculations of their utilities. The familiar supply/demand schedules for goods and services are the outcome of these myriad individual decisions. Money is added this model only as a technical device – that is, *only* as a medium of exchange – to facilitate the more efficient conduct of transactions. It is in this sense that money is a 'neutral veil' or 'vehicle' that has no efficacy other than to overcome the 'inconveniences of barter' which, in Jevons' famous late nineteenth century formulation, result from the absence of a 'double coincidence of wants'.[4] This approach contains a theory of the origins of money as the unintended consequence of individual rationality. In order to maximize their barter options, it is argued, agents will hold stocks of the most tradable commodities which, consequently, emerge spontaneously as media of exchange. Money has its origins as a commodity with exchange value which results from individual rational utility maximisation (Menger, 1982). This model of a 'natural' economy – or in Minsky's derogatory description, the 'village fair' (Minsky, 1984) – remains the foundation of the orthodox neoclassical, monetarist, and quantity theories of money (see Smithin, 1994 for an excellent accessible survey and critique of monetary theories). However, it is seriously flawed on both logical and empirical levels (see Ingham, 1996; 2000).

The first and most fundamental problem concerns the origins of the 'primary concept of a theory of money' (Keynes, 1930: 3) – that is, *abstract* money of account which makes possible price lists and debt contract. As I have argued elsewhere, the widespread use of a uniform money of account in the sense of the 'countability' of value (ie, £s and pence) cannot arise from myriad discrete *individual* calculations of the utility of tradable commodities (Ingham, 2000).[5] However, from the present standpoint, the most serious difficulty with the commodity-exchange, neutral medium of exchange theory of money is that the 'village fair' is a very inadequate analogy with which to grasp the complexity of the capitalist system. Given its 'real' analysis assumptions, orthodox economics has been compelled to explain the emergence of the capitalist credit-money form as the *direct* representation of 'real' commodities – most obviously in the gold standard or the real bills doctrine (Smithin, 1994; Ingham, 1996). This formulation is riddled with conceptual and theoretical difficulties; but monetary developments have rendered it more blatantly mistaken. Gradually over the twentieth century, formal precious metals standards have ceased to operate and the reserves that form the bases for the expansion of the money supply have been reduced exclusively to other authorities' issues of promises to pay (see note 7). But it is important to recognize that the relationship between the issue of state and bank 'promises to pay' and the precious metals which they supposedly represented was always a useful ideological fiction (Ingham, 2000).

Actually existing capitalism, as opposed to the ideal type of the natural barter economy, was consituted by a new form of 'dematerialized' credit-money. From the early beginnings in late medieval Italy, state and bank debts – that is, their promises to pay – became accepted means of payment. In other words, debts could be discharged with a higher 'quality' form of debt that was trusted and/or enforced. This transformation in the form of money required the depersonalization and negotiability of debt and entailed a significant social structural change (Weber, 1978; Ingham, 1999). It is precisely this fact – that money is constituted by a particular *social relation* of credit/debt – that mainstream economics, in its preoccupation with the calculation of the utility of *commodities*, has found it difficult to comprehend. Money is not a 'thing' that is exchanged for another 'thing'; it is rather a social relation (Simmel, 1978 [1904]: 177–8; Ingham, 1996; 2000).

It is a measure of Keynes's genius that he was able to resist his academic training and milieu of intellectual orthodoxy in monetary theory. Especially in his *A Treatise on Money*, Keynes explored the economic consequences of the fact that that the elasticity of production of the supply of modern state and bank credit money is much greater than that of precious metal coinage, which is ultimately limited by nature and the costs of mining and minting.[6] Capitalist banks do not simply intermediate – that is, act as neutral distributors of accumulated deposits of savings (deposits make loans). Rather they 'manufacture' money by the creation of debt (loans make deposits) according to agreed rules and practices.[7]

A number of important consequences follow from this understanding of capitalist credit-money. First, as money is constituted by social relations, and therefore its supply is determined by the social system for the production of money, it cannot be simply a neutral veil for the measurement of the value of goods and services and the facilitation of their exchange. In this orthodox view, any disequilibrium between money and goods (eg, inflation) is the result of various imperfections or irrationality on the part of economic agents – such as deliberate 'debasement' or 'exuberant' credit creation. In contrast, in the implicitly sociological Keynesian conception, the relation between money and goods is socially enacted and is the outcome of the conflict between the potential debtors and creditors; that is to say, the production of money involves a struggle between those wishing to expand value through the creation of credit-money and those concerned to limit this through fear of the inflationary consequences that will undermine its role as a store of abstract value (Ingham, 1998, 2000; Mirowski, 1991).[8] This trade-off and tension between the expansion of value through the elasticity of the credit-money supply and the breakdown of monetary stability is arguably the *central dynamic of the modern capitalist system*. There are three main sources of demand for the creation of bank-credit money – demand from the 'real' economy for investment and income (including consumer demand); from motives to finance speculative monetary transactions (as in the case of LTCM); and from states to meet their commitments. The attempts to manage this central dynamic have profound implications for class and inequality.

The expansion and stabilisation of capitalist credit-money and inequality: first order effects

At the risk of oversimplification, it can be argued that the regime for the governance of western capitalism after 1945 entailed the subordination of the interests of money-capital to those of the producers.[9] Not without good reason, it was held that the mismanagement of money was, in a large measure, responsible for the serious instability and ineffectiveness of the capitalist mode of production. In particular, the 1930s depression was considered to be result of the perverse deflationary policies that were designed to preserve the value of money. The change of regime to the managed domestic economy after 1945 lasted until the early 1970s. It was based – at least nominally – on broadly Keynesian principles that entailed the political control of international capital movements and a modification of the internal power structure of capital in favour of production and employment (Smithin, 1996).

By the late 1960s, this 'golden age' of steady growth and low inflation was coming to an end. The complexities of the crises need not concern us here beyond noting that it was not deflation, as in the 1930s, but inflation that arguably posed the more serious threat to capitalism – as Lenin had always maintained that it might do. Eventually, absolute priority was given to the stabilization of the value of money. In 1979, Volcker began his work at the Federal Reserve in the US (Greider, 1988), followed shortly by the first

Thatcher government's monetarist experiment and related reform of industrial relations in order to curb 'cost-push' inflation. The details of the policy shift over the period from the late 1970s are familiar; here I wish very briefly to sketch the main distributional consequences of the restoration of money-capital to what Schumpeter considered to be its natural place as the 'headquarters' of the capitalist system.

It must be emphasized that these consequences are not the result of discrete random perturbations of a tendency toward equilibrium and price stability in the monetary system that periodically require technical 'corrections' by 'experts'.[10] Rather, monetary stabilization must be seen as the effect of the restructuring of the social relations of the means by which capitalist credit money is produced; for example, most obviously in recent times by the creation of 'independent' central banks. Moreover, the production and stabilization of money is a *continuous* socially enacted process which involves, states, money and capital markets, banks, the financial press, economic theory etc.

There are two general consequences of monetary stabilization by states and their central banks, which in essence is intended to reward the holding of assets in money-forms and to punish the acquisition of assets financed by the creation of credit-money (the debtor position). First, the adjustment of the balance of power is seen directly in the rise in *real* interest rates and falling *real* wages and profits. Intentionally induced deflation has the the effect of 'putting money back where it belongs – in the pockets of the Rockefellers' (Henwood, 1997). Since the late 1970s, real interest rates have been at historically record high levels (Rowthorn, 1995); and only in 1998 did real wages wages in the USA, for example, return to their 1989 levels.[11] Even with the curbing of inflation and the resumption of economic expansion, the relative dominance of money-capital continues to operate with the persistence of high real interest rates.[12]

Furthermore, the enhancement of money-capital power also has indirect, but no less tangible results. For example, the rentier share of corporate surplus in the US rose from between 20 to 30%, during the dominance of productive capital and labour from 1950–1970, to between 60 and 70% from the 1980s onwards (the following account relies on Henwood, 1997: ch. 2). Henwood estimates that with the inclusion of corporate borrowing for defence against takeovers and stock/share buy-backs, both of which indicate enhanced money-capital power, the transfers or flows from non-financial to financial interests between 1985 and 1995 was equal to total capital expenditure in large US corporations. This shift is also evident in the growing dominance of financial sectors *within* the corporation during the transition from the mass production managerial control era, with its emphasis on sales and growth, to the current preoccupation with productivity, profitability and shareholder value (Fligstein, 1990) This shift from growth and overall production to productivity and returns to capital lies behind the 'downsizing' and 'delayering' that has taken place since the late 1980s and early 1990s and which, in turn, has had an impact on employment and overall levels of inequality.[13] Furthermore, changing income differentials also show the dominance of the financial sector. The

TUC's survey of the earnings settlements in the UK for the first quarter of 1998 showed that the financial sector earnings had grown by 10.3% as opposed to an overall 5.6% in the private and 2.6% in the public sector (TUC, 1998; see also Adonis and Pollard, 1997).

Second, it would appear that 'pure' financial activity increases relative to the production and exchange of goods and services during the ascendancy of money capital – that is to say, in Marx's notation, M-M_1 circuits expand in relation to M-C-M_1. Using the US Federal Reserve's flow of funds data, Henwood has estimated that such flows accounted for by non-financial firms rose from 25 to 40%, but that financial flows rose from 2 to over 50% of GDP. Overall debt – corporate and household, which can be taken as rough guide to the level of expansion of the financial sector, rose from 130 to 150% of GDP in the 1950s to over 250% in the early 1990s (Henwood, 1997; see also Guttman, 1994: 38).

As I suggested earlier, the ascendancy phase of money-capital is usually accompanied by potentially contradictory financial deregulation and the expansion of credit that ultimately destabilizes money and marks the beginning of a new cycle or swing. By the late 1990s, the expansion of household debt in the US had reached record levels and the question of whether this would result in inflation and/or the bursting of a speculative bubble continues to be keenly contested.[14] Whatever the outcome, however, the distributional effects of the growing dominance of finance are clear: growing levels of inequality in which the relative enrichment of the money-capitalist creditor classes accompanies the growing indebtedness of the poor (Henwood, 1997: 64–71). Moreover, there is considerable historical evidence to show that such 'financialization' phases in the periodic swings in the structural composition of capitalist activity (that is, from M-C-M_1 to M-M_1) is accompanied by increasing economic inequality and social polarization (see Fischer, 1996; Arrighi, 1994).[15] And if the value of money is threatened, its is the indebted whose positions will deteriorate during the stabilization period of higher interest rates.

In short, the monetary and financial organization of capitalism exerts an independent effect on social inequality. The producers and controllers of money in all its myriad forms, I would argue, comprise the the naturally dominant element in capitalism – not the owners of the means of *production*, as Marx maintained. Furthermore, the routine (second order) operation of the credit-money system locks-in and reinforces any existing level of inequality; capitalist money is yet another locus of the ubiquitous 'Matthew Effect'.

Money, inequality and second order 'Matthew Effects'

In typical circumstances, it is the relatively poor majority of debtor 'classes' that borrows from the minority of net creditors and the owners and controllers of the means for producing credit-money. Moreover, the 'social relations' of this credit production systematically and compounds the inequality of the credit relation.

Whether lending either consists in the simple intermediated transmission of actual savings or involves the creation of credit-money by the banking system through the sanctioning of debt, loans are priced in relation to a calculation of the degree of risk of default. Despite assurances to the contrary, and leaving aside the technical complexities, risk assessment always entails a degree of arbitrariness that is based on lender power. Three basic considerations are taken into account. First, risk increases with the length of the term of the loan; second, it is considered to vary with the purpose of the loan – the purchase of assets, especially if they provide collateral, is less risky than loans for consumption; and third, the credit-worthiness of the borrower is assessed. Apart from the very top levels of *haute finance*, credit-rating is now a formal and almost completely depersonalized process. It is based on information provided by the borrower and credit-rating agencies.

This existence of credit-rating and the production of a *stratification order of credit-risk* is an example of what economists refer to as 'market failure' – that is to say, when a single price does not 'clear' the market by bringing supply and demand into equilibrium.[16] A *single* interest rate that would be considered high enough by the lender to cover most risk would also deter trustworthy and low risk borrowers. In particular, such a single sufficiently high risk-proof interest rate would not attract those who already 'hath' and who might want to borrow for investment in $M\text{-}M_1$ deals. But these high rates would not deter the reckless and desperate who 'hath not', nor swindlers.[17] Consequently, credit is 'rationed' (Stiglitz and Weiss, 1981).

Thus, there are important structural assymetries in the credit 'market'. On the one hand, low risk 'high net worth' individuals receive favourable terms – 'to those that hath shall be given'. Moreover, at the very highest levels credit relations can involve a significant degree of lender dependency – as, for example, in the perceived need to rescue the LTCM hedge fund to protect the US banking system. As the adage has it: if you owe the bank £5,000 you're in trouble, but if the sum is £5m it's in trouble. On the other hand, the converse is more commonly the case at the other end of the scale. The past decade or so has seen a rapid growth in lending from outside the core banking and financial sector to 'non status' borrowers or those with 'impaired' credit-rating – the literally discredited, as Goffman would surely have noted. For example, in 1997 the Office of Fair Trading referred to the City Mortgage Corporation – one of the largest 'non status' lenders with over 30,000 borrowers – as 'deceitful and oppressive'. It operated a dual interest structure in which loans to the 'impaired' begin at 3% above the 'unimpaired', but also *doubled* on first and subsequent arrears (*Financial Times* July, 19, 1997).[18]

The Consumer Credit Act (1983) provides a code that is supposed to prevent 'exorbitant' interest rates. However, in the absence of statutory ceilings, which are difficult to impose in a capitalist market system where the producers of credit must be seen to be in control, there are obvious problems of interpretation and of debtors' access to legal redress. The law as it stands can also be evaded by stratagems such as that used by Cash Converter chain of shops. They claim not to lend money, but to 'buy' the clients goods with an option of repurchase after twenty one days. However, the goods are subject to a 'storage' charge of 30% of the value and an APR of over 2,000% for a maximum of two twenty eight day periods, after which time the goods are sold (*Guardian*, 17 January, 1998).[19]

At the most elementary level, the lack of a current bank account creates further inequality. For example, customers who pay by direct debit from a bank account for a variety of goods and services – especially gas, electricity and other utilities – receive discounts. 'Unbanked' workers might have to make use of Cash Centres to cash their pay cheques, but they will typically be charged an 'introduction fee' and between 5 and 9% of the value of each cheque. In 1998, the 10% of the population without a bank account cashed cheques to the value of over £1.5bn in 1,200 centres nationwide (*Observer*, 22 August, 1999).[20]

In very general terms, we might then refer to three types of credit relation and, therefore, 'class' positions in relation to the means of credit production. The top level is constituted by the essential capitalist practice of borrowing – as always, either by pooled accumulated savings or bank created money – in order to make more money. This ranges from typical corporate enterprise in the production of goods and services ($M\text{-}C\text{-}M_1$) to the speculative or arbitrage strategies ($M\text{-}M_1$) of individuals or groups – such as the hedge funds or affluent students who use the low interest loans available to them to make higher yielding investments.[21] The second category involves prudent borrowing for consumption in the sense that current income will service the interest – for example, mortgages, home improvements, car purchases etc. The third level comprises the unbanked 'excluded', 'non-status borrowers' who ignore Micawber's warning and become indebted to avoid poverty; and those at the bottom who are rejected even by the 'loan sharks' – that is, the totally discredited.[22]

Moreover, as disadvantaged areas become less attractive to the mainstream banking and financial system, this polarization also compounds regional inequalities; for example, bank branches close, middle class local businesses leave and shops and services decline. (Dymski and Veitch, 1992, 1993, quoted in Leyshon and Thrift, 1997). However, there is some evidence to suggest that, in the USA at least, banks are beginning to realize that it is in their interest to remain active in taking measures to revitalize disadvantaged areas in order to create more customers – especially credit-worthy debtors. However, in the main, it is here at Braudel's level of 'material life' that we find a recrudescence of grass roots financial organization and monetary alternatives.

Third order effects: resistance, 'grassroots finance', and the limits of monetary self-help

The history of capitalism shows clearly how the financially 'excluded' have sought to organize alternatives to either the disregard or predations of the mainstream banks and financial institutions.[23] If they prove successful and profitable, some of these initiatives are ultimately incorporated by the mainstream financial system. Recently in the UK, for example, many building societies have been 'demutualized' and taken on the normal capitalist practice of giving priority to the generation of profits for shareowners.

At the same time, however, new forms of grassroots money and finance have once again expanded across the capitalist world in the wake of the further concentration of the financial system and increased levels of economic and social inequality and financial exclusion. These developments have received good deal of academic and journalistic attention that can only be touched upon here. Rather, my major focus will be to raise some of the more general theoretical issues concerning the scope and limits of such alternatives. Do these initiatives fulfil the intention of countering exclusion and reducing inequality or are they ironically the basis for further 'Matthew Effects'? Currently, there are three main forms of alternative money and financial organization that occupy a marginal position *vis a vis* the mainstream system: local exchange trading systems/schemes (LETS); authentic local currencies; and various forms of 'micro-finance' such as credit unions.

Local Exchange Trading Systems/Schemes (LETS)

Since the original LETS was founded on Vancouver Island, Canada in 1983, they have spread rapidly across North America, Australia, New Zealand and Great Britain (Boyle, 1999; Bowring, 1998). In the UK, the first Norwich based scheme appeared in 1985 and although the number had only increased to five by 1992, there are now over 450 LETS (Bowring, 1998; Williams, 1996, 1998; Lee, 1996).[24]

Although LETS refer to local 'currencies', they are, strictly speaking, barter-credit associations in which offers and wants of goods and services are matched. Members are issued with LETS cheques, which shadow the national currency, but signal the locality ('Olivers' in Bath, 'Bobbins' in Manchester, 'Tales' in Canterbury etc). These media of exchange are placed in local collection boxes or posted directly to a central clearing house after the transaction has been completed, where members' accounts are credited or debited. This form of exchange occupies a position between simple barter and a fully developed money economy. LETS currencies are a money of account and media of exchange; but they do not function beyond the *direct representation* of the actual goods and services to be exchanged; that is to say, they conform precisely to the concept of money as the *neutral veil* in the orthodox economic model. LETS 'currencies' go some way towards overcoming the impediment to exchange of an absence of a double coincidence of wants. Within the limits imposed by the typical size of the systems, multilateral transactions and the separation in time of the matching of offers and wants is achieved.[25] (The average scheme has only 85 members and a £6,000 turnover (Williams, 1998); but Manchester had 7,000 members by early 1997 (Bowring, 1998: 93)). The successful operation of LETS requires frequent, regular trades and mechanisms have been developed to discourage 'hoarding', which might threaten the system as confidence in the use of LETS cheques, like all simple media of exchange, depends on a readiness to buy as well as to sell (Bowring, 1998: 97–98). In other words, LETS media of exchange are not stores of abstract value and means of unilateral payment/settlement, like full money.[26]

The benefits of LETS are yet to be thoroughly assessed; but it is clear that they are sources of both social and economic inclusion. Although a large proportion of the schemes' members are from the self-employed middle class who follow an environmental and alternative lifestyle ethos, the unemployed do participate disproportionately (Williams, 1998). However, both actual and potential 'Matthew Effects' are evident. Middle class resources such as tools and equipment or scarce skills and knowledge earn credits with relatively little expenditure of time; whereas the lower classes typically offer time-consuming, labour intensive services. Moreover, any significant expansion of LETS schemes would almost inevitably involve an interpenetration with the wider mainstream economy and would further enhance the position of the 'legal tender rich' middle class participants. Any direct connection with the mainstream economy could create dual system in which the local credit occupied a second class position. It is likely that the possessors of legal tender might only participate in LETS to the extent that it was to their advantage. For example, the middle classes' scarce skills and resources would generate sufficient LETS credits, at a very favourable rate of exchange, with which 'to hire from a gamut of unskilled – and typically female – LETS members, servants, who in addition to doing their own housework, are willing to perform domestic chores for the wealthy' (Bowring, 1998: 104). In other words, such a development would actually intensify structured inequality by creating a 'class' that occupied a dependent and subordinate position in relation to the local currency (see Bowring, 1998).

Local currencies

It has been suggested that any reinforcement of inequality by LETS might be avoided if their media of exchange were to be based on an alternative standard rather than merely shadowing legal tender. The *absolute* state monopoly of currency issue is relatively recent. Shortages of state money led to the growth of local currencies in provincial British towns as late as the early 19th century (Davies, 1996).[27] But today, the issue of a *freely circulating* local currencies, which are unrelated to any particular transaction and denominated in units of time, is much more prevalent outside the UK; for example, they are to be found in over thirty US cities.[28] The largest is in Ithaca (New York State), whose 'Hours' are used by over 2% of the population, including over 300 businesses, and have financed $1.5bn transactions (*The Wall Street Journal*, June 27, 1996). Some rather confused claims have been made for the time standard of value. It is argued, for example, that a unit of currency with this basis would not reproduce the inequalities between workers in the formal economy, 'since every hour worked ... is equivalent in value' (Bowring, 1998: 109). However, this outcome would depend entirely on the willingness of the possessors of the most marketable goods and skills to accept such an egalitarian non-market standard of value. There is some evidence that the time standard of value does encourage people to use non-market criteria in comparing the value of their time with that of others. But, as in Montpelier – the state capital of Vermont, '[a] lawyer could still opt to charge five Hours for an hour of work, while a babysitter might charge half an Hour ...' (*Economist*, June 28, 1997: 65). Again it is the interpenetration with the formal local economy that compromises the local currency's autonomy, which if it is to become more widely accepted requires an exchange rate with the legal tender (as of the mid-1990s, it was usually average hourly wage rate of $10).

As with LETS, the relatively narrow range of goods and services on offer reduces the liquidity of local currencies; in the words of another Vermont participant: 'You can only have so many massages and aromatherapies in your lifetime' (*Economist*, June 28, 1997: 65). But the insertion of local currencies into the formal economy, in order to expand the ranges of goods and services, is limited by their not being accepted as legal tender for the payment of taxes, which, moreover, might be assessed on the total of *both* local currency and legal tender transactions. The situation is by no means straightforward and to a large extent developments depend on the attitude of the tax authorities. If transactions remain tax free, the acceptance of local currency will be limited by the size of its sphere of circulation and liquidity. If these increase, local currency transactions will attract the attention of the tax authorities and central banks and limit their attraction and advantages.

In any event, unless they can be accumulated and lent, local currencies fulfill only the medium of exchange function of money and restrict their holders to a relatively passive role in the capitalist economy. Moreover, any accumulated repositories of local currencies would not be part of the central bank/banking system giro and, consequently, could not be used for 'manufacture' money, in the formal system, where bank lending creates money in the form of deposit account debt as I have outlined. Only in a very small minority of atypical cases – as in Harvey, North Dakota (population 2,300) – have local banks accepted deposits in local currency and then lent them on interest free (*The Wall Street Journal*, June 27, 1996). However, LETS and local currencies might have more effect were they to be more extensively integrated with existing self-help afforded by existing credit unions (Bowring, 1998).

Micro-finance and credit unions

Credit unions, which are the most extensive form of micro-finance in the advanced capitalist economies, are – usually non-profit making – mutual savings and lending associations. Apart from the UK, they are commonplace in the Anglo-American type economies. One in 4 Australians belongs to a credit union, but in the UK the figure is only 1 in 300. However, the number of unions is growing and there are now about 600 with 200,000 members and £104m share capital (*Guardian*, January 29, 1997). In the UK, there are two types of credit union: first, an understandably small number that cater mainly for the 'non status' borrowers who are excluded from the mainstream system; and, second, the majority of occupationally based unions. Current legislation, which was framed to prevent competition with existing banks and financial firms, requires that credit union members have a 'bond of association' – such as common occupation. Most police forces have a credit union and the London Cabbies' Pentecostal Union has £3.5m deposits.

Obviously, credit unions cannot be composed entirely of the dispossessed or excluded and this constraint is the source of particularly perverse 'Matthew Effects'. In the formal financial system, high income groups have excess savings over debt, whereas in lower income groups the converse is the case. However, Berthaud and Hinton (1989) found that this relation is reversed in credit unions where, in order to take advantage of the low interest rates, the higher income groups have excess borrowing over saving; and lower income groups save more than they borrow. As they stand, then, many credit unions effect transfers from the poor to the rich. In other words, inequality is reproduced entirely by the 'internal' operation of these particular financial relations.

However, the situation might be changing. In the first place, the New Labour government in the UK would like further to increase the number and scope of credit unions in its efforts to reduce financial exclusion and welfare dependency (*Financial Times*, November 4, 1998: 17). The government proposes to remove the limit credit union membership, which currently stands at 5,000, and to relax the rules on common bonds of association. Secondly, other forms of micro-credit are beginning to appear in this country. In a recent survey, the British Banking Association found 62 schemes in which banks, local businesses and advice organizations had created special loan funds for 'a wide range of people who fall outside the banks' conventional business finance system' (*Guardian*, May 11, 1999). However, it is not clear whether or not these are simply a means of mopping profitable opportunities that tend to be overlooked at the margins of conventional finance. Again, if these schemes remain outside the formal central bank-based giro, it will seriously limit the capacity to create the credit to 'include'. All indications are that the established banks would strongly resist any such competition, even if it was designed to include those they had already disregarded.[29]

Conclusions

Late nineteenth and early twentieth century classical sociology, which laid the foundations for all subsequent analysis of class and stratification, was based upon the analysis of capitalist market and property relations *in the sphere of the production and exchange of commodities in the so-called 'real' economy*. Here, money is seen as the measure or alienated embodiment of these social relations of production. However, theory on both these related levels – that is, the primacy of the 'real' relation of production and the epiphenomenal nature of money – is ultimately based on a one-sided and, I would argue, seriously defective understanding of the structure and operation of capitalism. Of the early social scientists, only Schumpeter really grasped the precise significance of the distinctive 'monetary side'.[30] What eventually became known as capitalism involved more than the formal freedoms of the labour market and the concentrated appropriation of the means of production. A further constitutive element, I would argue, is the institutionalized production of money capital in the form of credit money. 'Credit operations of whatever shape or kind do affect the workings of the monetary system; more important, they do affect the workings of the capitalist engine – so much so as to become an essential part of it *without which the rest cannot be understood at all*' (Schumpeter, 1994 [1954]: 318 emphasis added). As I have briefly sketched, capitalist money itself consists in the social relations that constitute the hierarchy of promises to pay that are produced and controlled by states and banking systems. In short, people are systematically related to the means and social relations of the production of money and three orders of the effects of these relations were outlined in a preliminary way.

It would be mistaken to press this line of argument too far; and it must be made clear that I am not claiming that the conventional emphasis on the 'material' side should be inverted. Rather, I would argue that 'class' in late twentieth century capitalism cannot be fully understood without an explication of the way its distinctive monetary and financial system exerts an autonomous effect on inequality. But, for those still wedded to, say, the Marxian notion of 'fictitious capital' (Harvey, 1982; Lipietz, 1985), or even attracted by the more recent concept of 'virtual' or 'postmodern' money (Leyshon and Thrift, 1997), perhaps a further reflection on the example of the British mortgagers might serve to emphasize the central argument. Ultimately, their class situation was produced by *two* relatively autonomous sets of capitalist social relations – those of the labour market and production process *and* those by which the supply and value of money is established. Money is not only an expression of class inequality – as either measure or store of wealth; the conditions of its creation are, rather, an integral part of 'the struggle for economic existence' (Weber, 1978: 108).

This elaboration of Weber's understanding of money raises a final and most difficult problem. In his sophisticated and sociologically informed interpretation of the Austrian economists' defence of the market as an arena of effective competition, Weber argued that money could never be merely 'a voucher for unspecified utilities' (Weber, 1978: 108). Rather, a stable purchasing power could only be established through the struggle between the producers and possessors of *both* money and goods.[31] Is it then possible to both regulate the means by which this struggle is enacted – or, indeed, the outcome – to the extent of 'financial citizenship', in which individuals would possess certain rights with regard to the social system by which money is produced and its value maintained? Whatever the intention of the current British government's policies on financial 'inclusion' and however sketchy they might be, it is nevertheless the case that citizenship is implied by the proposals for universal bank accounts, access to credit unions, stakeholder pensions, ISAs etc? For example, the replacement of the Conservative government's tax sheltered TESSAs with ISAs illustrates the tension in the notion of 'financial citizenship'. For a variety of motives, the Labour government decided to replace the tax exempt PEP and TESSA schemes, which had been introduced by previous Conservative governments, with Individual Savings Schemes (ISAs) whose greater emphasis on cash saving, as opposed to investment in equities, was thought to be more socially 'inclusive'. However, from the outset the major financial corporations and firms were extremely reluctant to participate because they considered that the simple cash savings scheme that the government wished to encourage would not generate an acceptable level of profit. ISAs have now been introduced, but it would appear that they have not had the intended impact of extending financial services to low earners (*Financial Times*, May 4, 1999). It would be ironic if this element of the government's attempt to sidestep past ideological antinomies, in its quest for a 'modern' transcendental form of distributive justice, should perhaps lead to the unveiling of the most acute expression of the old 'war' between class and citizenship (Marshall, 1950).

Notes

1 There are honourable exceptions, most obviously Simmel (1978 [1907]) and also Dodd (1994); and also a recent revival of interest. But I have argued that many of these do not go far enough in the analysis of the actual social production of money (Ingham, 1998)

2 At the time of its collapse, LCTM had on-balance sheet assets equal to at least 25 times its equity. In other words, its debts were 25 times greater than its capital (*Financial Times*, June 18, 1999).

3 The commodity theory of money is ultimately based on an ideological 'naturalization' of money as a precious commodity which, arguably, makes it easier to comprehend. Fundamentally, the quantity theory of money is based upon the commodity theory's metaphors of tangible objects and an inelasticity of production that is the result of natural/physical constraints. The more transparent social relation that constitutes credit-money is more difficult to subsume under this analysis as modern economic theory and central bankers discovered to their discomfort (see Ingham, 2000 and forthcoming).

4 Barter requires a double coincidence of wants – that is, A has chickens but wants ducks at the same time that B offers ducks but wants chickens. In a fundamental sense, money makes markets possible in the sense that there can be price lists that coordinate supply and demand. Strictly speaking, barter can only be bilateral and not decentralized, multilateral exchange separated in time and space, which requires at least a money of account (Ingham, 1996; 2000). Money *is* the 'invisible hand'.

5 The tobacco used as a medium of exchange in 17th century Louisiana only became 'money', Grierson (1977) argues, when its price was fixed at 3 shillings a pound. As shillings were not minted, they had a virtual existence as an abstract money of account.

6 See Keynes implicitly 'sociological' formulation of credit money creation: '[I]t is evident that there is no limit to the amount of bank money which the banks can safely create *provided that they move forward in step*. The words italicised are the clue to the behaviour of the system ... Each Bank Chairman sitting in his parlour may regard himself as the passive instrument of "outside forces" over which he has no control; yet the "outside forces" may be nothing but himself and his fellow chairmen, and certainly not his depositors.' (Keynes, 1930: 26–27). Here Keynes is stressing that the banks have the power to decide what the rules will be for the creation of credit money – that is to say, 'moving forward in step'.

7 In this regard, two issues have dominated economic theory in the 20th century. First, whether banks 'manufacture' money by lending that is relatively independent of any given level of incoming deposits. As late as 1921, the eminent economist Cannan, writing in the *Economic Journal*, argued, by analogy, that if a cloakroom attendant loaned out the deposited coats this would not involve the creation of more coats and, moreover, they would have to be recovered from the borrowers before the owners could wear them. But as Schumpeter explains, this is precisely what happens in banks – depositors and borrowers have simultaneous use of the 'same' money (Schumpeter, 1994 [1954]: 1113–1114). The bank credit money multiplier is now orthodoxy; but the nature of the process of credit-money creation remains the source of a second major dispute in economic monetary theory, and indeed in economics in general (see Wray, 1990; Smithin, 1994). On the one hand, monetarist and other orthodoxies whose intellectual position can be traced back to the earlier commodity and quantity theories of money (and the now abandoned deposits makes loans theory), maintain that the central bank can 'exogenously' fix the money supply quite rigidly, as they assume the mints did in the days of precious metal coinage. There are of course a range of devices and strategies by which central banks attempt to control the banking system's production of credit money. The two main ones are the purchase and sale of government securities to adjust the banking system's reserves; and the interest rate. However, the empirical details of how this actually occurs are unclear and have proved to be intractable problems for orthodox economic theory. Indeed, Friedman once suggested that, as money was neutral in the long term, this was not an important question and one might simply assume that the money was dropped into the economy by helicopter. (It has also been pointed out that this position was intellectually incoherent in the insistence on monetary neutrality and the vociferous advocacy of controlling the money *supply*.) On the other hand, the Post-Keynesian school and others maintain that money is relatively freely produced 'endogenously' in the banking system, as I have outlined above (see Wray 1990; Smithin 1994). In this view, money can only be controlled, if at all, by restricting demand through interest rates. The debacle of monetarism in the early 1980s, when the authorities found that they were unable to take the first step in controlling money with any certainty because they were unable precisely to define the various forms of money – M_1, M_2, ..., M_{10} etc, would seem to support the general case for 'endogeneity'. However, from a sociological standpoint the 'exogeneity-endogeneity' antinomy does not capture the complexity of the process of monetary creation which involves a struggle between two powerful agencies. According to the US central banker, Alan Holmes: 'In the real world banks extend credit, creating deposits in the process, and look for the reserves later. The question then becomes one of whether and how the Federal Reserve will accomodate the demand for reserves. In the very short run, the Federal Reserve has little or no choice about accomodating that demand; over time its influence can obviously be felt.' (quoted in Henwood, 1997: 220; see also Gardiner, 1993).

8 However, as we shall see, creditor classes, with an interest in purely financial and monetary deals often pursue potentially contradictory ends – for example, they press for both financial deregulation and monetary stabilization policies.

9 Of course, the production and control of money has been the most jealously guarded power of capital since states were 'alienated' to the bourgeoisie in national debts from the sixteenth century onwards (see Arrighi, 1994: 11–13). In England, the deal was sealed by the formation of the Bank of England in 1694. Notwithstanding some public accountability, there is no democratic control of capitalist banking, as Pauly has recently asked: *Who Elected the Bankers?* (1997).

10 That is to say, the standard orthodox 'rational expectations' economic equilibrium model, of which the 'theory' of 'reflexive modernization' would appear to be the sociological analogue (see Giddens, 1990).
11 For evidence on the long run historical pattern of the cycle or swing between high and low real interest rates and profits and wages, see Fischer (1996).
12 The emerging global consensus on what constitutes capitalist 'best practice' consists in low tax, high real interest rate, stable money regimes; flexible labour etc. This can be enforced by the impact of capital movements and foreign exchange markets. This is precisely why Keynes argued for controls on international capital movements (see Helleiner, 1994).
13 Most orthodox explanations place emphasis on the impact of technological change.
14 It is of great theoretical and practical significance that the supply of credit money continues to expand whilst inflation remains low. The continuance of this state of affairs now threatens the latest generation of macro-economic empirical generalizations (which tend be regarded almost as 'general laws'), such as NAIRU (non-accelerating inflation rate of unemployment), in the same way that the economic events of the 1970s challenged earlier ones. For example, 'stagflation' appeared to cast doubt on the unemployment/inflation tradeoff expressed by the 'Phillips Curve'.
15 In his analysis of Reagan's America in the 1980s, Phillips has argued that at least since the age of Habsberg Spain 'an excessive preoccupation and a tolerance of debt' has been accompanied increasing inequality and social polarization (Phillips, 1993). These ideas have been incorporated into Arrighi's dazzling structural history of capitalist development which integrates Smith, Marx, Marshall, Braudel, Hicks, Schumpeter and argues that such 'financialization' signals the end of accumulations cycles and the decline of the hegemonic power (Arrighi, 1994). Details aside, the importance of this work for our present concerns is that 'class' – broadly speaking – should not be seen exclusively as a function of the social relations of *production*.
16 At a global level, the power of the credit-raters such as Moodys and Standard and Poor has increased enormously (see Sinclair, 1994). As credit risk cannot be calculated on the basis of fixed and objectively verifiable probabilities, it entails the social construction of a symbolic status order. It is therefore surprising that sociologists have not given credit-rating more attention. For an analysis of the autonomous effect of a status order which created differences in the market price of a single good uniform quality, which according economic theory should not occur, see Podolny (1993).
17 This particular market failure is an example of what economists refer to as 'adverse selection' – in which a single price cannot discriminate between acceptable and unacceptable purchasers and is typical of the market for insurance in which there are many 'prices' in that the premium is related to the level of risk.
18 A quick comparison of the financial advice pages of the weekend broadsheet newspapers with the small ads for the 'non-status' money lenders in the tabloids shows the difference.
19 Unlike pawnbrokers, 'cash converters' do not return any excess profit from the sale after the deduction of interest charges. Although with their typical rates, it is very unlikely that their would be any net surplus!
20 In order to tackle fraud, the 1992 Cheques Act introduced the concept of 'account payee' as law; but this now makes the cashing of cheques by friends or pubs more difficult.
21 There are obviously pronounced cultural capital effects. These are now also closely related to the possession of the appropriate information and communication technology. Telephone and Internet banking and financial services reduce transaction costs and offer higher returns and will further increase 'financial polarization'.
22 These are approximately the same as Braudel's three levels of capitalism – the top level of the truly capitalist 'jungle' of predators; the intermediate, impersonal, level of the 'invisible hand' market; and the underlying level of 'material' life (Braudel, 1981, 1982, 1984).
23 Indeed, there is a long heterodox tradition in economic monetary theory which is related with the underconsumptionist view that economic stagnation is caused by insufficient demand which may be remedied by the production of money. These ideas were also often associated with populist critiques of the 'money powers'. Mainstream economics has generally regarded

proponents of this view as 'monetary cranks'; but Keynes, understandably, had some sympathy with such 'brave heretics' (Keynes, 1973[1936] ch. 23; see also Clark, 1989).

24 A two and a half year ESRC project – *Evaluating LETS as a Means of Tackling Social Exclusion* – was started in 1998 (Theresa.Aldridge@btinternet.com).

25 It is argued by the school of 'new monetary economics' that advances in information technology, by making it possible to deal almost instantaneously with enormous numbers of matched wants and offers of goods and services, might possibly transform the whole economy into what would be, in effect, a gigantic LETS scheme. See Mervyn King (Deputy Governor of the Bank of England) lecture to US Federal Reserve's Annual Symposium, August 1999 (*Financial Times*, 30 August, 1998; on 'new monetary economics, see Smithin 1994). Such thinking is associated with the view that technology might bring about the 'end of money'. But as I have noted this only applies, if at all, to 'money' as medium of exchange only and, in a typical category error, conflates the form of money with monetary *practice* (see Angell, 1997; and my reply 1998a).

26 LETS cheques are, in the terms of the early 19th century Banking versus Currency schools dispute on the nature of credit, 'real bills' in that they directly represent the actual exchange of real goods. The Banking School maintained that such transferable instruments of credit issued by banks were, in addition to commodity money, also 'money' insofar as they could be used as a means of payment.

27 It should be noted that the two major functions of money as media of exchange and means of payment/settlement were separated into two different forms in most advanced coinage money systems. The Romans used base metal media of exchange with a high velocity of circulation in small localized transactions; but they were not legal tender in the payment of taxes and the settlement of large debts.

28 US tax laws restrict credit barter schemes like LETS. Edgar Cahn, the Washington lawyer who developed the idea of 'Time Dollars' was able to persuade the US Inland Revenue Service that these were 'social' as opposed to 'economic' earnings and need not be taxed (*Guardian*, 22 March, 1995). In this system, 'Time Dollars' are paid to community volunteers who can then spend them on services for themselves and their families and so produce a kind of 'voluntary welfare multiplier'.

29 The relaxation of the 'bond of association' regulation in the US in 1982 led to great expansion of credit union membership, from 44m (assets $69bn) in 1980 to 71m (assets $316bn) in the late 1990s. However, in February 1998, the Supreme Court decided in favour of the banks' petition that the relaxation violated the original Federal Credit Union Act of 1934. It seems likely that new legislation will overturn the Court's decision; but the American Bankers Association are devising attractive schemes that would enable them to swallow up and control the credit unions assets (Leonard, 1998) ['Credit Unions vs. Banks', *Nolo's Legal Word*, March 5, 1998, www.nolo.com]. Of course, the net result might still be 'inclusion' albeit on the establishment's term and, moreover, after the unions have created a new class of the 'creditworthy'.

30 But given the force of economic orthodoxy even he was an ambivalent reluctant 'creditist' (Earley, 1994).

31 This is perhaps the clearest expression of Weber's argument that the formal rationality of capitalism had substantive bases. It is directly related to the 'socialist calculation debate' of the early twentieth century which retains a relevance for current debates on financial inclusion. For a recent exposition see O'Neill (1999: ch. 9).

References

Adonis, A. and Pollard, S., (1997), *A Class Act*, London: Hamish Hamilton.
Angell, I., (1997) 'Flip side of the coin', *Financial Times*, 22 December 1997.
Arrighi, G., (1994), *The Long Twentieth Century*, London: Verso.
Bowring, F., (1998) 'LETS: An Eco-Socialist Alternative?', *New Left Review*, 232: 91–111.

Boyle, D., (1999), *Funny Money: In Search of Alternative Cash*, London: Harper Collins, *British Journal of Sociology*, 50 (1): 77–96.

Braudel, F., (1985), *Civilization and Capitalism, Volume 2: The Wheels of Commerce*, London: Fontana.

Clark, D., (1989), 'Monetary cranks', in Eatwell *et al.* (eds), *The New Palgrave, Money*, London: Macmillan.

Crompton, R., (1998), *Social Stratification*, Cambridge: Polity Press.

Dodd, N., (1994), *The Sociology of Money*, Cambridge: Polity Press.

Earley, J., (1994), 'Joseph Schumpeter: A Frustrated "Creditist"', in Dymski, G. and Pollin, R. (eds), *New Perspectives in Monetary Macoeconomics*, Ann Arbor: University of Michigan Press, 337–351.

Fischer, D., (1996), *The Great Wave*, New York: Oxford University Press.

Fligstein, N., (1990), *The Transformation of Corporate Control*, Cambridge, M.: Harvard University Press.

Ganssman, H., (1988), 'Money – a symbolically generalised medium of communication? On the concept of money in recent sociology', *Economy and Society*, 17 (4): 285–315.

Gardiner, G., (1993), *Towards True Monetarism*, London: Dulwich Press.

Giddens, A., (1990), *The Consequences of Modernity*, Cambridge: Polity Press.

Grieder, W., (1987), *Secrets of the Temple*, New York: Simon and Schuster.

Grierson, P., (1977), *The Origins of Money*, London: London University, The Athlone Press.

Guttman, R., (1994), *How Credit Money Shapes the Economy*, New York: M.E. Sharpe.

Hahn, F., (1987), 'The Foundations of Monetary Theory', in deCecco, M. and Fitoussi, J. (eds), *Monetary Theory and Economic Institutions*, London: Macmillan, 21–43.

Harmes, A., (1998), 'Institutional investors and the reproduction of neoliberalism', *Review of International Political Economy*, 5 (1): 92–121.

Helleiner, E., (1994), *States and the Emergence of Global Finance*, Ithaca: Cornell University Press.

Henwood, D., (1997), *Wall Street*, London: Verso.

Ingham, G., (1996), 'Money is a Social Relation', *Review of Social Economy*, LIV (4): 507–529.

Ingham, G., (1998a), 'Still a lot of value left in money', *Financial Times*, 6 January 1998.

Ingham, G., (1998b), 'On the Underdevelopment of the "Sociology of Money"', *Acta Sociologica*, 41 (1): 3–18.

Ingham, G., (1999), 'Capitalism, Money and Banking: a Critique of recent Historical Sociology', *British Journal of Sociology*, 50 (1): 76–96.

Ingham, G., (2000), '"Babylonian Madness": On the Sociological and Historical "Origins" of Money', in Smithin, J. (ed.), *What is Money?*, London: Routledge.

Keynes, M., (1930), *A Treatise on Money*, London: Macmillan.

Lee, R., (1996), 'Moral Money?', *Environment and Planning*, 28 (8).

Leyshon, A. and Thrift, N., (1997), *Money/Space*, London: Routledge.

Marshall, T., (1963), 'Citizenship and Social Class', in *Sociology at the Crossroads*, Heineman: London.

Menger, K., (1892) 'On the Origins of Money', *Economic Journal*, 2: 239–255.

Minsky, H., (1982), 'The Financial Instability Hypothesis', in Kindleberger, C.P. and Laffargue, J-P. (eds), *Financial Crises*, Cambridge: Cambridge University Press.

Mirowski, P., 'Postmodernism and the Social theory of Value', *Journal of Post Keynesian Economics*, 13 (4): 565–582.

O'Neill, J., (1999), *The Market: Ethics, Knowledge and Politics*, London: Routledge.

Podolny, J., (1993), 'A Status-based Model of Market Competition', *American Journal of Sociology*, 98: 829–72.

Rogers, C., (1989), *Money, Interest and Capital*, Cambridge: Cambridge University Press.

Rowthorn, R., (1995), 'Capital Formation and Unemployment', *Oxford Review of Economic Policy*, 11 (1): 26–39.

Schumpeter, J., (1994 [1954]), *A History of Economic Analysis*, London: Routledge.

Simmel, G., (1978 [1907]), *The Philosophy of Money*, London: Routledge.

Sinclair, T., (1994), 'Passing judgement: credit rating processes as regulatory mechanisms of governance in the emerging world order', *Review of International Economy*, 1: 133–150.

Smithin, J., (1994), *Controversies in Monetary Economics: Ideas, Issues and Policy*, Aldershot: Edward Elgar.

Smithin, J., (1996) *Macroeconomic Policy and the Future of Capitalism*, Aldershot: Edward Elgar.

Stiglitz, J. and Weiss, A., (1981), 'Credit Rationing and Markets with Imperfect Information', *American Economic Review*, 71: 393–410.

Valdez, S., (1997), *An Introduction to Global Financial Markets*, London: Macmillan.

Weber, M., (1978), *Economy and Society*, Berkeley: University of California Press.

Weber, M., (1981 [1927]) *General Economic History*, New Brunswick, NJ: Transaction Publishers.

Williams, C., (1996), 'Informal Sector Responses to Unemployment: An Evaluation of the Potential of Local Exchange Trading Systems', *Work Employment and Society*, 10 (2).

Wray, R., (1990), *Money and Credit in Capitalist Economies*, Aldershot: Edward Elgar.

Social polarization in the electronic economy

Jan Pahl

Introduction

The previous chapter ended with the idea of 'financial citizenship', in which individuals would possess certain rights with regard to the system by which money is produced and its value maintained (Ingham, this volume, p. 80). Such rights might be expressed in terms of access to banking, credit and other financial services, that is to say, in terms of access to the means of consumption. Discussions about class increasingly identify consumption as a way of differentiating social groups (see for example, Crompton and Scott in this volume, and Pakulski and Waters, 1996). Bauman has argued that the poor of today are, first and foremost, those who cannot consume as much as other people: as 'flawed consumers' they are failing in one of the most crucial social duties of citizens in a consumer society (Bauman, 1998, 90).

This chapter is concerned with two of the processes which shape patterns of consumption within households. First, there are changes in financial services and in the forms which money can take. We are currently in the midst of a revolution in the ways in which ordinary people receive, hold and spend their money. Far more people than ever before now have bank and building society accounts, use cheque cards, credit cards, debit cards and smart cards, and pay their bills by direct debit or standing order. Their accounts are not just with traditional banks but with building societies and supermarkets, and they may be accessed by phone or through the Internet. All these developments, which are included within the term 'new forms of money', are creating a fast-growing electronic economy, in which money is increasingly abstract and invisible.

Secondly, there are the social and economic processes which shape financial arrangements within households. The disparity in incomes between men and women, particularly during the child rearing years, means that there has to be some sharing of resources if non-earners are not to have a lower standard of living than earners. Every household has to devise some arrangement by which incomes can be shared, joint bills paid and individual needs met. Even though many couples never consciously decide to organize their finances in one way or another, in every case there is a describable system of money management.

The development of new forms of money is creating new patterns of gender and class inequality and raising many questions. Until quite recently many men handed over a wage packet to their wives each week, social security payments came as cash, and cash was used for much bill-paying and most shopping. How have the financial arrangements of individuals and households adapted to the development of new forms of money? What is the position of those individuals and households who are still in the cash economy, or those for whom getting credit is problematic? Some wives may have gained the right to a credit card through the credit-worthiness of their husbands, but with the constraint that their spending will be subjected to the scrutiny of the main cardholder. What effect will this have on their use of credit?

The aim of this chapter is to present some tentative answers to these and other questions, using results from a recently completed study (Pahl, 1999). The hypothesis which underpinned the study was that new forms of money are creating a set of filters which enhance or constrain the access which individuals have to the market. Those who are credit-card-rich must be not only credit-worthy but also confident of their ability to manage the technology and to repay the debts which will be incurred. Individuals who are credit-card-poor may have failed to pass the scrutiny of the credit assessors, or they may simply lack the confidence to use the new forms of money. Thus spending money is no longer a simple cash transaction, but an electronic process, access to which is shaped by fundamental social and economic forces.

Previous research on couples and their money

Previous research has shown that some couples pool all their income, typically in a joint bank account, and attach considerable importance to financial equality. Other couples maintain independence in financial matters, dividing responsibility for the payment of joint bills and attaching importance to privacy and autonomy in financial matters. Some couples give overall financial control to one partner, while others divide finances into separate spheres, making each partner responsible for specific areas of spending. The most recent evidence, from the British Household Panel Survey, suggests that about half of all couples pool their incomes and share management of the pool. In about a third of couples finances are managed by the wife, while in about one sixth they are managed by the husband, typically with a housekeeping allowance being transferred to the wife. Finally, a small but growing number of couples hold and manage their money as though they were still two separate individuals (Laurie and Rose, 1994; Laurie, 1996).

The ways in which couples manage their money reflect a range of different variables. When money is short and making ends meet is hard, women typically manage finances on behalf of the household. At higher income levels, employment status becomes important. If only the husband is in employment he tends to control the money, often delegating the management of a part of it to his wife. The higher the proportion of the household income contributed by the wife, the more likely it is that she will control finances and have power in financial decisions (see, for example, Brannen and Wilson, 1987; Burgoyne and

Morison, 1997; Laurie and Rose, 1994; Goode, Callender and Lister, 1998; Morris and Ruane, 1989; Pahl, 1989 and 1995; Vogler and Pahl, 1993 and 1994; Wilson, 1987).

Crucially, this research has underlined the fact that the household cannot be treated as an unproblematic financial unit. Opening up the 'black box' of the domestic economy has shown that individuals can be poor even though the household has an adequate income. In general, men tend to have more personal spending money than women, especially in households where they control finances. Women are more likely than men to deprive themselves when money is short, and this situation is most likely to occur in low income households and in households with adequate incomes but strong male control of finances (Vogler and Pahl, 1994). Cross-national research has shown that in general women have different priorities for spending than men. Where women control household finances a higher proportion of household income is likely to be spent on the children and on collective expenditure for the household as a whole, compared with the situation when men control finances (Blumberg, 1988; Dwyer and Bruce, 1988; Pahl, 1989).

However, all this research essentially conceptualized money as cash. Over the past thirty years there have been dramatic changes in the ways in which ordinary people receive, hold and spend their money. The first credit card was launched in 1966, to be followed by store cards, debit cards, loyalty cards and smart or chargeable cards. Banking by telephone or computer began in the 1980s, with an accelerating expansion in the use of electronic banking services throughout the 1990s. The Credit Card Research Group produces information about the use of different types of credit and debit cards. In 1997 there were 37 million credit cards and 37 million debit cards in the United Kingdom. About 16% of retail expenditure involved the use of a credit card, and 91% a debit card (Credit Card Research Group, 1998). However, since then all these figures have increased, with the rise in the numbers of debit cards being particularly striking.

Research on the ways in which couples use bank accounts has suggested that the development of more complex forms of money management leads to a lessening of collective financial arrangements (Cheal, 1992; Treas, 1993). Even though opening a joint account is often a symbol of togetherness, many individuals within couples also maintain their own separate accounts, and these are legally available only to those whose names are specified as having access to them. Qualitative work carried out for the British Household Panel Study has shown that setting up banking systems, such as standing orders, feeder accounts and transfers between current and deposit accounts, tends to be a male activity, and can have the effect of reducing the access which women have to the financial resources of the couple (Laurie, 1996).

Most previous research on credit cards has been carried out by economists, who have not traditionally been concerned with financial arrangements within households. Their research has focused on the individual credit card user, on the development of user profiles, and on the exploration of broader economic issues. (See, for example, Brito and Hartley, 1995; Burton, 1994: Crook *et al.*, 1994; Duca and Whitesell, 1995; Feinberg *et al.*, 1992). Among mainstream economists interest has focused on the implications for the money supply of the increased use of credit cards (Begg *et al.*, 1994; Laidler, 1993). Psychologists have focused on the ways in which financial services are perceived by consumers (Lewis, Betts and Webley, 1997).

In the field of social policy, research on new forms of money has been concerned in particular with financial exclusion and with credit card default. This research has shown that in the late 1990s, two out of ten households did not have a current bank or building society account, three out of ten had no savings at all and about the same proportion had not had access to consumer credit facilities in the previous year. The situation is exacerbated by the fact that people who lack one type of financial product have an increased likelihood of being without other products as well (Kempson and Whyley, 1999). Credit card default is often the result of job loss, small business failure or changes in family circumstances (Ford, 1991; Kempson, 1994; Rowlingson and Kempson, 1994).

Research on the use of new forms of money within households has been taking place at the Centre for International Research on Communication and Information Technologies (CIRCIT) in Melbourne, Australia (Singh, 1997). This has shown how developments in banking technology are altering the ways in which couples manage their money. Different forms of money can be used for different kinds of payments, in a way which expresses not only what is being bought but also who is making the purchase. Singh concluded, 'The connections between banking and marriage are so critical that electronic banking technologies are altering the way in which money is managed and controlled within marriage' (Singh, 1997, 166).

This brief review of the existing literature suggests that most previous research on the control and allocation of money within marriage paid little attention to the implications of new forms of money. Most previous research on new forms of money focused on credit cards, and has been concerned with either individuals or households, but not with the complex social and economic processes which shape financial arrangements between individuals within households. The study reported here attempted to bridge this gap in the literature by exploring the ways in which new forms of money are changing the access which individuals have to the financial resources of the households in which they live.

Methods of the study

Money is a sensitive and private subject. All researchers know that asking individuals about their finances can feel more intrusive than asking about sexual relations. In an attempt to avoid some of the biases which can result from the inhibitions of respondents, three different sources of data were used in the study.

First, analyses of the 1993/4 Family Expenditure Survey (FES) provided quantitative data about the spending patterns of married couples (Office of National Statistics, 1996). The FES is a long-running continuous survey, using a random sample of households drawn from every county in the United Kingdom. Interviews take place in about 7000 households each year and involve all 'spenders' over the age of 16. Each respondent is asked to complete an expenditure diary over a two week period, recording every single item bought and noting if a credit card was used to make the purchase. Since the focus of this study was on married or as-married couples, the analysis began by selecting households containing a married couple. The FES does not identify stable cohabiting couples, so these could not be included in the analysis. In some cases crucial data was missing, so the total sample on which the analysis was based numbered 3676 couples.

Secondly, seven focus groups took place, involving 59 individuals in five different parts of England. Focus group members were selected to represent particular sub-groups of the population in terms of age and employment status, and every individual who took part was currently living as one of a couple, though their partners did not attend the focus group.

Thirdly, face-to-face interviews were carried out with 40 couples, in order to develop a more qualitative understanding of the ways in which individuals and couples managed their finances and made use of new forms of money. The focus of the study was on married or as-married couples and men and women were interviewed separately and privately. Both the focus groups and the interviews were tape-recorded and transcribed verbatim. For further details about the methods of the study see Pahl, 1999.

Social polarisation in a focus group

An argument which broke out in one of the focus groups may serve to set the scene for discussion of the quantitative data. It began after Henry, who was a telecommunications consultant and an enthusiast for all new forms of money, had dominated the discussion for some time. Jim, who was a retired headmaster from a disadvantaged part of the city, interrupted him:

> Jim. The thing that worries me is that people who don't want to move onto modern systems will eventually be penalized. Like standing orders – you may now get a discount if you operate one and if you want to pay cash for electricity you actually pay more. So you're penalized for trying to pay cash.
>
> Interviewer. How do you view the prospect of a cashless society?
>
> Henry. It's a natural consequence of living. We have got a credit card and I use it for buying things over the Internet. We don't like writing cheques – its too much of a faff. We see it as very much an enabling technology in our

house. My wife is a very independent lady. She uses telephone banking an awful lot. Now she's into Internet banking and most of our friends and acquaintances are like that.

This exchange was interesting in a number of different ways. Jim highlighted the penalties attached to remaining in the cash economy, while Henry was an example of the male technophile, for whom the electronic economy is so taken for granted that he sees it as 'a natural consequence of living'. When Jim replied to Henry's last remark he was thinking of all those people who live on social security benefits, paid through the Giro bank at the local Post Office:

Jim. But there are hundreds and thousands of people who are collecting their Giro through the Post Office, handling cash much of which is already committed. They don't have these choices. All electronic banking is going to be no use whatever, and if there are penalties for actually dealing with cash we're going to have a further disadvantaged, very large section of society.

Henry picked up the topic of people living on social security, but cleverly used it to advance his own argument. He referred to a recent proposal that social security benefits should be paid by means of a smart card, which claimants would be able charge up when the benefit was due.

Henry. But those same people, Jim, in two years are going to get a card from the Benefits Agency. The Benefits Agency have plans to make every person who's in receipt of unemployment benefit – they wont get a Giro, they'll get a card like this. It might not be VisaCash. They'll just stick it in any cash machine, the system knows that they are due a payment, and they've got the option to spend it or go to the bank and get their money. 'Cos it will save you and me, as taxpayers, millions of pounds.

In his reply Jim went back to the reality of life as he knew it, in a housing estate on the edge of a big city, and to the fact that many poor people find it easier to manage their finances in cash.

Jim. They get this wonderful card, to go to a wonderful machine, but that money's already heavily committed and more. I was in special education so I sort of fly the flag for the disadvantaged. An awful lot of people will not be able to handle it. Its hard enough having the practicalities of the cash on the table to divide it out, to make it last. But an electronic system, where you can't physically see the money – a lot of people still have the cocoa tins – there's the rent, there's the food, there's what I owe the club for those toys for Christmas.

An argument such as this highlights the extremes in terms of social polarization, but it does not tell us anything about the prevalence of particular patterns in the use of new forms of money. For that we turn to the quantitative data from the FES.

Patterns of credit card spending

Previous research has suggested that people prefer to use different forms of payment for purchases of different cost, with a trend away from cash towards credit cards as cost increases, except for very expensive items which tend to be paid for by cheque. There is also a trend over time away from cash and towards credit cards as a means of payment. Thus a survey of 2000 adults, carried out for Girobank, showed that cash was the preferred means of paying for items costing under £10. For purchases of £100, cash was preferred by 25% of those surveyed, down from 28% a year earlier, while cards were preferred by 43%, compared with 39% a year earlier. For purchases costing £1000 cheques remained the first choice for 46%, compared with 33% who said they would use a card and 10% who would use cash (Graham, 1997).

The new analyses of the FES data produced a similar pattern, with credit cards being used less often for items costing under £10 or over £1000, as Table 1 shows. Credit cards were most likely to be used for goods costing between £100 and £1000, where 15% of payments were made in this way. More detailed analyses, not shown in the table, revealed that the peak of credit card use came in the price range of £250 and £500, where 38% of payments involved credit cards.

Table 1 also underlines the enormous differences between men and women in the number and costs of the items which they buy. Women make many more low cost purchases than men, and many fewer high cost purchases: so nearly three quarters of items under £10 were bought by women compared with under two fifths of items over £1000. In general women's share of credit card

Table 1 Expenditure on items of different cost by use of credit cards and gender of purchaser

	Cost of item purchased in £			
	Under 10	10–100	100–1000	Over 1000
% of all items bought by credit card	6	12	15	8
% of all items bought by women	71	52	39	38
% of credit card purchases made by women	72	47	37	38
Total number of items bought	281,811	31,492	2,330	105

N = 3676

expenditure was similar to their share of total expenditure, though men were slightly more likely than women to use a credit card. The greatest gender difference came in the price range of £500 and £1000, where only 33% of all the credit card purchases were made by women.

Treating the sample as a whole, however, obscures variations between different sub-groups. The next stage in this exploration of the use of credit cards was to sub-divide all the couples in the sample according to employment status.

Employment patterns within households

Previous analyses had suggested that two aspects of employment were particularly relevant. These were, first, the employment status of women, with a distinction being made between full time, part time and no employment, and, secondly, household employment status, with distinctions being made between 'work rich' and 'work poor' households in particular. In order to examine the effects of these two aspects of employment, a variable was created which combined the employment situations of both the man and the woman. This involved re-coding the employment variables given by the FES to make six broad *household employment categories*.

Table 2 shows the six employment categories, giving the mean gross income for each partner in £ per week. The table also gives the mean expenditure by each partner in £ per week, as given in the FES expenditure diaries. It is important to remember that some expenditure, such as direct debits and standing orders, did not appear in the diaries and that couples differed in the extent to which they made use of these forms of payment. However, payments by cash, by cheque and by credit and debit card all appeared in the diaries. All the differences between men's income and women's income were highly significant, except in the 'Woman main earner' category. The expenditure differences would have been significant in some categories if outliers had been removed, particularly from men's expenditure. As it was, the differences between male expenditure and female expenditure were only significant in the case of 'Both full time' employed couples ($p < 0.001$) and 'Both retired' couples ($p < 0.01$).

The first category contained 857 couples where *both partners were in full time employment or self employed*; in a very few cases one or both worked part time. These were the households with the largest mean household incomes, and their expenditure was correspondingly high. Despite the fact that both partners were in full time work, the men had substantially higher incomes than the women, with mean gross incomes of £352 per week, compared with £243. However, despite their lower incomes, women spent more than men, with a mean expenditure of £201 compared to £179. The differences between income and expenditure shows that some financial transfers had taken place within these

Table 2 Income and expenditure for household employment categories

Mean gross income £ per week
Mean expenditure from FES diary £3 per week
± Standard error of means

Household employment categories	No. of couples	Men's income	Women's income	Men's expenditure	Women's expenditure
Both full time	857	352 ±8.0	243 ±5.6	179 ±8.8	201 ±7.7
Full time/part time	858	371 ±9.6	118 ±3.0	145 ±16.2	184 ±6.64
Full time/no paid work	688	412 ±16.6	44 ±2.3	152 ±11.9	161 ±7.9
Woman main earner	274	164 ±9.1	180 ±8.0	201 ±76.6	134 ±5.4
Both retired	848	164 ±4.7	60 ±2.3	135 ±13.0	99 ±3.9
Both unemployed	151	130 ±11.6	34 ±3.2	101 ±38.4	100 ±7.0

households between men and women. These were the 'work rich' couples, and only two fifths of them had dependent children.

The second category contained 858 couples where the *man was in full-time employment or self employed, while the woman in part-time employment*. As might be expected, there was a greater disparity between mean male and female incomes in this group, with mean male earnings of £371, compared with mean female earnings of £118 per week. Women continued to take a larger part in shopping, spending on average £184 per week compared with the men's average of £145. It seemed as if women in part-time employment had more time for doing the family shopping and less excuse for not doing it, compared with women in full-time employment. Over two thirds of these couples had dependent children.

The pattern is even clearer among the third category, which contained 688 couples where the *man was in full time employment or self employed, while the woman was 'unoccupied' or 'unemployed'*. Men in this category had the highest incomes of all at £412 per week. This may have reflected their responsibility as the sole breadwinner in a family with young children; it may be that having a full-time housewife at home enabled them to work longer and harder; or it may simply be that the high earnings of the man freed the woman from the need to take paid work. The women in this category had an average income of just £44 per week, coming partly from child benefit and benefits for disabled people, but also from interest on savings and investments. A few of these women were very wealthy indeed. Over three fifths of the couples in this category had dependent children.

The fourth category consisted of 274 couples where the *woman was the main earner*. This was the most heterogeneous of all the household employment categories, with some women employed full time, some part time and some self employed, while some of the men worked part time, but most had retired from paid work, or were unemployed or disabled. As Table 2 shows, male incomes were not so much less than female incomes in this category, but in general the woman was the only person in the labour market. Here men spent much more than women, which was probably a reflection of the extra time at their disposal. Many of these couples were approaching retirement and only a third had dependent children.

The fifth category contained 848 couples where *both partners were retired*. Here again mean incomes were low, especially for women, a consequence of the financial difference between the married man's retirement pension and that of his 'dependent' wife. Men's greater than average share of the expenditure in this group surely reflects the fact that going shopping is an activity which many elderly men enjoy. In addition, this is an age cohort in which men traditionally expected to control finances and in which many still give their wives a housekeeping allowance. As might be expected, very few of these couples had dependent children.

Finally, the sixth category consisted of 151 couples where *both partners were 'unemployed' and/or 'unoccupied'*. These were the poorest couples in the sample, as well as the poorest men and women on an individual basis: they might be described as the 'work poor'. Mean expenditure in this group was larger than mean income. However, further analysis showed that this discrepancy only applied to 15% of the group, and typically was the result of buying one expensive consumer good during the two weeks when they were keeping the expenditure diary (for further discussion of this issue see Pahl and Opit, 1999). Here men spent as much as women. This may be because when money was tight women cut back on spending in a way that men did not. On the other hand it may be that some unemployed men had taken on the job of doing the family shopping. Two thirds of these couples had dependent children.

In referring to Table 2 it is important to remember that the figures for income are gross, with net take home pay at a lower level, except among unemployed people. The figures for expenditure represent only expenditure recorded in the diaries; household bills paid by direct debit or standing order, which are likely to include mortgage repayments and some utility bills, will not appear here. So real household expenditure will usually be greater than the table suggests. Nevertheless Table 2 does underline the part which households play in the re-allocation of financial resources. In general women appeared to spend more than they earned, except where they were in full time paid work or were the main earner for the household, partly because their spending was more likely to appear in the expenditure diaries. By contrast men appeared to earn more than they spent, but this was partly because some large items of household expenditure, such as mortgage repayments, did not appear in this table.

Table 2 highlighted some of the differences which flow from employment status, both on a household and on an individual basis; it also underlined the rather different market experience of men and women. How were these differences translated into differences in spending involving credit cards?

Employment status, credit cards and spending

We have seen that employment status, both at an individual and at a household level, affects patterns of spending. Does the same apply to the use of credit cards?

Table 3 suggests that gender, employment status and age all have an impact on the use of credit cards. The table gives the percentage of men and women, in each employment category, who used a credit card to make a purchase over the two week period during which they kept the diary for the FES. Significance was tested by chi squared test, *N* being the number of households with expenditure on the item in the two week period.

The results suggest that between a quarter and a third of all those who took part in the survey used a credit card over this period, with men being slightly more likely than women to use cards. Differences in employment status were associated with differences in the use of credit cards. When the man and the

Table 3 Percentages of individuals using a credit card for making a purchase over a two week period by household employment categories

Household employment categories	Credit card used for a purchase Men %	*N*	Women %	*N*	Significance $p<$
Both full time	42	350	41	349	ns
Full time/part time	42	356	35	304	0.085
Full time/no paid work	37	256	25	170	0.001
Woman main earner	24	66	23	63	ns
Both retired	21	174	14	119	0.003
Both unemployed	6	9	7	12	ns
All	33	1221	28	1017	

woman were both in full time employment they were equally likely to have used a credit card. However, women in part time employment were less likely, and women without employment very significantly less likely to have used a credit card, by comparison with their employed husbands.

The table highlights the exclusion of unemployed people from the credit card economy, with only a very few individuals in this category using a credit card during the two weeks. This is consonant with research on access to credit more generally, which shows that low income households find it hard to obtain credit; if they are forced to borrow they tend to contact more expensive money lenders than the typical credit card company (Ford, 1991; Rowlingson, 1994). Table 3 provides quantitative evidence relevant to the debate between Henry, who represented work rich couples with Internet access, and Jim, who spoke for work poor couples in the disadvantaged parts of his city.

Table 3 also suggests that retired people are relatively excluded from the credit card economy. This may partly be a result of low income and lack of credit worthiness. But it may also be a consequence of a lack of financial confidence in new forms of money and of a general mistrust of getting into debt. There was a significant difference between men and women in this group, which may reflect the income differences revealed in Table 2.

In order to examine the interacting effects of different variables, we carried out a linear multiple regression analysis, with the dependent variables being total household expenditure, as recorded in the diaries, or total credit card expenditure. The independent variables were the man's gross income, the woman's gross income, the age of each partner, each partner's age at the end of full time education, and dummy variables representing being economically active and the presence of children in the household. The regression was carried out stepwise and significant results are shown in Tables 4 and 5.

Table 4 shows that the total household expenditure was correlated strongly with the man's gross income and the woman's gross income, and less strongly with the age at which the man ended full time education, with men who spent longer in full time education having higher household expenditure. The pattern for credit card expenditure was similar, but with one interesting difference. The beta values suggested that the relative effect of the man's income was only twice that of the woman's in estimating the overall expenditure, but three times that of the wife's income in estimating credit card expenditure. In other words, compared with total expenditure, credit card expenditure was more strongly influenced by male than female incomes.

We have already shown that employment patterns within the household had significant effects on spending. What could regression analyses tell us about the interactions between all the relevant variables? In order to answer this question we repeated the procedure, first, with households where both partners were in full time employment and, secondly, with those where only the man was in employment, while the woman was not in paid work.

The results are shown in Table 5. When both partners were in full time employment, only the two income variables proved to be relevant in explaining

Table 4 Regression analyses on total household expenditure and total credit card expenditure

	Standardized coefficients Beta	*t.*	Significance $p<$
Household expenditure			
Man's income	0.21	12.49	0.000
Woman's income	0.11	6.82	0.000
Man's age at end FT education	0.04	2.55	0.000
$r^2 = 0.08$			
Credit card expenditure			
Constant	0.33	−6.80	0.000
Man's income	0.12	20.10	0.000
Woman's income	0.09	7.82	0.000
Man's age at end FT education	0.06	5.33	0.000
Man's age		3.85	0.000
$r^2 = 0.17$			

total household expenditure, with the income of the wife having marginally more impact that that of the husband. However, the pattern was different for credit card expenditure. Here the man's income was the more significant of the two income variables, with his age at the end of full time education and his current age also being important: households in which the man was older when he ended full time education tended to spend more by credit card.

When only the man was in employment, as might be expected, his income was by far the most significant variable in terms of the total household expenditure, though once again his age at the end of full time education was also important. It was perhaps surprising to find that the wife's income also appeared in the regression results, since the average income for this group of women was quite small: this finding may represent the high spending of a few affluent women who did not have paid work because they had independent incomes of their own.

However, when the regression analysis was repeated for credit card expenditure only the man's income and his age at the end of full time education were significant. Once again there was a contrast between total expenditure and credit card expenditure, with the latter being more closely related to men's than women's incomes. The association between credit card expenditure and the man's age at the end of full time education may reflect the greater confidence which better educated men have in using new forms of money.

In order to learn more about the processes which shaped these patterns we turn next to two case studies from the interviews.

Table 5 Regression analyses on total household expenditure and total credit card expenditure for households with two and one earners

	Standardized Coefficients Beta	$t.$	Significance $p<$
Both FT: household expenditure			
Constant		5.19	0.000
Woman's income	0.26	8.00	0.000
Man's income	0.24	7.27	0.000
r^2 0.17			
Both FT: credit card expenditure			
Constant		−4.42	
Man's income	0.23	6.22	0.000
Woman's income	0.14	4.25	0.000
Man's age at end FT education	0.12	3.55	0.000
Man's age	0.08	2.43	0.015
$r^2=0.13$			
FT/no paid work: household expenditure			
Man's income	0.45	12.45	0.000
Man's age at end FT education	0.08	2.35	0.019
Woman's income	0.07	1.97	0.050
$r^2=0.25$			
FT/no paid work: credit card expenditure			
Constant		−3.73	0.000
Man's income	0.47	13.56	0.000
Man's age at end FT education	0.12	3.33	0.001
$r^2=0.27$			

An unemployed couple with credit card debts

Table 3 showed that unemployed people were the group most likely to be excluded from the credit card economy. Tom and Teresa, both aged 25, unemployed and with two young children, were finding it hard to make ends meet. Their current financial problems were exacerbated by the fact that when she had been in employment Teresa had used her Visa card to pay for their holiday. They had taken out money up to and above her credit limit and were still paying off what they owed.

When asked about their financial arrangements, Tom and Teresa chose the option, 'We pool all our money and manage our household finances jointly', but in the separate interviews both said that Teresa was really responsible for making ends meet: when family income is low women tend to get the job of making ends meet, and many women will deprive themselves if there is not enough money to go round (Vogler and Pahl, 1994). Tom said, 'I leave it all up to her'. Teresa said,

> I have to remind him that there's things to pay and that he can't just go out and squander money. I get very worried about money, you see. If I haven't paid something I won't sleep. I have to pay my bills. And whatever I've got left I'll live on it. I can live on like a fiver a week, if I have to. But he says things like, 'We only live once'. But I think you have to pay bills to survive.

Tom explained his attitude in terms of his family of origin:

> I'm not really money oriented. The family that I've been with hasn't really been money oriented. Whereas she, Teresa, should I say, she's from that different area and class. So she's got more responsibility with money than what I have. I'm quite glad she's there, because if she wasn't there, I'd spend all me money.

Teresa was indignant about the interest she was paying on the outstanding debt on her credit card, but her remarks made it clear that she did not conceptualize this debt in the same way as the credit card company.

> I think it's ridiculous. I don't think you should have to pay interest on any cards or your accounts. They get enough money out of you as it is. I mean I've only got £500 over the limit and some people have got thousands and thousands on it.
>
> Q What do you feel when you're using your credit card?
>
> I don't really know I'm doing it. Like I say, it's a piece of plastic and it's not like handing cash over. No, its plastic money. It's lies. You don't feel you're spending anything.

When the interviewer asked Tom whether he was thinking of getting a new credit card, it became clear that he, too, had a carefree approach to credit card debt:

> Um ... yes and no. 'Yes' because the simple fact is, like I say, it's as good as money, and you've got it on you whenever you need it. 'No' because there's sometimes you can overspend money, without knowing.
>
> Q What did you feel when you had a card and you used it?
>
> I thought, 'Yeah, I've got this credit card here, and now I can go buy what I want, when I want'. Because I know, if I want something, that I will definitely get it. Most definitely.

Teresa and Tom were operating the system of financial management which in previous research has been described as 'wife management' or the 'whole wage system'. This system is characteristic of low income families. As in this example, the man's lack of involvement in financial matters can serve to protect his personal spending money and keep the woman's struggles to make ends meet off the agenda (Vogler, 1998). For this couple, and especially for Tom, new forms of money, such as credit cards, offer an opportunity for personal spending which can undermine the woman's struggle to make ends meet for the household as a whole.

A breadwinner husband who controlled finances

A contrasting picture was presented by those couples where the husband was in full time employment, while the wife was had no paid work, or only a part time job. Table 3 showed that among those couples the man was significantly more likely than the woman to have used a credit card over the two weeks when the expenditure diaries were being kept. Derek and Helen fell into this category. He had left school at 18 and was an estate agent, while she had left school at 16 and now worked part time in an office. They had three teenage children. There was a great disparity in their salaries, since she earned under £10,000, while he received at least £42,000 per annum gross, and may have earned much more, since this was the top point on the salary scale from which respondents were invited to identify how much they earned.

Both saw him as the main earner and both considered that he controlled the family finances. They had a joint account, into which his salary was paid, while her salary was paid into her own account. She described how their system worked, and it was clear that, like many women in her situation, she did not feel comfortable about spending 'his' money:

> We have a joint account into which his money goes and the household expenditure is made from. So I'm very strict with myself about what I spend money from that account on. It won't be on things for me, because I have my own account for that. And it gives me a sense of independence to be able to do that.

Derek confirmed what she had said,

> I mean, basically, I provide the money. She has her own independence now, but most of the money that comes into the household is mine. And the money that Helen earns, I don't touch at all. Dare I say absolute pin money or whatever. It's a bit of a chauvinistic statement that, but I'm not ashamed.

They had a joint Visa card, which he paid out of their joint account, and a joint debit card, and she had several store cards, which she paid from her own account. He also had an American Express card. In the past she had had her own Barclaycard, but Derek had disapproved of the fact that she was paying high interest rates on her outstanding balance. She described what happened:

> Derek said to me, 'Look, you're paying through the nose on your Barclaycard – really high interest rates. I'm going to get you transferred to the Cooperative Bank'. Well I wasn't too keen, to be honest with you, because my Barclaycard I'd had since I was at work. So it was my sort of account, in my name. I didn't want to be second named on his account. Silly sort of thing really. So I sort of kicked my heels over this one for a little bit, cutting my nose to spite my face, and in the end sort of gave in. So now Derek gets the statements on our joint Visa card. Which in a way I don't really like, because he knows now what I'm spending with my credit card. I like to have some sort of mysteries in my life.

In his own separate interview, Derek described the same incident, but threw rather a different light on it:

> Helen was Barclaycard and she had about £1500 on there. She was being charged 17 or 18%, which is dire. They were offering a freebie at the Co-op, so I applied for a card, got her balance transferred over and they paid off the Barclaycard. Cut that up, and got rid of it at a special incentive rate of 6% for the first six months. I paid some of it for her, but I didn't pay the whole lot off, because – perhaps it's my thing – I've never discussed it with her as a discipline thing, that yes, I could pay it off, because I bring the money in. But it's important for Helen to contribute towards it, because she spent the money, you see.

The story of her credit card reflects a more general situation in which he ultimately controlled finances. When asked about making a major purchasing decision, she said,

> We would discuss it. But I would have to say, ultimately the decision would lie with Derek. And I think that boils down to the fact that he earns the money. It's as simple as that.

Derek and Helen were operating the system of financial management described in previous research as 'male controlled pooling', but with a strong ideology of the male as breadwinner, which is reflected in his control of finances and Helen's feeling that she has no right to spend 'his' money on herself. The dispute about her credit card illustrated his power to control the discussion (Vogler, 1998). This couple underlined the point that two individuals living in the same household can have access to different amounts of money, can vary in their right to spend that money, and can have different standards of living. They may also keep secrets from each other.

Conclusions

The patterns which emerged from the research were complex, but they suggested an increasing social polarisation in which social class *per se* was less important than income, gender and education. Those who were making full use of new forms of money tended to be 'work rich', in that they belonged to households with more than one earner, 'credit rich', in that their credit rating was secure, and 'education rich', in that they were confident of their ability to control their finances and to manipulate the financial market place for their own advantage. The Mathew effect is still very much in evidence: 'For unto everyone that hath shall be given, and he shall have abundance: but from him that hath not shall be taken away even that which he hath' (Mathew, 25, 29).

At the other extreme, some individuals were more or less excluded from the electronic economy. Like Tom and Teresa, they tended to be 'work poor', typically living in households without a regular earner, 'credit poor', in that it was hard for them to get any sort of loan, and 'education poor', in that they did not fully understand the rules of the new world of personal finance. It was significant that the regression analyses highlighted the man's age at the end of full time education in explaining the use of credit cards: the increasing complexity of the financial services sector is making it harder than ever for poor people to manage their finances efficiently. If in the future full citizenship depends on access to banking, credit and other financial services, those who remain in the cash economy are likely to be increasingly penalised.

There are also implications for debates about financial exclusion. Recent analyses of the Family Resources Survey have produced very similar results to those reported here. The risk of financial exclusion has been shown to be highest among people on low incomes, those claiming means tested benefits, those who left school before the age of sixteen, those living in rented accommodation, members of the Pakistani and Bangladeshi communities and people living in the most deprived local authorities (Kempson and Whyley, 1999). Concern about financial exclusion has become a focus for government policy, with initiatives in financial education and advice, in the extension of banking services and in access to affordable credit, for example through credit unions (Oppenheim, 1998; Treasury Committee, 1999a and 1999b).

Gender has emerged as another important issue. Within marriage new forms of money are having an impact on the relative financial power of men and women. Men were more likely to use credit cards than women, while women whose credit worthiness depended on their husband's income used cards less often and spent less with them than women in full time employment. As the example of Derek and Helen showed, even invisible money can feel like 'his money' as opposed to 'my money'. Women without employment, and older women, were significantly less likely to use credit cards than their partners.

In the near future credit cards are likely to be superseded by increasingly sophisticated smart cards, by the extension of telephone and Internet banking and by the development of e-commerce. Results from the focus groups and interviews suggested that men were more confident than women in using these new technologies (see also Singh, 1998). From this perspective, access to the electronic economy can be seen as another source of power, and one which will advantage some members of households and disadvantage others. The man who keeps the accounts for the couple on his computer spread sheet is likely to have more power in financial matters than the woman who simply gives him the information to enter on that spread sheet. The coming of the electronic economy may be altering the balance of financial power between men and women within marriage, to the advantage of men (see also Singh, 1998).

In the global economy of the future financial citizenship is likely to depend on credit ratings and on access to information and communication technology. As this chapter has shown, access to the electronic economy is stratified by income, employment status, gender and education. New forms of money may be changing the ways in which couples manage their finances, but they are also reproducing, and in some cases reinforcing, some very traditional inequalities within and between households.

Acknowledgements

This research was funded by the Joseph Rowntree Foundation and the University of Kent at Canterbury: I am pleased to have this opportunity to acknowledge their support. I am very grateful to all those who worked on the project, and to the members of the Advisory Group, who were immensely helpful and generous. I would also like to thank the Data Archive at the University of Essex and the Office of National Statistics for making the Family Expenditure Survey available to researchers. Professor Lou Opit worked on the analyses of the FES until four days before his death in May 1998: this chapter is dedicated to him, with my love.

References

Bauman, Z., (1998), *Work, Consumerism and the New Poor*, Buckingham: Open University Press.

Begg, D., Fischer, S. and Dombusch, R., (1994), *Economics*, London: McGraw Hill.

Blumberg, R., (1991), *Gender, Family and Economy: the Triple Overlap*, Newbury Park, California: Sage.

Brannen, J. and Wilson, G., (1987), *Give and Take in Families: Studies in Resource Distribution*, London: Allen and Unwin.

Brito, D. and Hartley, P., (1995), Consumer rationality and credit cards, *Journal of Political Economy*, 103 (2): 400–433.

Burgoyne, C. and Morison, V., (1997), Money in re-marriage: keeping things separate – but simple, *Sociological Review*, 45: 363–395.

Burton, D., (1994), *Financial Services and the Consumer*, London: Routledge.

Cheal, D., (1992), Changing household financial strategies, *Human Ecology*, 21: 197–213.

Credit Card Research Group, (1998), *What's On the Cards?* London: Credit Card Research Group.

Crook, J., Thomas, L. and Hamilton, R., (1994), Credit cards – haves, have nots and cannot haves, *Service Industries Journal*, 14 (4): 204–215.

Duca, J. and Whitesell, W., (1995), Credit cards and money demand – a cross sectional study, *Journal of Money, Credit and Banking*, 27 (2): 604–623.

Dwyer, D. and Bruce, J., (1988). *A Home Divided: Women and Income in the Third World*, Paolo Alto, California: Stanford University Press.

Feinberg, R.A., Westgate, L.S. and Burroughs, W.J., (1992), Credit cards and social identity, *Semiotica*, 91 (1–2): 99–108.

Ford, J., (1991), *Consuming Credit: Debt and Poverty in the UK*, London: Child Poverty Action Group.

Goode, J., Callender, C. and Lister, R., (1998), *Purse or Wallet? Gender Inequalities and Income Distribution within Families on Benefits*, London: Policy Studies Institute.

Graham, G., (1997), Cash still prefered for small payments, *Financial Times*, 9 June.

Kempson, E., (1994), *Outside the Banking System: a Review of Households without a Current Account*. London: HMSO.

Kempson, E. and Whyley, C., (1999), *Kept out or Opted out? Understanding and Combating Financial Exclusion*, Bristol University: Policy Press.

Laidler, D., (1993), *The Demand for Money*, London: Harper Collins.

Laurie, H., (1996), *Women's Employment Decisions and Financial Arrangements within the Household*, University of Essex: PhD Thesis.

Laurie, H. and Rose, D., (1994), Divisions and allocations within households, in Buck, N., Gershuny, J., Rose, D. and Scott, J. (eds), *Changing Households: the British Household Panel Survey 1990–1992*, Colchester: University of Essex.

Lewis, A., Betts, H. and Webley, P., (1997), *Financial Services: a Literature Review of Consumer Attitudes, Preferences and Perceptions*, Bath: University of Bath School of Social Sciences.

Morris, L. and Ruane, S., (1989), *Household Finance Management and the Labour Market*, Aldershot: Avebury.

Office of National Statistics, (1996), *Family Expenditure Survey*, London: HMSO.

Oppenheim, C., (1998), *An Inclusive Society: Strategies for Tackling Poverty*, London: Institute for Public Policy Research.

Pahl, J., (1989), *Money and Marriage*, London: Macmillan.

Pahl, J., (1995), His money, her money: recent research on financial organisation in marriage, *Journal of Economic Psychology*, 163.

Pahl, J., (1999), *Invisible Money: Family Finances in the Electronic Economy*, Bristol: Policy Press.

Pahl, J. and Opit, L., (1999), Patterns of exclusion in the electronic economy, in Bradshaw, J. and Sainsbury, R. (eds), *Researching Poverty, vol. 2, Aldershot*: Ashgate.

Pakulski, J. and Waters, M., (1996), The re-shaping and dissolution of social class in advanced society, *Theory and Society*, 25: 667–691.

Rowlingson, K., (1994), *Moneylenders and their Customers*, London: Policy Studies Institute.

Rowlingson, K. and Kempson, E., (1994), *Paying with Plastic: a Study of Credit Card Debt*, London: Policy Studies Institute.

Singh, S., (1997), *Marriage Money: the Social Shaping of Money in Marriage and Banking*, St Leonards, NSW, Australia: Allen and Unwin.

Singh, S., (1998), *Gender, Design and Internet Commerce*, Centre for International Research on Communication and Information Technologies, Melbourne, Australia: RMIT University.

Treas, J., (1993), Money in the bank, American Sociological Review, 58, 723–734.

Treasury Committee, (1999a), *Third Report: Financial Services Regulation*, HC 1998–99 73-I, London: HMSO.

Treasury Committee, (1999b), *Third Report: Financial Services Regulation*, HC 1998–99 73-II, London: HMSO.

Vogler, C., (1998), Money in the household: some underlying issues of power, *Sociological Review*, 46 (4): 687–713.

Vogler, C. and Pahl, J., (1993), Social and economic change and the organisation of money in marriage, *Work, Employment and Society* 7 (1): 71–95.

Vogler, C. and Pahl, J., (1994), Money, power and inequality within marriage, *Sociological Review*, 42 (2): 263–288.

Wilson, G., (1987), *Money in the Family*, Aldershot: Avebury.

Logics of urban polarization: the view from below

Loïc Wacquant

> All social phenomena are, to some degree, the work of collective will, and collective will implies choice between different possible options ... The realm of the social is the realm of modality.
>
> Marcel Mauss, *Les civilisations. Eléments et formes* (1929)

This chapter analyses the major modalities whereby new forms of urban inequality and marginality are spreading throughout the advanced societies of the capitalist West, fuelling the process of polarization 'from below', as it were, by multiplying social positions and entrapping populations situated at an increasing remove from the middle and upper tiers of the class structure. The argument unfolds in two steps.

First, I sketch a compact characterization of what I take to be a *new regime of urban marginality*. This regime has been ascendant for the past three decades or so, since the close of the Fordist era defined by standardized industrial production, mass consumption, and a Keynesian social contract binding them together under the tutelage of the social welfare state. Yet its full impact lies ahead of us because its advent is tied to the most advanced sectors of our economies – this is why I refer to it as 'advanced marginality'. It is not a residue from the past, as theories of de-industrialization and skills or spatial mismatch would have it, but a harbinger of the future. Identifying the distinctive properties of this consolidating regime of urban marginality linked to the ascendant mode of capitalist growth helps us pinpoint what exactly is new about the 'new poverty' of which the city is the site and fount and why old remedies of more economic growth and an extended wage labour sphere are largely without effect.

Second, I turn to the question that implicitly informs or explicitly guides European debates on the resurgence of destitution, division, and tension in the transforming metropolis: namely, are we witnessing an *epochal convergence of urban poverty regimes across the Atlantic*? I argue that, contrary to superficial journalistic portraits and hasty scholarly pronouncements, we are not: although it is fuelled by common structural forces, urban relegation follows different social and spatial dynamics on the two continents that correspond to the distinct state structures, paths of civic incorporation, and urban legacies of the Old and New Worlds. Lumping these variegated dynamics under the catch-all phrase of 'Americanization' (or one of its partial derivatives, such as racialization, ghettoization, or multiculturalism, as many analysts of the urban scene have been wont to do) is neither empirically illuminating, nor analytically fruitful. The combined resurgence of inequality and rising hegemony of U.S.-rooted concepts across the globe should not blind us to persistent divergences in the ways societies produce, organize, and react to urban polarization, *even as its structural sources are similar* across societies. At the same time, European state élites must beware of pursuing public policies inspired by neoliberalism that reinforce blind market sanctions in the allocation of space, jobs, and people, and tend to isolate distinct urban zones and populations, thereby encouraging them to pursue divergent and even oppositional life strategies that can set off self-reinforcing cycles of social involution not unlike those that underlay segmentation and ghettoization in the United States.

This chapter, then, is an effort to diagnose the broad social forces and forms with which our current urban predicament is pregnant and that promise to feed polarization in the metropolis of tomorrow – unless we exercise our 'collective will', as Marcel Mauss urged, and act to check mechanisms and steer trends in a different direction. It stresses that, for all the talk of urban rebirth and prosperity that accompanies the millenarist celebration of 2000, for those consigned to the lower reaches of the dualizing occupational structure and the declining neighbourhoods of formerly industrial cities, the prosperity of the 'new economy' has yet to come and the rosy promise of the 'information age' remains a bitter fairy tale.

Symptoms of advanced marginality in the city

The close of the twentieth century is witnessing a momentous transformation of the roots, makeup, and consequences of urban poverty in Western society. Along with the accelerating economic modernization caused by the global restructuring of capitalism, the crystallization of a new international division of labour (fostered by the frantic velocity of financial flows and increased mobility of workers across porous national boundaries), and the growth of novel knowledge-intensive industries based on revolutionary information technologies and spawning a dual occupational structure, has come what one might call the *modernization of misery* – the rise of a new regime of urban inequality and marginality that contrasts with that prevailing during the three decades of the postwar (for a fuller argument, see Wacquant, 1996a).

Where poverty in the Western metropolis used to be largely residual or cyclical, embedded in working class communities, geographically diffuse and considered remediable by means of further market expansion, it now appears to be increasingly long-term if not permanent, disconnected from macroeconomic trends, and fixated upon disreputable neighbourhoods of relegation in which social isolation and alienation feed upon each other as the chasm between those consigned there and the rest of society deepens. The consolidation of this new regime of urban marginality is treading diverse routes and taking different forms in the various countries of the First World. In the United States and the United Kingdom, it has been greatly facilitated by the policy of wholesale state retrenchment pursued by conservative and liberal parties alike over the past decades. The American pattern is also highly peculiar for the rigid and stubborn spatial and social ostracization imposed upon blacks in the major urban centres. In other nations with strong corporatist or social-democratic welfare states and far less segregated cities, such as northern Europe and Scandinavia, the onset of advanced marginality has been partly attenuated but not wholly deflected. And it has become embroiled with the vexed question of the integration of Third World migrants and refugees, as expressed in the anguish over the crystallization of immigrant 'ghettos' gripping the continent from Marseille to München and Brussels to Brindisi (see Hadjimichalis and Sadler, 1995; Mingione, 1996).

Whatever the label used to designate it – 'underclass' in America and Great Britain, 'new poverty' in the Netherlands, Germany, and Northern Italy, 'exclusion' in France, Belgium, and Nordic countries – the telltale signs of the new marginality are immediately familiar to even the casual observer of the Western metropolis: homeless men and families vainly scrambling about for shelter, beggars on public transportation spinning heart-rending tales of personal disaster and dereliction, soup kitchens teeming with not only drifters but also the unemployed and the under-employed; the surge in predatory crime and the booming of informal (and more often than not illegal) street economies spearheaded by the trade in drugs; the despondency and rage of youths shut out from gainful employment and the bitterness of older workers made obsolete by deindustrialization and technological upgrading; the sense of retrogression, despair, and insecurity that pervades poor neighbourhoods locked in a seemingly unstoppable downward spiral of deterioration; and mounting ethnoracial violence, xenophobia, and hostility towards and amongst the poor, as expressed for instance in the proliferation of police and penal measures against loitering and assorted 'sub-criminal behaviors' amounting to a 'criminology of intolerance' (Young, 1999, pp. 121–140). Everywhere state élites and public policy experts have become acutely concerned with preventing or containing the 'disorders' brewing within and around expanding enclaves of urban decline and abandonment. Thus the sprouting of research on urban decline and destitution supported by various national and transnational bodies, including the European Commission (with its Targeted Socio-Economic Program on exclusion and integration), the OECD, and even NATO on the European side, and major philanthropic foundations on American shores.

Four structural logics fuel the new urban marginality

But the distinctive structural properties of 'modernized misery' are much less evident than its concrete manifestations. Schematically, the emerging regime of marginality may be characterized as the product of four logics that jointly reshape the features of urban poverty in rich societies and foster the multiplication of positions situated at or near the bottom of the social and spatial hierarchy. These features stand in stark contrast with the commanding traits of poverty in the era of Fordist expansion from the close of World War II to the mid-seventies.

(i) Macrosocial dynamic – occupational dualization and the resurgence of social inequality

The new urban marginality results not from economic backwardness, sluggishness, or decline but from *rising inequality in the context of overall economic advancement* and prosperity.

Arguably thc most puzzling attribute of the new marginality indeed is that it is spreading in an era of capricious but sturdy growth that has brought about spectacular material betterment for the more privileged members of First World societies. Notwithstanding ritual talk of 'crisis' among politicians for the better part of two decades, all leading capitalist countries have seen their GNP expand and collective wealth increase rapidly since the 'oil shocks' of the 70s. Opulence and indigence, luxury and penury, copiousness and impecuousness have flourished right alongside each other. Thus the city of Hamburg, by some measurements the richest in Europe, sports both the highest proportion of millionaires and the highest incidence of public assistance receipt in Germany, while New York City is home to the largest upper class on the planet but also to the single greatest army of the homeless and destitute in the Western hemisphere (Mollenkopf and Castells, 1991).

The two phenomena, though apparently contradictory, are in point of fact linked. For the novel forms of productivity- and profit-seeking in the 'high-tech', degraded manufacturing, and business and financial service sectors that drive *fin-de-siècle* capitalism are splitting the work force and polarizing access to, and rewards from, employment. Post-industrial modernization translates, on the one hand, into the multiplication of highly skilled and rewarded positions for university-trained professional and technical staff and, on the other, into the deskilling and outright elimination of millions of jobs as well as swelling of casual employment slots for uneducated workers (Sassen, 1991; Carnoy *et al.*, 1993). The growing concentration of wealth, in the form both income and property, at the top of the class structure has even spawned a vigorous demand for a post-industrial brand of urban domestics supplied mostly by cheap immigrant labour that caters to the full gamut of household needs of the new corporate nobility: driving children to and from school, walking the dog, cooking, cleaning, as well as provisioning the home and providing personal security. What is more, today jobless production and growth in many economic sectors is not a utopian possibility but a bittersweet reality. Witness the virtual emptying of the harbour of Rotterdam, perhaps the most modern in the world and a major contributor to the rise of unemployment in this Dutch city above the 20% mark by the early 90s.

The more the revamped capitalist economy advances, the wider and deeper the reach of the new marginality, and the more plentiful the ranks of those thrown in the throes of misery with little respite or recourse, even as official unemployment drops and income rises in the country. In 1994, the U.S. Census Bureau reported that the American poverty rate had risen to a ten-year high of 15.1% (for a staggering total of 40 million poor persons) despite two years of robust economic expansion. Five years later, the poverty rate in large cities has barely budged in spite of the longest phase of economic growth in national history and the lowest official employment rate in three decades. Meanwhile the European Union officially tallies a record 52 million poor, 17 million unemployed, and 3 million homeless – and counting – in the face of renewed economic growth and improved global competitiveness. As major multinational firms such as Renault and Michelin in France turn in unprecedented profits and see their stock value zoom up, they also 'turn out' workers by the thousands.

Put differently, advanced marginality appears to have been 'decoupled' from cyclical fluctuations in the national economy. The consequence is that upswings in aggregate income and employment have little beneficial effect upon life chances in the neighbourhoods of relegation of Europe and the United States while downswings cause further deterioration and distress within them. Unless this disconnection is somehow remedied, further economic growth promises to produce more urban dislocation among those thrust and trapped at the bottom of the emerging urban order.

(ii) Economic dynamic – the desocialization of wage labour

The new urban marginality is the by-product of a double transformation of the sphere of work. The one is quantitative and entails the elimination of millions of low-skilled jobs under the combined press of automation and foreign labour competition. The other is qualitative, involving the degradation and dispersion of basic conditions of employment, remuneration, and social insurance for all but the most protected wage workers. The two combine to feed the process of polarization from below.

From the time when Friedrich Engels wrote his classic exposé on the condition of the working class in Manchester's factories to the crisis of the great industrial heartlands of Euro-American capitalism a century-and-a-half later, it was rightly assumed that expanding wage labour supplied a viable and efficacious solution to the problem of urban poverty. Under the new economic regime, that assumption is at best dubious and at worst plain wrong. First, a significant *fraction of the working class has been rendered redundant* and composes an 'absolute surplus population' that will likely never find work again. This is particularly true of older industrial workers laid off due to plant shutdowns and relocation: they are unlikely to have or acquire the skills and contacts needed to reconvert themselves into pliable service workers. At any rate, given the loosening of the functional linkage between macroeconomic activity and social conditions in the poor enclaves of the First World metropolis, and considering the productivity increases permitted by automation and computerization, even miraculous rates of growth could not absorb back into the workforce those who have been deproletarianized, that is, durably and forcibly expelled from the wage labour market to be replaced by a combination of machines, cheap immigrant labour, and foreign workers (Rifkin, 1995).

Second, and more importantly, the character of the wage-labour relation itself has changed over the past two decades in a manner such that it no longer grants foolproof protection against the menace of poverty even to those who enter it. With the expansion of part-time, 'flextime', and temporary work that carry fewer benefits, the erosion of union protection, the diffusion of two-tier pay scales, the resurgence of sweatshops, piece rates and famine wages, and the growing privatization of social goods such as health coverage, *the wage labour contract itself has become a source of fragmentation and precariousness* rather than social homogeneity and security for those consigned to the peripheral segments of the employment sphere (eg, European Economic Community, 1989; Mabit, 1995; MacDonald and Sirianni, 1996). During the golden age of Fordism, wage labour tended to homogenize the work force by creating commonalities of fate along a linear lifecourse pegged on the '40–50–60' schema: forty hours of employment a week for about fifty weeks of the year until one retires at age sixty. With the onset of 'desocialized wage labour', employment no longer supplies a common temporal and social framework because the terms of the labour contract are increasingly diverse and personalized, job tenures are short and unstable, and a growing number of positions do not carry with them protection from material deprivation, illness, joblessness, not to mention adequate retirement. In short, where economic growth and the correlative expansion of the wage sector used to provide the universal cure against poverty and polarization, today they are part of the malady.

(iii) Political dynamic – the reconstruction of welfare states

The fragmentation and desocialization of labour are not the only factors fuelling the rise of the new urban poverty. For, alongside with market forces, welfare states are major producers and shapers of urban inequality and marginality. States not only deploy programmes and policies designed to 'mop up' the most glaring consequences of poverty and to cushion (or not) its social and spatial impact. They also help determine who gets relegated, how, where, and for how long. States are major engines of stratification in their own right and nowhere more so than at the bottom of the sociospatial order (Esping-Andersen, 1993): they provide or preclude access to adequate schooling and job training; they set conditions for labour market entry and exit via administrative rules for hiring, firing, and retirement; they distribute (or fail to distribute) basic subsistence goods, such as housing, and supplementary income; they actively support or hinder certain family and household arrangements; and they co-determine both the material intensity and the geographical exclusivity and density of misery through a welter of administrative and fiscal schemes.

The *retrenchment and disarticulation of the welfare state* are two major causes of the social deterioration and destitution visible in the metropolis of advanced societies. This is particularly obvious in the United States, where the population covered by social insurance schemes has shrunk for two decades while programmes targeted to the poor were cut and then turned into instruments of surveillance and control. The recent 'welfare reform' concocted by the Republican congress and signed into law by President Clinton in the summer of 1996 is emblematic of this logic (Wacquant, 1997a). It replaces the right to public aid with the obligation to work, if necessary at insecure jobs and for substandard wages, for all able-bodied persons, including young mothers with dependent children. It drastically diminishes funding for assistance and creates a lifetime cap on public support. Lastly, it transfers administrative responsibility from the federal government to the fifty states and their counties, thus aggravating already existing inequalities in access to welfare and accelerating the incipient privatization of social policy.

A similar logic of curtailment and devolution has presided over wholesale or piecemeal modifications of social transfer systems in the United Kingdom, Germany, Italy, and France. Even the Netherlands and Scandinavian countries have implemented measures designed to reduce access to public support and to stem the growth of social budgets. Everywhere the mantra of 'globalization' and the fiscal strictures imposed by the Maastricht treaty have served to justify these measures and to excuse social disinvestment in formerly working-class areas highly dependent on state provision of public goods. The growing shortcomings of national welfare schemes has spurred regional and local authorities to institute their own stop-gap support programmes (especially in response to homelessness and long-term unemployment), which in turn has increased the administrative complexity, heterogeneity, and inequality of social provision.

Now, the irrelevance of the 'national state' has become a commonplace of intellectual conversation the world over. It is fashionable nowadays to bemoan the incapacity of central political institutions to check the mounting social dislocations consequent upon global capitalist restructuring. But large and persistent discrepancies in the incidence and persistence of poverty, as well as in the living standards, (im)mobility, and spatial distinctiveness of the urban poor in different countries suggest that news of the passing of the national welfare state has been greatly exaggerated. As of the late 1980s, tax and transfer programmes lifted most poor households near the median national income level in the Netherlands (62%) and France (52%); in West Germany only a third of poor families escaped poverty thanks for government support and in the United States virtually none. Extreme destitution has been eliminated among children in Scandinavian countries while it plagues one child in six (and every other black child) in the United States (these data are drawn from McFate, Lawson, and Wilson, 1995; a more analytical overview on this question is Kangas, 1991). States do make a difference – that is, when they care to. Therefore it is imperative to bring them back to the epicentre of the comparative sociology of marginality and polarization as *generative* as well as *remedial* institutions.

(iv) Spatial dynamic – concentration and stigmatization

In the postwar decades of industrial expansion, poverty in the metropolis was broadly distributed throughout working-class districts and tended to affect a cross-section of manual and unskilled labourers. By contrast, the new marginality displays a distinct tendency to conglomerate in and coalesce around 'hard core', 'no-go' areas that are clearly identified – by their own residents no less than by outsiders – as urban hellholes rife with deprivation, immorality, and violence where only the outcasts of society would brook living.

Nantua in Philadelphia, Moss Side in Manchester, Gutleutviertel in Hamburg, Brixton in London, Niewe Westen in Rotterdam, Les Minguettes in Lyon's suburbs and Bobigny in the Parisian periphery: these entrenched quarters of misery have 'made a name' for themselves as repositories for all the urban ills of the age, places to be shunned, feared, and deprecated. It matters little that the discourses of demonization that have mushroomed about them often have only tenuous connections to the reality of everyday life in them. A *pervading territorial stigma* is firmly affixed upon the residents of such neighbourhoods of socioeconomic exile that adds its burden to the disrepute of poverty and the resurging prejudice against ethnoracial minorities and immigrants (an excellent analysis of this process of public stigmatization is offered by Damer [1989] in the case of Glasgow).

Along with territorial stigmatization comes a sharp diminution of the sense of communality that used to characterize older working-class locales. Now the neighbourhood no longer offers a shield against the insecurities and pressures of the outside world, a familiar and reaffirming landscape suffused with collective meanings and forms of mutuality. It turns into an empty space of competition and conflict, a danger-filled battleground for the daily contest of survival and escape. This weakening of territorially-based communal bonds, in turn, fuels a retreat into the sphere of privatized consumption and strategies of distancing ('I am not one of them') that further undermine local solidarities and confirm deprecatory perceptions of the neighbourhood. We must remain alert to the possibility that this may be a transitional (or cyclical) phenomenon eventually leading to the spatial deconcentration or diffusion of urban marginality. But for those presently consigned at the bottom of the hierarchical system of places that compose the new spatial order of the city, the future is now. Relatedly, it must be stressed that such neighbourhoods of relegation are creatures of state policies in matters of housing, city, and regional planning. At bottom, then, their emergence, consolidation, and eventual dispersion are essentially political issues.

The specter of transatlantic convergence

One question is at the back of everyone's mind when it comes to the deterioration of social conditions and life chances in the Old World metropolis: does the rise of this new marginality signal a structural rapprochement between Europe and the United States on the model of the latter (see, for instance, Cross, 1992; Musterd, 1994; van Kempen and Marcuse, 1998; Haüßerman, Kronauer, and Siebel, in press). Framed in such simplistic, either/or, terms, the question hardly admits of an analytically rigorous answer. For regimes of urban marginality are complex and capricious beasts; they are composed of imperfectly articulated ensembles of institutional mechanisms tying together economy, state, place, and society that do not evolve in unison and, moreover, differ significantly from country to country with national conceptions and institutions of citizenship. It is therefore necessary first to rephrase this query.

If by convergence, one means the wholesale 'Americanization' of urban patterns of exclusion in the European city leading down the path of *ghettoization* of the kind imposed upon Afro-Americans since they urbanized at the beginning of this century (ie, the formation of a segmented, parallel, sociospatial formation serving the dual purpose of exploitation and ostracization of a bounded ethnoracial category), then the answer is clearly negative (Wacquant, 1996b). Contrary to first impressions and superficial, media-driven accounts, the changeover of the continental metropolis has not triggered a process of ghettoization: it is not spawning culturally uniform sociospatial ensembles based on the forcible relegation of stigmatized populations to enclaves where these populations evolve group- and place-specific organizations that substitute for and duplicate the institutional framework of the broader society, if at an inferior and incomplete level.

There is no Turkish ghetto in Berlin, no Arab ghetto in Marseilles, no Surinamese ghetto in Rotterdam, and no Caribbean ghetto in Liverpool. Residential or commercial clusters fuelled by ethnic affinity do exist in all these cities. Discrimination and violence against immigrants (or putative immigrants) are also brute facts of life in all major urban centres of Europe (Wrench and Solomos, 1993; Björgo and White, 1993). Combined with their typically lower class distribution and higher rates of joblessness, this explains the disproportionate representation of foreign-origin populations in urban territories of exile. But discrimination and even segregation is not ghettoization. Such immigrant concentrations as exist are not the product of the institutional encasement of the group premised on rigid spatial confinement –

as evidenced by rising rates of intermarriage and spatial diffusion when education and class position improve (Tribalat, 1995). Indeed, if anything characterizes the neighbourhoods of relegation that have sprouted across the continent as mechanisms of working-class reproduction floundered, it is their extreme ethnic heterogeneity as well as their incapacity to supply the basic needs and encompass the daily round of their inhabitants – two properties that make them *anti-ghettos*.

If convergence implies that *self-reinforcing cycles of ecological disrepair, social deprivation and violence*, eventuating in spatial emptying and institutional abandonment, are now operative on the continent, then again the answer is negative because European areas of urban exile which forms nodes of polarization, as it were, remain, with few exceptions (such as Southern Italian cities), deeply penetrated by the state. The kind of 'triage' and purposive desertion of urban areas to 'economize' on public services that has befallen the American metropolis is unimaginable in the European political context with its fine-grained bureaucratic monitoring of the national territory. At the same time, there can be no question that the capacity of European states to govern territories of relegation is being severely tested and may prove unequal to the task if recent trends toward the spatial concentration of persistent joblessness continue unabated (Engbersen, 1997).

Finally, if convergence is intended, more modestly, to spotlight the *growing salience of ethnoracial divisions and tensions* in the European metropolis, then the answer is a qualified and provisional yes, albeit with the following strong provisos. First, this does not necessarily imply that a process of 'racialization' of space is underway and that the societies of the Old World are witnessing the formation of 'minorities' in the sense of ethnic communities mobilized and recognized *as such* in the public sphere. Second, ethnoracial conflict is not a novel phenomenon in the European city: it has surged forth repeatedly in the past century during periods of rapid social and economic restructuring – which means also that there is little that is distinctively 'American' about it (Moore, 1989; Noiriel, 1989). Lastly, and contrary to the American pattern, putatively racial strife in the cities of the Old World is fuelled not by the growing *gap* between immigrants and natives but by their greater *propinquity* in social and physical space. Ethnonational exclusivism is a nativist reaction to abrupt downward mobility by the autochthonous working class before it expresses a profound ideological switch to a racist (or racialist) register. Notwithstanding faddish blanket pronouncements about the 'globalization of race', the increased salience of ethnicity in European public discourse and everyday life pertains as much to a politics of class as to a politics of identity.

Coping with advanced marginality: the turn to the penal state

In their effort to tackle emergent forms of urban relegation, nation-states face a three-pronged alternative. The first, middle-ground, option consists in *patching up* the existing programmes of the welfare state. Clearly, this is not doing the job, or the problems posed by advanced marginality would not be so pressing today. One might even argue that such piecemeal and increasingly local responses to the disruptions caused by urban polarization help perpetuate the latter insofar as they fuel bureaucratic cacophony and inefficiency.

The second, regressive and repressive, solution is to *criminalize poverty via the punitive containment of the poor* in increasingly isolated and stigmatized neighbourhoods, on the one hand, and in jails and prisons, on the other. This is the route taken by the United States following the ghetto riots of the 60s (Rothman, 1995). It is no happenstance if the stupendous expansion of the carceral sector of the American state – the imprisoned population has quadrupled in twenty-five years and corrections departments risen to the rank of third largest employer of the country even as crime levels remained *grosso modo* constant over that period – has taken place just as casual (under)-employment spread and public assistance waned before being 'reformed' into a system of forced employment. For the atrophy of the social state and the hypertrophy of the penal state are two correlative and complementary transformations that partake of the institution of a new government of misery whose function is precisely to impose desocialized wage labour as a norm of citizenship while providing a functional substitute for the ghetto as a mechanism of racial control (Wacquant, 1998).

While the United States are truly exceptional for the zeal with which they have embraced this 'solution' to social polarization and for the scale on which they have implemented it, the temptation to rely on the police and carceral institutions to stem the effects of social insecurity generated by the spread of precarious work and the retrenchment of social welfare is present throughout Europe. This can be seen in the spectacular rise of incarceration rates among most member countries of the European Union over the past two decades; the massive over-representation, within the imprisoned population, of non-European immigrants and of people of colour, as well as of drug dealers and addicts who are rejects from the labour market; the hardening of penal policies, more openly turned towards incapacitation, as over rehabilitation, and tacitly guided by the principle of 'lesser eligibility'; and in the overpopulation of carceral establishments, which reduces imprisonment to its function of warehousing of the undesirable. Recent shifts in public discourses on urban disorder reveal a similar drift towards a penal treatment of poverty and of the dislocations which, paradoxically, arise from having truncated the capacity for social intervention of the state. One is thus founded to predict that a 'downward' convergence of Europe on the social front, entailing further deregulation of the labour market and continued unraveling of the collective safety net, will ineluctably result in an 'upward' convergence on the penal front and a new burst of carceral inflation throughout the continent (Wacquant, 1999).

Despite the colossal social and fiscal costs of the mass confinement of poor and disruptive populations, imprisonment remains a seductive stop-gap solution to mounting urban dislocations even in the most liberal societies (Christie, 1997). But, aside from the powerful political and cultural obstacles that stand in the way of the wholesale carceralization of misery inherent in the makeup of social-democratic states in Europe, punitive containment leaves untouched the root causes of the new poverty. The third, progressive, response to urban polarization from below points to a fundamental *reconstruction of the welfare state* that would put its structure and policies in accord with the emerging economic and social conditions. Radical innovations, such as the institution of a citizen's wage (or unconditional income grant) that would sever subsistence from work, expand access to education through the lifecourse, and effectively guarantee universal access to essential public goods such as housing, health, and transportation, are needed to expand social rights and check the deleterious effects of the mutation of wage-labour (Van Parijs, 1996). In the end, this third option is the only viable response to the challenge that advanced marginality poses to democratic societies as they prepare to cross the threshold of the new millennium.

Acknowledgements

This is the revised and expanded version of a text previously published as 'Urban Marginality in the Coming Millennium', *Urban Studies*, 36–10, September 1998, pp. 1639–1647. I would like to thank the participants to the ESRC Seminar on Social Polarization at Leicester for their cogent critiques and queries.

References

Björgo, T. and White, R. (eds), (1993), *Racist Violence in Europe*, New York: St Martin's.

Carnoy, M. *et al.*, (1993), *The New Global Economy in the Information Age*, Baltimore: Johns Hopkins University Press.

Christie, N., (1998), 'Eléments de géographie pénale', *Actes de la recherche en sciences sociales*, 124 (September): 68–74.

Cross, M. (ed.), (1992), *Ethnic Minorities and Industrial Change in Europe and North America*, Cambridge: Cambridge University Press.

Damer, S., (1989), *From Moorepark to 'Wine Alley': The Rise and Fall of a Glasgow Housing Scheme*, Edinburgh: Edinburgh University Press.

Engbersen, G., (1997), *In de schaduw van morgen. Stedelijke marginaliteit in Nederland*, Amsterdam: Boom.

Esping-Andersen, G. (ed.), (1993), *Changing Classes: Stratification and Mobility in Post-Industrial Societies*, Newbury Park: Sage.

European Economic Community, (1989), *Underground Economy and Irregular Forms of Employment: Synthesis Report and Country Monograpies*, Brussels: mimeo.

Hadjimichalis, C. and Sadler, D. (eds), (1995), *Europe at the Margins: New Mosaics of Inequality*, New York: Wiley and Sons.

Haüßerman, H., Kronauer, M. and Siebel, W. (eds), (in press), *Die Neue Armut und Exklusion in der Stadt*, Frankfurt: Suhrkamp.

Kangas, O., (1991), *The Politics of Social Rights*, Stockholm: Institute for Social Research.

Mabit, R. (ed.), (1995), *Le travail dans vingt ans. Rapport de la Commission présidée par Jean Boissonnat*. Paris: Odile Jacob.

MacDonald, C.L. and Sirianni, C. (eds), (1996), *Working in the Service Economy*, Philadelphia: Temple University Press.

McFate, K., Lawson, R. and Wilson, W.J. (eds), (1995), *Poverty, Inequality, and Future of Social Policy*, New York: Russell Sage Foundation.

Mingione, E. (ed.), (1996), *Urban Poverty and the Underclass*, Oxford: Basil Blackwell.

Mollenkopf, J.H. and Castells, M. (eds), (1991), *Dual City: Restructuring New York*, New York: Russell Sage Foundation.

Moore, R., (1989), 'Ethnic Division and Class in Western Europe', in Scase, R. (ed.), *Industrial Societies: Crisis and Division in Western Capitalism and State Socialism*, London: Allen and Unwin.

Musterd, S. (ed.), (1994), Special issue on 'A Rising European Underclass?', *Built Environment*, 20–3, 1994.

Noiriel, G., *Le Creuset français*, Paris: Editions du Seuil.

Rifkin, J., (1995), *The End of Work: The Decline of the Global Work Force and the Dawn of the Post-Market Era*, New York: G.P. Putnam's Sons.

Rothman, D., (1995), 'American Criminal Justice Policies in the 1990s', in Blomberg, T.G. and Cohen, S. (eds), *Punishment and Social Control*. New York: Aldine de Gruyter.

Sassen, S., (1991), *The Global City: New York, London, Tokyo*, Princeton: Princeton University Press.

Tribalat, N., (1995), *Faire France. Une enquête sur les immigrés et leurs enfants*, Paris: La découverte.

Van Kempen, R. and Marcuse, P. (eds), (1998), *The New Spatial Order of Cities*, Cambridge: Blackwell.

Van Parijs, P., (1996), *Refonder la solidarité*, Paris: Editions du Cerf.

Wacquant, L., (1996a), 'The Rise of Advanced Marginality: Notes on Its Nature and Implications', *Acta sociologica*, 39 (2): 121–139.

Wacquant, L., (1996b), 'Red Belt, Black Belt: Racial Division, Class Inequality, and the State in the French Urban Periphery and the American Ghetto', in Mingione, E. (ed.), *Urban Poverty and the Underclass*, Oxford: Basil Blackwell.

Wacquant, L., (1997a), 'Les pauvres en pâture: la nouvelle politique de la misère en Amérique', *Hérodote*, 85 (Spring): 21–33.

Wacquant, L., (1998), 'L'ascension de l'Etat pénal en Amérique', *Actes de la recherche en sciences sociales*, 124 (September): 7–26.

Wacquant, L., (1999), *Les Prisons de la misère*, Paris: Editions Liber-Raisons d'agir.

Wrench, J. and Solomos, J. (eds), (1993), *Racism and Migration in Western Europe*, New York: Berg.

Young, J., (1999), *The Exclusive Society: Social Exclusion, Crime, and Difference in Late Modernity*, London: Sage.

Employment, unemployment and social polarization: young people and cyclical transitions

Robert MacDonald and Jane Marsh

Introduction

This chapter discusses changes in the nature and distribution of work, employment and unemployment and how these impact upon processes of social polarisation. It does so by focusing upon a social group – young people – and a place – one local labour market in the Northeast of England – which illustrates these social and economic developments very clearly. From the age of sixteen, young people undertake transitions which are not only crucial for their own individual biographies and life-chances thereafter but also for the ways in which social classes are reproduced or reconstituted. The locality discussed – Teesside – is in many ways typical of Old Industrial Regions in other parts of the UK and Europe and demonstrates changes in the world of work in dramatic fashion. It has also been the site for qualitative research with young people carried out by one of the authors in the earlier part of the decade and is now the location for an on-going research project which we are jointly undertaking.

The *first* section describes the restructuring of the local economy and the patterns of employment, unemployment and social polarization which prevail at the end of the 1990s. The *second* part describes the research projects which provide the empirical material for discussion. The *third* section documents the deleterious impact of local socio-economic change upon the first steps that school-leavers take in the labour market, whilst the *fourth* part explores the longer-term experiences of young people in a polarized labour market, particularly in respect of unemployment, youth training schemes, the New Deal, marginal jobs and informal work. The *fifth* section characterizes these experiences in terms of 'cyclical transitions' and the chapter concludes by outlining some new directions for research on young people, social polarization and exclusion in the context of current national policy agendas and contemporary debates about class analysis.

The changing shape of work & unemployment in Teesside

In 1989 Huw Beynon and his colleagues published a short piece on the economic fortunes of Teesside. Drawing upon a comment of one of their interviewees, they titled the paper '*It's all falling apart here*'. Ten years later the story is still not a happy one and prospects for worthwhile work remain poor for many Teessiders, despite general improvements in the national economy and the implementation in Teesside of a series of policy measures designed to regenerate the local economy.

The speed and scope of the economic decline of a place which, as recently as the 1960s, was world-famous for its industrial success, is remarkable. There can be few other places which demonstrate such a change in economic fortunes as vividly. Whilst we are suggesting that Teesside can be used as a case study to explore more general and wider processes of social and economic change, it should be acknowledged that there are some things which make it atypical of other declining industrial regions.

It cannot be claimed, for instance, that the reason for its weakened industrial strength lies in capital under-investment (prior to the late 1970s Teesside's chemical and steel industries received enormous input), nor can it be explained in terms of conflictual industrial relations (the area has been typified by its lack of Trade Union militancy: see Hudson, 1989a). And unlike other comparable regions the mainstays of employment were to be found in a narrow range of heavy industries (steel, chemicals and heavy engineering) with little tradition of small and medium sized enterprise development or of diversification into other industrial sectors. In terms of its social composition (eg, its relatively small non-white, ethnic population) it is also different from, say, the English Midlands or Northwest. Nevertheless, the processes and experiences we will describe here will be at least familiar to observers of other Old Industrial Regions in other parts of the UK and Europe (Hudson, 1989b) and will provide the context necessary for the subsequent discussion of the way that such changes in the world of work have been experienced and responded to by local people.

In 1965, the conurbation had an unemployment rate of 1.5%. Full employment for men in relatively well-paid, long-term and skilled jobs provided the economic security which underpinned social reproduction, cohesion and stability. As a result of fierce global competition, shifting policies towards nationalized industries and over-concentration in a narrow industrial base, restructuring and redundancy on a massive scale ensued (MacDonald and Coffield, 1991). Between 1975 and 1986 one-quarter of all jobs and one-half of all manufacturing jobs were lost (Cleveland County Council, 1986). In the 1980s Teesside became notorious for having some of the highest levels of unemployment in mainland Britain and joblessness persists at high levels in the late 1990s.

In June 1999, around one in ten of the workforce were unemployed, compared with one in twenty nationally (Tees Valley Joint Strategy Unit,

1999a). This official figure for Teesside unemployment disguises quite dramatic differences at a more local level. Some local authority wards have very low levels of unemployment. These tend to be areas of private owner-occupation, such as Ingleby Barwick in Stockton, which is mainly comprised of one large, new, 'dormitory' estate and which has 3% male unemployment (about the lowest in Teesside). Nearby Parkfield lies at the other end of the local spectrum of social polarization: an area of council-owned properties with the highest rate of male unemployment at 27% (see Byrne, 1995, for a discussion of the way that patterns of housing tenure consolidate patterns of work polarization in Teesside).

And of course these are estimates only of those officially counted as unemployed (ie, people in receipt of unemployment-related benefits). If we add in those who are counted as 'jobless' (ie, those who are on various training schemes, those ineligible for benefits and those classed as economically inactive, but who would take up jobs if they were available) we find even more striking examples of how structural economic changes have blighted the locality. In one of the wards, which we call 'Orchard Bank', in our current research site (see below), nearly half of all working age men are 'jobless' (Tees Valley Joint Strategy Unit, 1999b). Beneath ward level the picture is even more desperate with local community leaders reporting that around 80% of men living on one street in Orchard Bank are unemployed.

The locality has as well experienced some positive employment developments over the past decade or so. As with other parts of Northeast England, Teesside has successfully attracted inward investment from other parts of the world. The Samsung electronics plant is perhaps the biggest and best known recent example of Far East employment creation. Recent closures and redundancies of similar plants in the Northeast of England – such as Fujitsu at Darlington and Siemens in North Tyneside – remind us, however, to remain cautious in estimating the long-term benefit of such developments for places like Teesside.

There have been increases in the numbers in service sector employment during the 1980s and '90s, which have partly offset the decline in manufacturing employment and limited the growth of unemployment. Related to this, the local TEC predicts a continuing decline in rates of male economic activity and increasing labour market participation by women over the next decade. Currently, half of all female employment is part-time and women are reported to be taking 80% of new jobs, the majority of which are again part-time and in the service sector (Teesside TEC, 1995). The TEC – in an unusually candid moment – acknowledges that many of the new jobs which might erode some of this local worklessness will be 'part-time, low-paid, low status, temporary contract positions and will be unattractive to many people' (1995, p. 45).

The decline in manufacturing industry and full-time employment (particularly for men) and the increase in service sector and part-time employment (particularly for women) are well established trends of the UK economy. The persistent structural unemployment which has beleaguered this *local* labour market may be less familiar to those who only receive reports of the state of the *national* economy and hear of month-by-month reductions in aggregate unemployment figures. It is predicted that unemployment will remain a significant problem into the 21st century (Cleveland County Council, 1992).

Researching youth on Teesside

The research drawn upon in this chapter is of two sorts. First, from the late 1980s to mid-1990s one of the authors undertook a series of related studies into various aspects of informal economic activity and the changing culture of work in Teesside. The primary motivation was to explore and understand the work that young people – and adults – undertook *outside* of standard employment through such things as volunteering, self-employment in small firms, working in co-operatives and community businesses, and in 'fiddly jobs'. The aims, design, methodology and results of these studies are published in detail elsewhere (MacDonald, 1991, 1994, 1996a, 1996b; MacDonald and Coffield, 1991).[1]

In brief, the methodology was qualitative involving semi-structured interviews with individuals and small groups, and various episodes of participant observation, conducted over four years. In total, over 300 hundred informants participated in the research. This sample was not selected randomly and therefore cannot necessarily be considered to be representative. Rather, research participants were recruited purposively, via various agencies and through a 'snowballing' technique, in order to gain access to experiences of non-standard and informal working. Around half of these were teenagers and young adults and it is their experiences which are drawn upon most heavily in the empirical discussions here.

The second research project of relevance to this chapter is, at the time of writing, currently being undertaken by both authors as part of the ESRC's *Youth, Citizenship and Social Change* research programme.[2] It builds upon the findings and conclusions of MacDonald's earlier research and is again located in Teesside. Its central aim is to interrogate empirically the usefulness of underclass theories in explaining the experiences and circumstances of young people in an area of high unemployment, crime and single-parenthood and, if these are found wanting, to develop more persuasive theoretical accounts of, and policy responses towards, social exclusion. The methodology is also qualitative, involving semi-structured interviews with 80 young men and women aged 15 to 25 years, together with some periods of participant observation with particularly interesting groups of young people (eg, the persistently unemployed, those with 'criminal careers', young single parents) and a series of interviews with local 'stake-holders' (professional workers who, in various capacities, have contact with 'excluded' young people). A few early insights from this research are included in the central sections of this chapter, but it is mainly alluded to in the final part where new directions for research on young people, social polarization and exclusion are discussed.

Restructured youth transitions

Perhaps the key interest of youth sociologists in the UK over the past fifteen years has been the description and analysis of the transitions – the staged movements between various institutional statuses and experiences – that young people make as they leave school, pass through their late teenage years and into adulthood (eg, Banks *et al.*, 1992). The primary focus has been upon school-to-work transitions and how these have been restructured as a consequence of the virtual collapse of the youth labour market in the early 1980s, the subsequent expansion of youth training and further education provision and the 'reform' (ie, virtual elimination) of welfare support for under-18 year olds. As Craine (1997) points out, sociologists have deployed a series of adjectives – 'long', 'broken', 'extended', 'fractured', 'uneasy', 'protracted' – to try to capture the changes which have as a consequence been wrought in youth transitions. Central to many of these accounts is the view that changes in the world of work, education and training have extended the youth phase.

The experiences of young people as they make transitions from school into the labour market are particularly revealing of the way that Teesside's economy has changed.[3] They can show us how – within the space of a generation or so – work opportunities have been dramatically recast.[4] This focus on youth also allows us to examine the processes which *establish* the polarization of the workforce into those who tend to have decent work opportunities and prospects and those who tend not to (Bates and Riseborough, 1993; Bynner *et al.*, 1997).

Surveys of youth transitions over the past decade (eg, Banks *et al.*, 1992) tell us that these processes begin with the first steps that school-leavers take. Those who enter employment or continued education at 16 are more likely to make 'successful' transitions in the longer term (for instance, into the primary labour market of decent jobs) whereas those who enter unemployment and/or youth training at compulsory school leaving age are more likely to encounter repeat spells of unemployment and/or involvement in a peripheral labour market of more insecure employment (Williamson, 1993; Furlong and Cartmel, 1997).

Each year local Careers Services collect the first destination statistics for school-leavers. The most recently available figures for Teesside describe how the landscape of post-16 opportunities is now constructed for local young people (Future Steps, 1998). These figures are presented in Table 1. The category 'not available' refers to young people who are not available for work because they are, for instance, acting as carers, in custody or looking after their own children.

It is useful to contrast these figures with destination statistics from previous decades in order to get a sense of the way that youth transitions have been

Table 1 First destinations for Teesside and Middlesbrough 16 year olds, 1998 (percentages)

	Teesside	Middlesbrough
Full-time Education	55	48
Employment	7	5
Training	14	15
Unemployment	9	12
Not Available	10	18
Moved Away	1	1
Not Known	04	2

Source: Future Steps, 1998

reshaped within this local economy. Twenty-five years ago – when the 'working-class kids' in Paul Willis's famous study were 'learning to labour' (Willis, 1977) – the most common destination was a job or apprenticeship, with 55% of 16 year olds following this path: the same proportion that now 'stay on' in education. Youth training schemes and expanded further education provision in colleges and sixth-forms now soak up many of those who would, in previous decades, have moved into work in the dockyards, steel mills, chemical plants, shops or offices. This level of post-16 educational participation is still low by national standards but it represents a substantial increase in an area with little widespread tradition of non-compulsory education and which contains some of the worst levels of educational achievement in the country. In the area in which we are undertaking our current research around one in five young people leave school with no qualifications; in two of the secondary schools less than 5% leave with five or more A–C grades at GCSE, against a national average of almost 50% (DfEE, 1998).

Of course, care needs to be taken when reading these first destination statistics. There is considerable variation recorded between towns in Teesside, as the figures for Middlesbrough indicate. Most noteworthy in this respect are the lower numbers in Middlesbrough moving into full-time education (48%) and higher proportions of people becoming unemployed or classified as 'unavailable' for work (together amounting to as many as 30%). Our current research suggests that various wards and neighbourhoods display even greater variation in patterns of post-16 destination. Perhaps the greatest limitation of these figures, however, is that they only provide a snap-shot of the first destination post-school and give no indication of the longer-term careers of young people.

The sharp decline in employment opportunities for school-leavers is dramatic and may be considered depressing. Conversely, it could be argued that the related increase in participation in post-16 education represents an opening up of new routes of transition for working-class young people who previously have tended to move into the labour market as quickly as they can.

Our research interviews would suggest that for many of this group a job at 16 would have been preferred and that college participation is strongly, if not wholly, motivated by the *lack* of employment opportunities when they leave school.

Despite the depressed nature of their local labour market some Teesside school-leavers *do* avoid social and economic insecurity in their early careers and make 'successful' transitions into mainstream employment. Many of these will be those from more socially advantaged, affluent families and neighbourhoods who are still able to trade on cultural capital and trade in educational qualifications for relatively secure and rewarding employment. Perhaps the widening of access to Further and Higher Education (FE and HE) has set in place new routes to more secure and rewarding futures for some working-class young women and men?

This is one question that our current research will be investigating. Local levels of graduate un- and under-employment, however, remind us not to overstate the benefits of lengthened educational participation and nor is it certain that this wider social access will be maintained in the situation where students, rather than the state, bear most of the financial costs of HE. There is also some evidence from the early stages of our current research that participation in FE may often be short-lived (with significant proportions not completing the courses for which they enrolled) and, in some cases, motivated as much by a simple concern to do *anything* other than join those of their cohort who become unemployed or enter training schemes of debatable worth.

Young people's paths through a polarized labour market

So what happens to these people who experience 'unsuccessful' transitions, who do not successfully pursue continued education or secure access to gainful employment, who end up on the wrong side of polarized labour markets? Youth cohort surveys tell us that these people are most likely to have either become unemployed immediately after leaving school or to have entered training schemes which are likely to lead them into unemployment. The following section concentrates on the long-term experiences of teenagers and young adults in respect of training and related schemes, unemployment and various forms of marginal work. It draws primarily upon the research completed by MacDonald in the mid-1990s (1991, 1994, 1996a, 1996b; MacDonald and Coffield, 1991).

Status Zer0, youth training and the New Deal

Participation in government training or 'make-work' schemes was an extremely common feature of young people's biographies and it was rare to come across individuals who had not enrolled for at least one from the array of varieties and acronyms on offer. Whilst local training agencies are happy to quote figures for the numbers of young people who have entered or completed a training course or who have gained a National Vocational Qualification (NVQ) in the process, they tend to be more reticent about the employment (or other outcomes) of youth training schemes.

There continues to be a general political consensus that insists that such schemes are valuable in transferring youth from school to the workplace. The Labour government's New Deal programme consolidates the thinking which lay behind the multifarious youth unemployment schemes set in place by previous Conservative administrations: that the problem of youth unemployment is a problem of the young unemployed, of the quality of the labour supplied to potential employers, rather than a problem of the diminishing demand for youth labour. Under the New Deal, this problem, it is implied, can be resolved by cajoling young people into temporary schemes for work participation, environmental action, volunteering, self-employment and training which will induce in their young participants the sorts of experiences, outlooks and behaviours required by eager employers (see Convery, 1997). In the context where this government seems to be rehashing the policies of the 1980s (albeit in extended form) it is worth repeating the simple question often asked then by critics of such schemes: training for what?

Steve Craine (1997) followed the fortunes of a group of school-leavers in a high unemployment area of Manchester through the 1980s. Many of them took part in youth and, later, adult training programmes and between them they accumulated 60 years worth of participation on schemes. Only one person found a job as a result. The situation in Teesside seems to be better but is by no means glorious. Official figures gained through personal correspondence with local TEC staff suggest that only around one-third of youth trainees move into a job afterwards, with the majority returning to unemployment.

Howard Williamson and his colleagues have described those young people who are not in employment, education or training as occupying Status Zer0; a group who have simply 'gone missing' from official registers of young people and become 'lost' in the process of transition (Williamson, 1997; Istance, Rees and Williamson, 1994). Since the 1988 Social Security Act, those who are in this category who are under 18 year olds are not normally entitled to unemployment benefits. Some young people will be in receipt of the Youth Training Bridging Allowance (£15 per week) if they are 'between schemes' and a small number in particular hardship will be eligible for Job Seekers Allowance payments. The clear majority of Status Zer0 youth will, however, have no obvious source of legitimate income – no wages, no training allowance, no college grants, no dole money – and will either be forced into longer-term dependency upon family or will seek ways to earn a living in less legitimate ways.

The Social Exclusion Unit (1999) has recently estimated that 161,000 16 to 19 year olds occupy Status Zer0 nationally. Announcing this new report, Baroness Blackstone (an Education Minister) described these young people as 'a lost generation ... [who] find themselves on a fast track to social exclusion'

(*The Guardian*, 14 July 1999). Whilst acknowledging the issue of Status Zer0, neither the local Training and Enterprise Council nor the local Careers Service publish an equivalent figure for Teesside. However, given the numbers officially recorded as unemployed by the Careers Service (see Table 1), and the high proportions officially deemed 'unavailable' or 'unknown', it is possible that nearly 1 in 4 young people in Teesside (and nearly 1 in 3 in Middlesbrough) enter Status Zer0 a few months after they have left school.

Once young people have reached the age of 18 and have claimed Jobseekers' Allowance for six months they are eligible for entry to the New Deal for Young People programme. The New Deal for unemployed 18 to 25 year olds became active in Spring 1998 and, at the time of writing, it is not possible to estimate quantitatively the success of this programme in terms of its core aim of moving young people 'from welfare to work'. What our research *has* revealed is that, already, New Deal staff are beginning to present a reconfigured measure of success of the programme in terms of its contribution to the *employability* rather than the *employment* of young adults. In other words, in the view of the New Deal Managers and Advisors that we have interviewed recently, the programme will be deemed to have worked if it is has made its participants *more likely* to get employment (or otherwise leave the unemployment register) by instilling in them certain work disciplines, habits and outlooks and generally making them more 'work ready' (to borrow their phrase). How this will be judged and who will make the judgement is unclear but it is perhaps not surprising that professionals who are aware of the limitations of the local labour market are nervous about measuring the success of their efforts in terms of getting unemployed young people into jobs. Already some young people in Teesside are in the process of entering their second cycle of New Deal participation, having completed the programme, failed to find work and received Jobseekers' Allowance for a few more months.

Marginal jobs and informal work

The discussion so far has concentrated on young people's encounters with unemployment, training schemes and the New Deal. Of course, the transitions of young Teessiders are not wholly bereft of experiences of work – far from it. In a minority of cases, training schemes did lead directly into jobs. More frequently employment was disconnected from training scheme participation (in terms of both time and the nature of the subsequent job). Overall, the jobs that young adults went into tended to be of the sort that Huw Beynon (1997: 31) has called 'hyphenated work' – short-term, part-time, low-paid, low-skilled, dead-end employment often in service sector 'Mcjobs' (eg, serving in fast-food 'restaurants', bars and shops). Occasionally informants got routine machinist work in the textile industry or packing work in local food processing factories. In our current research we are exploring in more detail the nature of the employment available to young people and their perception and experiences of it. In previous studies the focus was purposefully upon the work that young adults did *outside* of standard employment and the following passages summarize some of this (see MacDonald, 1994, 1996a, 1996b for fuller accounts).

Some young people started their own small businesses or co-operatives and were lauded by Prince Charles, government ministers and enterprise agencies as budding 'young entrepreneurs' (MacDonald and Coffield, 1991) albeit, though, with very limited commercial success in the long-term (MacDonald, 1996b). This entrepreneurship was forced by the lack of real alternatives (Storey and Strange, 1992) and typified by general experiences we can describe as survival self-employment. Business failure led the vast majority back to the unemployment and benefit dependence which first motivated their enterprises. Their self-exploitative 'enterprise culture' was as wasteful – of individual hopes and energies, of working lives and state grants and allowances – as the alleged dependency culture which government intended it to replace.

Others volunteered, preferring work without pay to the idleness of unemployment (MacDonald, 1996b). Indeed, a few risked losing their unemployment benefits because of their volunteering. Although we might classify these 'unemployed' volunteers as part of the economically surplus population, their care work was vital to agencies trying to fill the gaps left by cut-backs in social service provision. In this sense, it is hard to class them as 'unemployable' but they became long-term unemployed because of the inability of their local labour market to provide these and other sorts of work as employment.

Some engaged in 'fiddly work' (MacDonald, 1994; Jordan *et al.*, 1992). They did these risky, sometimes dangerous, always poorly remunerated, irregular scraps of work because of 'need not greed', as one Department of Social Security fraud manager candidly put it. Interviewees described in detail the various needs which this sort of poor work partially met. It was needed in order to maintain personal self-respect and identity in the context of work careers full of unemployment. It was valued because it could demonstrate to families, future employers and a society that labelled them as literally useless that they were willing to work. They were unhappy to be perceived as idle, unproductive, unemployable. It allowed them to maintain contact with the neighbourhood sub-cultures which distributed both fiddly and proper jobs and to retain the work disciplines necessary for employment. Finally, and most obviously, it helped to alleviate the poverty faced by benefit-dependent households. In these senses, fiddly work was informed by quite conservative and moral considerations. Even those who had never done it largely understood and condoned those who had. A few interviewees had embarked upon quasi-criminal careers (eg, in petty drug dealing) which intermingled with the search for more legitimate work. A small number moved away to seek their fortunes in more prosperous parts of the country or overseas in semi-nomadic careers, hunting temporary, casual jobs in the service and agricultural sectors of European economies. Other local people will have developed responses unrecorded by these studies.

There was one, inescapable conclusion which cut across all these studies. Young adults wanted work and were extraordinarily dogged and enterprising in their search for it amidst the economic wreckage of their local labour market. They remained attached to durable, mainstream attitudes which valued work as the key source of self-respect, as the principal definer of personal identity, as a social (and in many cases moral) duty, as the foundation upon which to build sustainable family lives and respectable futures. Indeed, the way that they stubbornly clung on to orientations to work which are now possibly obsolescent might be regarded as remarkable given the limited supply of decent work around.

Cyclical transitions

From these studies we can see that regular employment does not feature highly in the working lives of the young people that moved into unemployment and training schemes in the early 1990s in Teesside. What as recently as the 1960s were regarded as, secure, safe and normal transitions for working-class young people from the school at 16 into working-class jobs have been replaced by transitions in which the movement to working-class adulthood is no longer framed by standard employment but rather by the cyclical movement through various types of informal work, marginal jobs, unemployment and government schemes. The participants in Craine's ethnography describe this gloomy series of encounters as the 'Black Magic Roundabout' (1997).

'Cyclical' is used here to denote the lack of any sense of progression or forward movement normally associated with notions of 'career' or 'transition'. The biographies that interviewees outlined certainly contained numerous and different labour market statuses patterned over time (and often within quite a short work history) but that these were somehow linked together, providing stepping stones upwards and onwards towards improved occupational locations was not the case. Rather, time spent participating in one or other of the various 'options' available would usually end, sooner or later, with a return to unemployment (and then, after a period, fresh participation in a new scheme, low-level job or short-lived college course, and so on and so on).

For those young adults who entered Status Zer0, who failed to find durable employment post-school or training scheme, circulation through various permutations of these casualized and marginal economic activities became the norm. It is these people who most directly experience the negative effects of the social and economic polarization of British labour markets whose 'outstanding characteristics have become flexibility and insecurity' (Brown, 1997: 9). Moreover, there seems to be little opportunity to jump off the Black Magic Roundabout, to find more promising routes out of peripheral sub-employment. One useful and unusual aspect of the earlier research was that it explored the longer-term outcomes of youth transitions as people entered their mid-twenties and, in a few cases, their thirties. What this has shown is that early labour market marginality can harden very quickly into apparently permanent exclusion where the chances of a return to the mainstream of 'proper jobs' seem very slim. Let us give one example from previous fieldwork.

Malcolm had left school at 16 in the late 1970s and took part first of all in YOP (the Youth Opportunities Programme). By the age of 29, when last interviewed, he had worked his way through JIG (the Job Interview Guarantee Scheme), YWS (the Young Workers Scheme), CP (the Community Programme), ET (Employment Training) and various Job Clubs. He was now running a small business through the Enterprise Allowance Scheme (EAS) which offered advice to others about how to cope with unemployment, but nobody had yet taken advantage of his services. He didn't seem to be 'unemployable' (he had done much unpaid voluntary work for local welfare agencies) but he had never had a 'proper job'. Whether his *whole* working life will be constructed through engagements with schemes like this, or whether some unexpected work opportunity will come his way, is of course impossible to know. High unemployment persists and a generation of young people – and now adults – have never been included in the mainstream social and economic life of this locality. In this context what is more certain is that without long-term and imaginative effort to create new and more permanent employment, government schemes (with whatever appellation and acronym) are most likely to *sustain* rather than combat the marginal and cyclical transitions we have described.

New directions for research on young people, social polarization and exclusion

This chapter has attempted to illustrate how the economic restructuring of one locality has had enormous consequences upon the transitions that its young residents make. The most obvious and dramatic change has been the virtual removal of opportunities for regular, standard employment for young people in their late teenage years and early adulthood. Transitions for working-class young people are now framed by often reluctant participation in post-16 education courses and a range of schemes of debateable efficacy (most recently the New Deal), interspersed with recurrent periods of unemployment, marginal employment and informal work. These cyclical transitions describe the way that the polarization of opportunities for rewarding and worthwhile work are established for one particularly important group – working-class young people taking their first steps in the labour market – and how these early experiences impact upon longer-term life-chances.

The chapter has also shown how early then continued experience of these cyclical transitions can transform labour market marginality into what *appears* to be almost permanent socio-economic exclusion. A number of writers have taken evidence of this sort to suggest that we are witnessing the emergence of an underclass of people who, in the context of persistently high unemployment, have become detached from the normal working, social and moral life of their communities (Murray, 1990, 1994; Field, 1989; Dahrendorf, 1987; Smith, 1992).

We would argue that such underclass theses are mistaken (see MacDonald, 1997 for a fuller discussion). Even in such promising territory for 'underclass hunting', it was very difficult to locate evidence for the existence of a distinct, deviant underclass *culture* (see Murray, 1990, 1994; Green, 1992). Nor was it easy to locate individuals who had become wholly cut off and *structurally* excised from the labour market (Runcimann, 1990; Robinson and Gregson, 1992; Westergaard, 1992; Gallie, 1994). Even in the desperate economic circumstances described here, these most marginal of workers (young people with very little in the way of cultural capital) seemed able to resist falling into complete economic inactivity and permanent worklessness, as underclass theses suggest would be the case (e.g. Dahrendorf, 1987; Wilkinson, 1995).[5] Young people remained *attached* to work: they retained personal *values* which stressed its moral and social worth *and* they were able to maintain, sporadically, the *practice* of working (albeit in jobs and informal economic activities which were usually precarious and unrewarding).

It would seem that in poor areas of Britain there is *not* a class of people *beneath* the lowest class of the gainfully employed population almost *permanently* kept there by separate cultural outlooks and activities or by the structures of the labour market (see Roberts, 1997; MacDonald, 1997), but a restructuring of the lower levels of the labour market typified by cyclical *movements* around peripheral work and unemployment. Unemployment, job insecurity and underemployment have become common *working-class* experiences rather than the preserve of an underclass separated from and beneath them. Our informants were experiencing first-hand these cyclical movements between peripheral, non-standard work and unemployment typical of British labour markets in the 1990s.

A number of labour market studies in the 1990s have pointed to the same phenomena. Daniel (1990) has drawn attention to the flows in and out of the stock of unemployed. Quoting Daniel's work, Cornford argues that there are 'almost as many poor people trapped in low paid work as on benefits ... but what low income figures do not reveal are the *movements* between these groups' (1992: 61, our emphasis). Wintour (1996) quotes Department of Employment research which demonstrates that half Britain's unemployed find jobs, lose them again within a year and return to claiming benefit (the figure for the North of England was 66% reclaiming within a year). Will Hutton (1996) reports a study by Jarvis and Jenkins which estimates that over half the British workforce will be employed as part-timers, self-employed or temporary by the year 2000. It highlights the 'churning' of the poor and sometimes unemployed around these different, destandardized forms of work. Most recently, White and Forth (1998) report that three-quarters of the unemployed in their sample were able to find work during the mid-1990s but their major route out of unemployment was through 'flexible' temporary, part-time or self-employed positions which tended not to lead into better or more permanent jobs (and for many resulted in a return to unemployment).

These conclusions lead us away from 'underclass hunting' toward closer, more detailed consideration of the way that the labour market structures unequal opportunities for participation in worthwhile work for different social groups. Lydia Morris's research in Hartlepool, which sits next to Teesside, has also been useful in exploring social polarization in economically declining local labour markets (Morris, 1992, 1993, 1994; Morris and Irwin, 1992). She too questions the fastness of the divide between the economically inactive *unemployed* (the putative 'underclass') and those *underemployed* in 'new' types of casualized, non-standard work (Hakim, 1987, 1989, 1990):

> [B]oth groups are clearly disadvantaged ... and there is probably some movement ... between them. The existence of an underemployed group, which seems likely to have grown given the changing patterns of employment throughout the 1980s, calls attention away from non-employment and towards the structure and operations of the labour market. The 'underclass' of the non-employed and state dependent then appears as an extreme position in the broader context ... (Morris, 1994: 162).

Thus, a focus upon the way that work in all its forms is now organized and experienced in particular localities can give a picture of social polarization and exclusion better than can underclass theories which focus only upon those *perceived* to be permanently deprived of work.

In Britain in the latter part of the 1990s sociological, political and policy debates about the so-called underclass have in large part given way to a new research and policy agenda concerned with the social exclusion of disadvantaged social groups and deprived local areas (eg, Social Exclusion Unit, 1998; Madanipour *et al.*, 1998; Lawless *et al.*, 1998; Jones Finer and Nellis, 1998; Jordan, 1998; Perri 6, 1997; Cousins, 1997). The 'New Labour' government, borrowing from European Community policy analyses and prescriptions, has made the combatting of social exclusion – particularly as it effects various disadvantaged groups such as young people and single mothers – the main priority of domestic policy. It has declared that the growth of an underclass is 'the greatest social crisis of our times' (*The Guardian*, 15 August 1997) and has set out a range of New Deal programmes (first for under-25s, then for lone parents, those over-25, the over 50s and communities) as the centre-piece of its endeavours to combat social exclusion.

Spurred by this new political and policy interest (and associated research funding opportunities), the late 1990s has witnessed a landslide of academic contributions to the analysis of social exclusion. Because of its size it is impossible to review in any detail here but some of its general concerns and foci can be noted. These include: the development of suitable definitions and indicators of social exclusion and deprivation (Atkinson, 1998; Barry, 1998; Lee and Murie, 1998; Bhalla and Lapeyre, 1997); the delineation and ranking of localities troubled by exclusion (Room, 1995; Howarth *et al.*, 1998; Glennerster *et al.*, 1999; Social Exclusion Unit, 1998); as well as more critical and theoretical debates about the intellectual heritage of the concept, its various meanings and its usefulness, or otherwise, in describing and theorizing aspects of poverty and inequality (eg, Levitas, 1996; Jordan, 1998).

To date, there have been relatively few academic studies published which have drawn upon these political and policy agendas to explore exactly how social exclusion is generated for, experienced by and responded to by the individuals and poor neighbourhoods said to suffer from it (for notable exceptions see: Smith and Stewart, 1998; Pleace, 1998; Gilroy and Speak, 1998). The research with which we are currently engaged has this aim. Although the concept of social exclusion shares some of the problems of recent underclass theory – in particular, it remains an ill-defined, inexact concept which desperately requires empirical application, critique and refinement (Atkinson, 1998) – we would argue that the new social exclusion policy and research agenda has value for the sociological investigation of work, (un)employment and social polarization in three important respects.

Firstly, unlike more static concepts like the 'underclass', social exclusion does imply social and economic *processes* whereby some people *become* included and others do not. This opens up room for more detailed explorations of the way that social structural constraints (eg, as reflected by the realities of growing up in an area of high unemployment) interact with individual agency (eg, as displayed in the decisions and steps taken by young people into and through the labour market) to create social exclusion/inclusion. Our on-going, qualitative research adopts a biographical approach in order to understand how individuals make sense of their changing fortunes and experiences between the ages of 15 and 25 years. Its design allows us to compare the hopes, expectations and outlooks of school-leavers embarking on transitions to adulthood, with detailed accounts of people in their mid-twenties as they look back upon their youth transitions and try to make sense of the experiences they have encountered and paths they have taken.

Secondly, the concept of social exclusion acknowledges that the problems that young people in areas like Teesside face are not *solely* concerned with issues of jobs and unemployment, even if opportunities for decent work and decent incomes are arguably the most crucial aspect of social polarisation processes. Government policy sees social exclusion as a multi-faceted experience in which a variety of social problems cluster together in an area, sometimes experienced simultaneously and in combination by individuals from that area (eg, poor housing, high crime rates, low educational attainment, worklessness, poor health) (Social Exclusion Unit, 1998).

Our current project explores how different dimensions of young people's transitions interact with each other in the creation of different outcomes for them in their mid-twenties. For instance, we are exploring how aspects of housing transitions (eg, leaving the parental home, experiences of homelessness, forced dependency upon parents for accommodation), of family transitions (eg, forming stable partnerships, becoming young parents) and of school-to-work transitions impact upon each other in the processes of social inclusion and exclusion. Similarly, because we adopt a broad conceptualization of 'work' we are able to investigate how, over time, engagement with various types of licit and illicit work and work-like activity evolve into different sort of work 'careers' for young adults (eg, mainstream employment careers, marginal careers of sub-employment and informal work, criminal careers of acquisitive crime, drug-use and drug-dealing).[6]

Thirdly, the new social exclusion policy agenda recognizes the importance of *locality*. Focussed academic research can uncover how the local socio-economic and cultural conditions of a place impact upon processes of social polarization and exclusion. The spatial patterning and polarization of work, employment and unemployment – with national figures masking regional disparities in joblessness, regional averages hiding local labour market differences, local labour market statistics concealing vastly different circumstances at ward and even neighbourhood level – reminds us of the importance of disaggregating statistical trends and rates of unemployment if our analytical impetus is an ethnographic one: to understand how individuals encounter, experience and respond to the work opportunities, or lack of them, that prevail in their localities. At the time of writing this chapter, youth unemployment in the United Kingdom was announced to be at its lowest for 25 years. The celebratory national press stories which accompanied the release of these figures must seem baffling to the young women and men in our studies who continue to search for rewarding, meaningful work.

The cyclical and marginal transitions of the young people described in this chapter cannot be understood properly without close reference to the way that the local labour market has been recast over the past thirty years. Our current research has an even sharper local focus and explores young people's transitions within one particularly deprived area of Teesside (which we are calling East Kelby). The sprawling local authority housing estates of East Kelby feature high in the rankings in current indexes of local deprivation (Mason, 1999). All five of its wards are described as 'poverty wards' (Glennerster *et al.*, 1999). A recent report which drew upon surveys of resident dissatisfaction claimed that one of these, which we call Primrose Vale, is 'the most miserable place in England' (Burrows and Rhodes, 1998). Because of its high rates of crime, unemployment and single-parenthood, Kelby itself was selected by Charles Murray (1994) as indicative of the emergence of what he called the 'New Rabble' underclass.

Through our qualitative research we are asking whether the grim statistical descriptions and negative labels – which are applied by academics and social commentators to a place they have often never visited – make sense to the young people who actually live here; in doing so, we are investigating how they perceive and experience the social phenomena listed under the tag of social exclusion. This more nuanced, ethnographic approach also allows for an appreciation of the diverse ways in which young people negotiate their local social and economic landscapes and how it is that young people from the same physical and socio-economic place seem to make transitions which result in such polarized outcomes. For instance, we have so far interviewed three young adults from Primrose Vale. The first is participating in New Deal in the hope that it will lead to a job in management after three years of unemployment. The second is well-advanced in a criminal career which is intertwined with his long-term heroin use. The third is studying for a PhD at a nearby University.

The concept of social exclusion, therefore, presents possibilities for a sociological analysis of young people's transitions which is tied into important, current policy developments. We would also suggest that the sort of research questions and methodological approach that we have described in this chapter offer some promising lines of inquiry for the sociological analysis of social polarisation and class inequalities.

Reflecting on her study of the experience of employment change in Hartlepool, Lydia Morris commented how the 'concept of class [as developed in conventional, mainstream British sociology] ... has seemed of little relevance to this work' (Morris, 1996: 184). Her focus upon rapid changes in the local employment structure (eg, the growth and spread of long-term unemployment) *and* upon people's changing employment histories *within* this shifting structure (biographies of repeated unemployment, sub-employment and insecure employment) raised problems for the more static and cross-sectional approaches to mapping class inequalities and the consequences of class position which have tended to dominate in UK sociology (Crompton, 1998). Drawing upon the findings of her study, Morris describes how conventional approaches to class analysis (designating individuals to particular social classes according to their *occupation*) are often unable to capture patterns of labour market disadvantage for people whose employment status *changes* repeatedly over time, in the context of structural unemployment and job insecurity. This standard approach to class designation (by occupation) faces a further problem when the individuals studied are long-term unemployed or have *never* worked in standard employment, as was true for many in our studies.

Bill Jordan and Marcus Redley in an important review of debates about social polarisation, welfare dependency and the underclass, decry the lack of academic attention paid to the actual activities of the marginal poor and call for 'a new orientation in research on social exclusion' which would investigate '... the[ir] survival strategies and cultures of resistance' (1994: 156). We would echo this call. If we are interested in *processes* of social polarisation and exclusion and – more widely – processes of class formation, then the sort of research questions and methods suggested in this chapter would seem appropriate (see Crompton, 1998).[7] A case-study approach in a particular locality can reveal in detail the way that social and economic institutions (changing arrangements of schooling, further education, training schemes and the labour market) operate to polarize opportunities for young people from different class backgrounds. A focus on the transitions made through *these* opportunity structures allows for an examination of a critically important life-phase – the late teenage years and early adulthood – in which social classes are reproduced or reconfigured. Coupled with an ethnographic method, this sort of study can provide for a more subjective understanding of the lived experience of class inequalities: how structural processes of social polarization and exclusion are made sense of 'from below' by the social actors involved in them. In our case, it also allows for empirical assessment of the underclass thesis and – potentially – the development of more persuasive theoretical accounts of social polarization, exclusion and the changing world of work and unemployment.

Acknowledgment

The authors are grateful to Rosemary Crompton for her helpful comments on earlier versions of this paper.

Notes

1 This research commenced at the University of Durham, in collaboration with F. Coffield, and was originally sponsored by the Economic and Social Research Council (grants XC05750014 and R000231976) and supported later by the University of Teesside. The support of these organizations is gratefully acknowledged, as is the assistance of all the people who took part in the studies. All names have been changed.

2 Our project, entitled *Youth, the 'Underclass' and Social Exclusion*, began in January 1999 and concludes in December 2000 (grant reference number L134251024). The support of the ESRC and the University of Teesside is, again, gratefully acknowledged.

3 The focus of this paper is upon teenagers and young adults. Their experiences are particularly illuminating of new patterns of transition and exclusion. They, of course, are not the only group to experience the changes in the worlds of work and unemployment that are outlined. The research sample for MacDonald's earlier studies ranged in age from 16 to over 70 years and the accounts gathered from people further up the age range (about self-employment, fiddly jobs and so on) were very similar to those collected from young people.

4 The extent of the restructuring of the local economy was revealed most dramatically when interviews with older research participants were compared with the accounts given by young people. The opening interview question asked informants to recount what they had done since leaving school. Eric, who was 61, used over one hour of audio-tape with his answer. He detailed a work biography commencing at 14 when he started work at a local steel foundry. Over the next forty years he worked for the same firm, moving up the occupational ladder until he reached senior supervisor level. He had recently been made redundant and was attempting to become self-employed. The same question asked of those in their late teens would typically receive a one-word answer: 'nowt'.

5 There is not the room here to provide a full review of different conceptions of the 'underclass' (see Westergaard, 1992), nor is there the opportunity fully to review the various strengths and weaknesses in their approaches and within the underclass debate more generally. Morris's 1994 book and the triumvirate of articles in *British Journal of Sociology* – by Marshall, Roberts and Burgoyne (1996), Morris and Scott (1996), and Crompton (1996) – provide very useful, critical coverage of the more sociological approach to understanding the underclass in terms of labour market changes.

6 This interest in the broad range of 'careers' evolved by excluded young people is being most directly pursued in another current research project. *Young People, Exclusion and Alternative Careers* is funded by the Joseph Rowntree Foundation and is being carried out in another part of this locality by Les Johnston, Paul Mason, Louise Ridley, Colin Webster and Robert MacDonald, all from the University of Teesside.

7 Rosemary Crompton (1998) describes various approaches to the analysis of class which have developed in UK sociology and notes how survey-based, 'employment aggregate' perspectives tend to present a relatively static picture of the *consequences* of designated class/employment positions. Like Morris (1996), Crompton suggests that case-study approaches can allow for a more dynamic picture of the way that class *processes* operate in particular localities for particular groups – some of which, like young people and the long-term unemployed, are inadequately theorized in 'employment aggregate' studies.

References

Atkinson, A., (1998), 'Social Exclusion, Poverty and Unemployment', in Atkinson, A. and Hills, J. (eds), *Exclusion, Employment and Opportunity*, CASE Paper 4, London: CASE.

Banks, M. *et al.*, (1992), *Careers and Identities*, Milton Keynes: Open University Press.

Bates, I. and Riseborough, G. (eds), (1993), *Youth and Inequality*, Buckingham: Open University Press.

Beynon, H., (1997), 'The Changing Practices of Work', in Brown, R. (ed.), *The Changing Shape of Work*, Basingstoke: MacMillan.

Beynon, H. *et al.*, (1989), '"It's all falling apart here": Coming to terms with the Future in Teesside', in Cooke, P. (ed.), *Localities: The Changing Face of Urban Britain*, London: Routledge.

Bhalla, A. and Lapeyre, F., (1997), 'Social Exclusion: Towards an Analytical and Operational Framework', *Development and Change*, 28: 413–433.

Brown, R., (1997), 'Flexibility and Security: Contradictions in the Contemporary Labour Market', in Brown, R. (ed), *The Changing Shape of Work*, Basingstoke: MacMillan.

Byrne, D., (1995), 'Deindustrialisation and dispossession: an examination of social division in the industrial city', *Sociology*, 29: 95–115.

Bynner, J. *et al.*, (1997), *Twenty-Somethings in the 1990s*, Aldershot: Ashgate.

Cleveland County Council, (1986), *Cleveland Structure Plan: People and Jobs*, Economic Development and Planning Department, Middlesbrough: Cleveland County Council.

Cleveland County Council, (1992), *Review of the Assisted Areas of Great Britain: A Response to the DTI Consultation Paper from the Local Authorities in Cleveland County*, Middlesbrough.

Convery, P., (1997), 'The New Deal Gets Real', *Working Brief*, 88: 7–18.

Cornford, J., (1992), 'Policy Issues and the Underclass Debate', in Smith, D. (ed.), *Understanding the Underclass*, London: Policy Studies Institute.

Cousins, C., (1997), 'Social Exclusion in Europe', *Policy and Practice*, 26 (2): 127–146.

Craine, S., (1997), 'The Black Magic Roundabout: Cyclical Transitions, Social Exclusion and Alternative Careers', in MacDonald, R. (ed.), *Youth, the 'Underclass' and Social Exclusion*, London: Routledge.

Crompton, R., (1996), 'The fragmentation of class analysis', *British Journal of Sociology*, 47: 56–67.

Crompton, R., (1998), *Class and Stratification*, Cambridge: Polity Press (2nd edition).

Dahrendorf, R., (1987), *The Underclass and the Future of Britain*, 10th Annual Lecture, Windsor.

Daniel, W.W., (1990), *The Unemployed Flow*, London: Policy Studies Institute.

DfEE, (1998), *Secondary School Performance Tables*, London: Department for Education and Employment.

Field, F., (1989), *Losing Out*, Oxford: Blackwell.

Furlong, A. and Cartmel, F., (1997), *Young People and Social Change: Individualization and Risk in Late Modernity*, Buckingham: Open University Press.

Future Steps, (1998), *First Destinations of 1998 School-leavers*, Stockton-on-Tees: Future Steps.

Gallie, D., (1994), 'Are the Unemployed an Underclass? Some Evidence from the Social Change and Economic Life Initiative', *Sociology*, 28 (3): 737–757.

Gilroy, R. and Speak, S., (1998), 'Barriers, Boxes and Catapults: Social Exclusion and Everyday Life', in Madanipour, A., Cars, G. and Allen, J. (eds), *Social Exclusion in European Cities: Processes, Experiences and Responses*, London: Jessica Kingsley/RSA.

Glennerster, H., Lupton, R., Noden, P. and Power, A., (1999), *Poverty, Social Exclusion and Neighbourhood: Studying the Area Bases of Social Exclusion*, CASE paper 22, London: CASE.

Green, D., (1992) 'Liberty, Policy and the Underclass', in Smith, D. (ed.), *Understanding the Underclass*, London: Policy Studies Institute.

Hakim, C., (1987), 'Trends in the Flexible Workforce', *Employment Gazette*, 95 (11): 549–60.

Hakim, C., (1989), 'Workforce Restructuring, Social Insurance Coverage and the Black Economy', *Journal of Social Policy*, 18 (4): 471–503.

Hakim, C., (1990), 'Core and Periphery in Employers' Workforce Strategies: evidence from the 1987 ELUS Survey', *Work, Employment and Society*, 4 (2): 157–188.

Howarth, C., Kennay, P., Palmer, G. and Street, C., (1998), *Monitoring Poverty and Social Exclusion: Labour's Inheritance*, York: JRF.

Hudson, R., (1989a), *Wrecking a Region*, London: Pion Press.

Hudson, R., (1989b), 'Labour Market Changes and New Forms of Work in Old Industrial Regions', *Environment and Planning*, 7: 5–30.

Istance, D., Rees, G. and Williamson, H., (1994), *Young People Not in Education, Training or Employment in South Glamorgan*, Cardiff: South Glamorgan Training and Enterprise.

Jones Finer, C. and Nellis, M. (eds), (1998), *Crime and Social Exclusion*, Oxford: Blackwell.

Jordan, B., (1998), *A Theory of Poverty and Social Exclusion*, Cambridge: Polity Press.

Jordan, B. *et al.*, (1992), *Trapped in Poverty?*, London: Routledge.

Jordan, B. and Redley, P., (1994), 'Polarisation, the underclass and the welfare state', *Work, Employment and Society*, 8 (2): 153–76.

Lawless, P., Martin, R. and Hardy, S., (1998), *Unemployment and Social Exclusion: Landscapes of Labour Inequality*, London: Jessica Kingsley/RSA.

Lee, P. and Murie, A., (1998), 'Targeting Social Exclusion: Targeting Deprivation Through Housing Tenure is Flawed', *New Economy*, 5 (2): 89–93.

Levitas, R., (1996), 'The Concept of Social Exclusion and the New Durheimian Hegemony', *Critical Social Policy*, 46: 5–21.

MacDonald, R., (1991), 'Risky Business? Youth in the Enterprise Culture', *Journal of Education Policy*, 6 (3): 255–269.

MacDonald, R., (1994), 'Fiddly Jobs, Undeclared Working and the 'Something for Nothing Society', *Work, Employment and Society*, 10 (3): 431–47.

MacDonald, R., (1996a), 'Labours of Love: Voluntary Working in a Depressed Local Economy', *Journal of Social Policy*, 25 (1): 19–38.

MacDonald, R., (1996b), 'Welfare Dependency, the Enterprise Culture and Self-employed Survival', *Work, Employment and Society*, 10 (3): 431–47.

MacDonald, R., (1997), 'Youth, Social Exclusion and the Millennium', in MacDonald, R. (ed.), *Youth, the 'Underclass' and Social Exclusion*, London: Routledge.

MacDonald, R. and Coffield, F., (1991), *Risky Business? Youth and the Enterprise Culture*, Basingstoke: Falmer Press.

Madanipour, A., Cars, G. and Allen, J. (eds), (1998), *Social Exclusion in European Cities: Processes, Experiences and Responses*, London: Jessica Kingsley/RSA.

Marshall, G., Roberts, S. and Burgoyne, C., (1996), 'Social class and underclass in Britain and the USA', *British Journal of Sociology*, 47: 22–44.

Mason, S., (1999), 'Patterns of Area Deprivation', in Hills, J. (ed), *Persistent Poverty and Lifetime Inequality: the evidence*, CASE Report 5, London: CASE/HM Treasury.

Morris, L., (1992), 'Social segregation and the long-term unemployed in Hartlepool', *Sociological Review*, 40: 344–369.

Morris, L., (1993), 'Is there a British Underclass?', *International Journal of Urban and Regional Research*, 17 (3): 404–13.

Morris, L., (1994), *Dangerous Classes: the Underclass and Social Citizenship*, London: Routledge.

Morris, L., (1996), 'Classes, underclasses and the labour market', in Lee, D. and Turner, B. (eds), *Conflicts About Class: Debating Inequality in Late Industrialism*, London: Longman.

Morris, L. and Irwin, S., (1992), 'Employment histories and the concept of an underclass', *Sociology*, 26: 401–420.

Morris, L. and Scott, J., (1996), 'The Attenuation of Class Analysis: some comments on G. Marshall, S. Roberts and C. Burgoyne ...', *British Journal of Sociology*, 47: 45–56.

Murray, C., (1990), *The Emerging British Underclass*, London: Institute of Economic Affairs.

Murray, C., (1994), *Underclass: the Crisis Deepens*, London: Institute of Economic Affairs.

Perri 6, (1997), 'Social Exclusion: Time to be Optimistic', in *The Wealth and Poverty of Newtorks: Tackling Social Exclusion*, Demos Collection 12, London: Demos.

Pleace, N., (1998), 'Single Homelessness as Social Exclusion: the Unique and the Extreme', in Jones Finer, C. and Nellis, M. (eds), *Crime and Social Exclusion*, Oxford: Blackwell.

Roberts, K., (1997), 'Is There a Youth Underclass? The Evidence from Youth Research', in MacDonald, R. (ed.), 1997 *Youth, the Underclass and Social Exclusion*, London: Routledge.

Robinson, F. and Gregson, N., (1992), 'The Underclass – A Class Apart?', *Critical Social Policy*, 34 (Summer): 38–51.

Room, G. (ed.), (1995), *Beyond the Threshold: The Measurement and Analysis of Social Exclusion*, Bristol: Policy Press.

Runcimann, W.G., (1990), 'How many classes are there in contemporary British society?', *Sociology*, 24: 378–96.

Smith, D. (ed.), (1992), *Understanding the Underclass*, London: Policy Studies Institute.

Smith, D. and Stewart, J., (1998), 'Probation and Social Exclusion', in Jones Finer, C. and Nellis, M. (eds), *Crime and Social Exclusion*, Oxford: Blackwell.

Social Exclusion Unit, (1998), *Bringing Britain Together: A National Strategy for Neighbourhood Renewal*, CM 4045, London: Social Exclusion Unit.

Social Exclusion Unit, (1999), *Bridging the Gap: New Opportunites for 16–18 Year Olds Not in Education, Employment or Training*, Cm 4405, London: Social Exclusion Unit.

Storey, D. and Strange, A., (1992), 'New Players in the Enterprise Culture?', in Caley, K. *et al.* (eds), *Small Enterprise Development*, London: Paul Chapman Publishing.

Teesside Training and Enterprise Council, (1995), *Labour Market Assessment*, Middlesbrough: Teesside TEC.

Tees Valley Joint Strategy Unit, (1999a), 'Unemployment Rates and Numbers Registered as Unemployed in June 1999', Darlington: Tees Valley Joint Strategy Unit; (www.teesvalley-jsu.gov.uk).

Tees Valley Joint Strategy Unit, (1999b), 'Unemployment in June 1999 for Borough Wards', Darlington: Tees Valley Joint Strategy Unit; (www.teesvalley-jsu.gov.uk).

Westergaard, J., (1992), 'About and beyond the underclass: some notes on influences of social climate on British Sociology', *Sociology*, 26: 575–587.

White, M. and Forth, J., (1998), *Pathways Through Unemployment: Where do they lead?* Joseph Rowntree Foundation, Findings Series no. 568, York: JRF.

Wilkinson, C., (1995), *The Drop Out Society: Young People at the Margin*, Leicester: Youth Work Press.

Williamson, H., (1993), 'Youth Policy in the United Kingdom and the Marginalisation of Young People', *Youth and Policy*, 40: 33–48.

Wintour, P., (1996), 'Think yuo're safe when you've finally got a job?', *The Observer*, 1 September.

Williamson, H., (1997), 'Status Zero Youth and the "Underclass": Some Considerations', in MacDonald, R. (ed.), *Youth, the 'Underclass' and Social Exclusion*, London: Routledge.

Willis, P., (1977), *Learning to Labour*, London: Saxon House.

Late twentieth century workplace relations: class struggle without classes

Paul Edwards

> 'Strong' class explanation entails the view that class ... must at some point be understood as a property of **social relationships** *per se* and is not simply reducible to the situations and actions of individuals (Lee, 1996: 245, emboldening added).

This chapter follows through the logic of Lee's argument, giving particular attention to the issue of social relationships. It argues that Lee's statement needs to be emboldened analytically as well as stylistically. If we accept that classes exist in the strong sense we need a theory which (1) addresses the dynamics of relationships and (2) does so by seeing class as the product of relations at the point of production. Lee, like many other writers, wishes to abandon all forms of Marxism and thereby loses a means of developing such a theory. Gubbay (1997) has provided a critique of various Weberian views of class and has indicated in very broad terms the outlines of an alternative. The present task is to extend the critique but more importantly to show how the alternative works and how it adds analytical purchase to the debate on class. In particular, the focus is on the linkages between class theory and the employment relationship, and how they are changing.

The core idea – that workplace relations are a central element of class – used to be asserted with some confidence by writers of most analytical persuasions. From the side of class theory, Goldthorpe's (1980: 39) well-known statement is that classes combine occupational categories whose members share similar sources of income and positions 'within the systems of authority and control governing the process of production'. (This was repeated in 1992 with explicit emphasis on 'positions defined by employment relations in the labour market': Goldthorpe and Marshall, 1992: 381). The importance of systems of authority and control could not be plainer. From the side of workplace studies, class was a common part of the rhetoric. Books with titles like *Class at Work* (Littler and Salaman, 1984) appeared, and analysts routinely said that day-to-day relationships within the workplace were related to class. Nichols and Beynon's (1977) study is sub-titled, 'class relations and the modern factory'. And at the end of their detailed observational study of strikes in an engineering factory Batstone *et al.* (1978: 218) argue that strikes as part of power relations between management and workers 'may have a class significance in that they constitute one means whereby class relations are modified'.

Since perhaps the mid-1980s, fewer statements of this kind seem to have appeared. The decline of trade unions and the collapse of traditional heavy industries such as coal and steel, where the language of class seemed to have day-to-day meaning, undermined the relevance of class terminology. The attack on collectivism under Conservative governments from 1979 to 1997 was self-evident. Then there was the rise of human resource management, with its linked claims to improve communication between management and worker, to replace the collectivism of unions with the individualism of performance appraisal and merit pay, and to move from the narrow job specifications of Taylorism to work force involvement, commitment and even 'empowerment'. As Carter (1997: 6) remarks, 'as a result of these changes, class perspectives ... look increasingly old-fashioned and inappropriate'.

Such developments did not mean that critical accounts of new management techniques disappeared. On the contrary, arguments that they entail a new form of control, often more insidious and subtle than the methods of the past, abound (Sewell and Wilkinson, 1992). Yet many of these arguments suggest than such control is achieved because workers are treated as atomized individuals who lack any collective organization through which to question managerial language. Any resistance becomes that of the individual seeking personal integrity. Casey's (1995) study of an American high technology company identifies various types of individual response. There are for example the 'defensive self', who complains about the company, feels confused, but still puts in long hours, and the 'colluded self' who displays total dedication and who may be an over-conformist. Old class-based solidarities are contrasted with the present: 'under present corporate conditions, class-based resistance is evident only in a remnant form among the defensive selves. The displaced remainder opt for capitulation and consumption' (p. 180).

Yet even such extreme developments (to the limited extent to which they are in any way typical of advanced capitalism, an important qualification often neglected in the more sweeping and historicist accounts like Casey's) can be seen as the product of class relations. The most appropriate concept is 'class struggle without classes' (Thompson, 1978; see Edwards, 1990a, for a previous discussion). This concept has not been much discussed in the sociological debates on class and is not for example mentioned in the Lee and Turner (1996) volume. The core of this idea is two-fold: that classes exist as a result of the fundamental processes around the system of production, and can thus be identified independently of any beliefs among class actors; and that relations between members of classes are a form of class struggle even when people do not use the language themselves.

Burawoy's arrow is a useful device to move forward. Burawoy (1985: 122) argued that studies of the state were over-politicized in the sense that the state was analysed independently of the underlying relations of production. At the same time, study of the workplace was under-politicized because the influence of the state on workplace regimes was neglected. The arrow was the concept of 'a politics of production', which could be directed in turn at these two targets. (Note in passing that Gubbay, 1997, sees the need to integrate analysis of the state within analysis of management and labour, rather than bringing it in as a separate force, as part of a future Marxist programme. Burawoy and many others (see Edwards, 1986) have already addressed the point). I begin with the importance of relations of production in understanding class theory. I then point the arrow at the workplace to address the role of class in workplace relationships. Finally, I try to link the two issues together, and in doing so comment on Carter's (1995, 1997) re-assessment of class theory.

Class and the production process

There are two approaches to class analysis which ought to complement each other. The first is the grouping of the population into classes and the comparison of the life chances of these groups (what Halsey *et al.*, 1980: 1 nicely call Political Arithmetic). The second is the analysis of the social processes which bring these groups into being and which generate change in their composition (Political Economy). This second approach tends to be associated with Marxism but is not the property of Marxists. A materialist yet non-Marxist analysis is perfectly feasible (Edwards, 1986). Yet proper criticism of Marxism has tended to lead to rejection of any study of social processes. Appropriately understood, such study is not only valid in its own terms but is also the necessary underpinning to a class-as-classification approach.

Goldthorpe and Marshall's delimitation of class analysis

It is convenient to use the definition of class analysis offered by Goldthorpe and Marshall (1992: 383–4). According to them, there are four things which class analysis does not entail though they would be found in most Marxist versions.

Goldthorpe and Marshall's third and fourth points require little discussion. They are that (a) their version of class analysis entails no theory of class-based collective action, 'according to which individuals holding similar positions within the class structure will thereby automatically develop a shared consciousness of their position'; and (b) we must reject any theory in which political action is the unmediated expression of class interests. Who could disagree?

The first point is that class analysis has 'no theory of history according to which class conflict serves as the engine of social change, so that at the crisis point of successive developmental stages a particular class... takes on its "mission" of transforming society through revolutionary action'. The latter part of the statement (the 'so that' phrase) characterizes classical Marxism and some more recent writers (notably Wright, 1985: 114–18). Yet a proper rejection of its determinism and historicism does not damage the first part of the statement. The classes recognized in Political Arithmetic have to come from somewhere, and it is reasonable to argue that they are generated through the development of the mode of production.

Second, class analysis as Goldthorpe and Marshall 'understand it implies no theory of class exploitation, according to which all class relations must be necessarily and exclusively antagonistic'; although they see 'conflict as being inherent within class relations' they do not see this as 'entailing exploitation as understood in Marxist discourse'. They are far from alone in this view. Lee (1996: 249–50) for example wishes to reject Marx's view that the accumulation of capital is possible only through the appropriation of surplus value in production. 'As bankers already recognize ... capital is *any* accumulated and administered fund of money'.

There are two problems here. First, does anyone seriously argue that class relations are *exclusively* antagonistic? A range of Marxist writers on the labour process (notably Friedman, 1977; Burawoy, 1979; Hyman, 1987) argue that any labour process requires a minimum of co-operation. Yet all these writers are also clear that consent is built on exploitation. For Friedman, managerial strategies are strategies of control in that they represent the pursuit of the interests of capitalists in maintaining control over and thus the exploitation of workers. Burawoy's starting question is why workers co-operate in their own exploitation. There is exploitation because of the extraction of surplus value, but this is hidden in various ways and overlaid with certain institutions, such as grievance procedures and collective bargaining, in which workers' interests are genuinely represented.

It is not clear how writers such as Goldthorpe and Marshall can argue that, to use their word, conflict is inherent in class relations without having some theory of exploitation. They are saying that it is more than simply likely or a possible concomitant of differing objectives. But why should the mere fact of there being different market and work situations mean that their occupants are necessarily in a state of conflict? Surely we need some idea of the relationship between them being antagonistic and hence some idea of exploitation, that is that the relationship is structurally one of opposed interests? As argued elsewhere (Edwards, 1986: 22–4), we need some such theory, for otherwise the statement that conflict is *inherent* in class relationships is merely rhetorical.

At this point one could be diverted into a debate on the meaning of production and surplus value, and indeed during the 1970s there was intense debate among Marxists as to which were the truly productive classes. But this would be to confuse levels of analysis. The generation of surplus value in the production process does not directly create observable classes. It is one of the underlying dynamics of society, but it needs to be complemented with other levels of analysis.

This brings us to the second problem mentioned above, the issue of exploitation, where again levels of analysis can be confused. Lee is quite correct that money (often in very large amounts) can be made in the non-productive sphere. But in what sense is the money actually made? For everyone making a profit there must be someone somewhere making a loss. Claims on commodities are simply being exchanged. The only source of new value is indeed the production process.

Giddens seems to be one of the few writers to address this point. Thus his original (1973) theory of class was, despite protestations to the contrary, firmly Weberian in identifying different forms of market and work situation. In particular it resolved the problem of the middle classes by arguing that capitalist society has three main forms of market capacity, ownership of capital, educational credentials, and labour power. Three classes then emerge around these capacities. But Giddens (1973: 135) also wanted to say that class conflict is inherent, but like Goldthorpe and Marshall he had no means of saying why this was so. Returning to the topic in 1981 (pp. 297–311), Giddens now discusses control of the labour contract as a central element in capitalism. He is thus at least aware of the need for a theory of exploitation. However, he admits that his initial definition was inadequate but offers no improvement. Moreover, if relations around the labour contract are now central, does this not generate two classes and put Giddens back in the problem from which he was so keen in 1973 to escape?

There is a further and more complex issue with Giddens's position. Giddens, like Wright (1985), sees ownership of each asset as involving exploitation. Yet it is now well-established that ownership of educational assets does not necessarily mean that the owners exploit those without these assets: there may be conflicts in the market between the two groups, but having education does not necessarily mean that one can in any precise sense exploit those who lack it (Carchedi, 1987; Gubbay, 1997; Savage *et al.*, 1992: 15).

Levels of analysis

This is where the idea of class struggle without classes comes in. The key passage in Thompson (1978: 49) reads:

> people find themselves in a society structured in determined ways (crucially but not exclusively in productive relations), they experience exploitation (or the need to maintain power over whom they exploit), they identify points of antagonistic interest, they commence to struggle around these issues and in the process of struggling they discover themselves as classes.

Thus class action is contingent on all kinds of historical circumstances and is not to be derived directly from material interests. Moreover, groups may struggle against others without seeing this as class struggle. For Thompson, classes in eighteenth-century England were engaged in class relationships as, for example, when agricultural labourers disputed their rights to land use and as ruling classes used the law, for example the notorious Black Act of 1723 (see Thompson, 1977), to restrain what they saw as disruption from the dangerous classes. Such struggle, though not defined in explicitly class terms, was class struggle because it entailed relationships around exploitation.

Katznelson (1986) offers a framework which complements these points. He distinguishes four levels of analysis: structure (the underlying development of a mode of production); the social organisation of society (the particular way in which a given society operates with, for example, important historical differences between, say, France and Germany); class as disposition (the actions and beliefs of individuals); and collective action as organised and self-conscious. There is no necessary linkage between these levels in the sense that organized action necessarily follows from a shared structural position. But, says Katznelson (1986: 6) in a key remark, possibilities for action are structurally constrained: the structural aspect of class

> exerts a 'determining' effect on culture and collective action in no more, but also no less, than the sense of Raymond Williams's definition of determination as 'not just the setting of limits' but 'also the exertion of pressures'.[1]

Figure 1 portrays Katznelson's version of the structure-formation-consciousness-action model. The heavy arrows pointing upwards identify the 'exertion of pressures' from below. The lighter arrows pointing downwards suggest that weaker forces can flow in the opposite direction, as discussed below.

Thus those who adopt what I would define as a materialist view agree with Goldthorpe and Marshall and many others that structure does not define interests still less actual behaviour: the arrows represent forces and influences, not determinate chains of causation. Yet materialists go further in saying that links between the four levels are not merely contingent or accidental. The

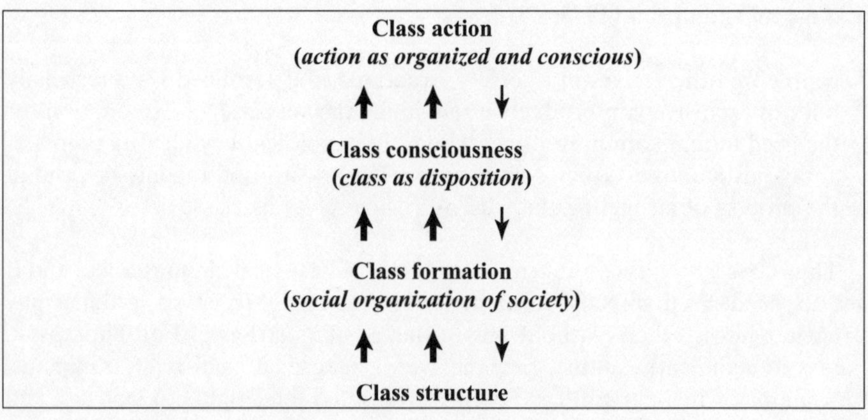

Figure 1 *The basis of class theory*

structural level constrains what is possible at more concrete levels of action. As a mode of production develops it exerts pressures towards the elimination of some positions in the class structure and the creation of new ones. Examples would be the rise of accountancy towards the end of the nineteenth century, which reflected the growth of large-scale enterprises and the need for capitalists and managers to develop indirect means of measuring performance in place of the direct observation which served when enterprises were smaller (Larson, 1980). As Stark (1980) argues, new occupational groups were active in the creation of their new places, for example through the creation of professional associations. It is also true that not all groups have been successful in establishing claims to professional status (see Armstrong, 1984) and that the position of groups such as accountants varies sharply between countries (Armstrong, 1989). There is nothing pre-determined about the rise of new groups. But the process is not just one of contingency. As Savage *et al.* (1992: 4) remark, an explanation in terms of social closure does not explain why some groups have the power to secure closure. The resources generated by change in the mode of production provided the power, but it then had to be used by social actors.

As for forces operating downwards in Figure 1, even defenders of strict historical materialism, notably Cohen (1978: 231–4), argue that 'bases need superstructures'. That is, to operate effectively an economic system benefits from superstructures, of which law is the standard example. A second example is the banking system, which is where Lee's point about banks has force. Banks assist commercial transactions in many ways, and their 'superstructural presence' helps to sustain the base. However, although superstructures may 'help' bases, concrete institutions emerge for all kinds of particular reasons and their effects can destabilize as well as stabilize the system.

Burawoy's (1979) analysis of his American plant offers a useful illustration of the point. Burawoy explains the rise of what he calls the internal state (a system of the workplace rule of law involving grievance procedures and collective bargaining) in terms of the benefits which it bestows on the generation of consent. Burawoy correctly argues that the internal state must have some autonomy from management for otherwise it would be seen as its creature; the result was that the wider legitimacy of management was strengthened by the operation of the superstructure. Yet the account is unduly functionalist in suggesting that the system arose because of its consent-enhancing properties. It can be rendered in functional rather than functionalist terms (to use the useful distinction introduced by Cohen, 1978: 249–96). Historical evidence (eg, Schatz, 1983) shows that rights against arbitrary discipline were central to unions' demands and that they were often resisted by firms. The internal state was not the automatic result of the 'need' for order. The establishment of the 'internal state' can be explained in terms of the pattern of class struggle during the 1930s, with employers fearing the loss of their authority and desperate to root out or neutralize a communist threat (which they greatly but understandably exaggerated). They were thus willing to cede certain trade union demands, notably for seniority in place of arbitrary powers of hiring and firing. Seniority was not a capitalist device. But its unintended consequence was that it reduced workers' collective identity and formed part of what Brody (1980) characterizes as a workplace rule of law: workplace law gave workers certain rights but also contained their ability to use their collective power. As Haiven (1994) has shown, North American systems, when compared to their British counterparts, gave unions with a weak shopfloor presence valuable rights but also meant that others with more shopfloor power were unable to exercise it.

The fact that, since Burawoy was writing, many firms have dismantled their internal states suggests that they may also entail costs as well as benefits to the employer. It is now commonplace to see such states as promoting inflexibility and as contributing to the vulnerability of the U.S. to Japanese competition (see Cappelli *et al.*, 1997, for a clear review). These 'superstructures' did not simply support the base but also generated tendencies such as excessively formalized internal labour markets which could destabilize as well as stabilize the base.

The conclusion from this example is four-fold. First, structures exert pressures but whether and how these are met is uncertain. Second, institutions such as collective bargaining which emerge in response to such needs exert influences back on structures. But, third, such stabilization can lead to direct costs for employers (as when they have to accede to worker demands) and also to indirect ones (such as inflexibility).[2] It is the relationship between the conflicting pressures of bases and superstructures which drives a pattern of regulation but this relationship is necessarily indeterminate and there is no set destination for the journey. Fourth, levels of analysis are important, for Burawoy moves too readily between America (in fact, a particular and unusual part of America, namely, unionized manufacturing) and capitalism. Seniority systems have less of a role in most other countries. Similarly, Savage *et al.* (1992: 51) argue that the American capitalist class developed in particular ways reflecting the professionalization and rationalization of management, whereas different processes were at work in Britain.[3]

With concepts such as exploitation and levels of analysis (wherein the more fundamental levels exert pressures and constraints on the more concrete) it is possible to develop a view of class in terms of relationships. The core contribution is to explain the processes which generate the groupings that Goldthorpean class analysis can then analyse. By what means do occupational categories arise, and through what processes do they have shared or differing sets of market and work situations? What is it about doctors or accountants which makes them a distinct group and puts them in one class rather than another? As is now widely argued, to deny that this is a valid question is surely to render class analysis narrow and to prevent it from dealing with changes in the class structure as new groupings emerge.

Class processes in the 1990s

Stability and change

It is commonly argued that management, for example, is undergoing substantial change through delayering, new information technologies and so on. In the words of Scarbrough (1998: 712) it is increasingly easy to 'eliminate middle management'. The traditional class position of managers would then be called into question. Yet such changes should be seen as reflecting new twists in class relationships rather than their collapse. What class schemas need, though, a fuller recognition of the dynamic nature of class relationships.

We saw above that students of 'new' workplaces, such as Casey, identify a breakdown of traditional class identities. The first point is that new forms of work organization are much less common than the more heady theories would suggest. Surveys find that advanced forms of teamworking and 'high commitment' are practised in perhaps 2% of European workplaces (European Foundation, 1997). Case studies (summarized by Geary, 1995) also find that change tends to be limited and patchy and that 'new' forms of labour management often depend on 'old' patterns of loyalty rather than being a sharp break from them. Thus in many workplaces there are recognizable continuities with the past.

Perhaps most importantly, those who diagnose extreme change confuse particular features of class with its general nature. It is true that the mean size of workplaces has fallen, that patterns of working time have changed, and that the composition of the work force has also altered. It is also true that restructuring has changed the contours of workplace relationships. Since the strike is often seen as the epitome of working class workplace action, trends here are particularly important. Britain used to be seen as peculiarly strike-prone. Yet strikes were concentrated in only three sectors: coal, the docks and cars. So it was never the case that the strike was the everyday experience of the majority of the working class: accounts of post-industrialism are exaggerated because they start from the wrong benchmark. It is also the case that formerly strike-free sectors, notably education and public services, are now more strike-prone. By the early 1990s there were more strikes in the odd official category of 'public administration, sanitary services and education' than in the whole of manufacturing (Edwards, 1995: 442). This change in the distribution of strikes can be related to the changing organization of work, with education and public sector workers being more subject to the budgetary controls that were formerly a feature of the private sector. To take one instance, studies of redundancy show that, when individuals are the focus, managers, administrators and clerical workers are close to the national average in their experience of redundancy (Field, 1997); analysis of establishments shows the same in respect of establishments in the education, health and government sectors (J. Smith *et al.*, 1999). Thus objective economic conditions underlie but do not determine changing strike patterns. In many countries strike rates have risen during the

1990s, Korea being a case in point. Finally, declining strike rates in Britain reflect unemployment and managerial policy, among other influences. To see such trends as evidence of individualism would be wrong.

It is common to find commentators diagnosing new problems. The management writer Charles Handy (1995: 23) identifies what he calls the paradoxes of our times and he makes the sweeping assertion, relying only on the authority of another guru, Peter Drucker, that the means of production are 'now literally owned by the workers because those means are in their heads and at their fingertips' (ie, the means of production now comprise knowledge and skills rather than capital equipment). Yet the paradoxes of uncertainty that Handy identifies have surely been with us for a long time. Indeed, the kind of analysis suggested above would say that this must be so, for capitalism is a fundamentally contradiction-ridden system. As for the claim that ownership of the means of production has slipped, 'literally', into the hands of the workers, it is of interest only as an example of the historicm of punditry (cf. Goldthorpe's, 1971, demolition of the recrudescence of historicism). The position of managers and of shopfloor workers illustrate these observations.

Managerial functions and the service class

Goldthorpe (1995: 314–16) has recently clarified his view of class. It is based on the concept of employment relations, with the primary division being between employers, the self-employed and employees. Within the latter group, the key distinction is between those with a service relationship and those with a labour contract. This approach is contrasted to a 'work centred' one in which the nature of work tasks and the autonomy enjoyed by individuals is central. The key differences between labour contract and service relationships are as follows:

> Employment relationships regulated by a labour contract entail a relatively short-term and specific exchange of money for effort. Employees supply more-or-less discrete amounts of labour, under the supervision of the employer or of the employer's agents, in return for wages ... In contrast, employment relationships within a bureaucratic context involve a longer-term and generally more diffuse exchange. Employees render service to their employing organisations in return for 'compensation', which takes the form not only of rewards for work done, through a salary and various perquisites, but also comprises important *prospective* elements – for example, salary increments on an established scale, assurances of security, ... and, above all, well-defined career opportunities. [Employees are likely to be required to] exercise *delegated authority* or *specialised knowledge and expertise* [and thus] their performance will depend on the degree of moral commitment that they feel towards the organisation (Erikson and Goldthorpe, 1993: 41–2, emphasis original).

The following discussion considers possible amendment to this view, in the light of evidence that employees in service positions may be losing such key benefits as career opportunities and of many arguments that the emphasis on the bureaucratic career is now out-moded. I suggest that fundamental amendment is not in fact required to the empirical assessment of the service class.

But there is a more basic point which suggests that the argument needs roots. Goldthorpe (1995: 318) denies that the way in which class structures develop is a valid aspect of sociological inquiry because the factors involved are highly diverse and often specific to particular countries. Yet two questions are arguably valid. First, at a structural level, what is it about the service class that means that they display commitment, how is trust generated, and whom and what are they serving? What in short are the conditions which create a distinct service relationship? In answering this question, Armstrong (1987, 1989) addressed the agency problem: given that the service class acts for others and enjoys delegated authority, how does the principal ensure that these agents act in appropriate ways? The answer lies in a mixture of trust and the monitoring of performance. Trust could, in turn, be increased through training, indoctrination or social assimilation (Fox, 1974).

In many ways Armstrong's broadly Marxian argument parallels Goldthorpe in stressing the relational aspects of service occupations, in contrast to much managerial writing which tries to specify the essence of management in terms of specific tasks. It differs in that Armstrong sets out to consider who is being served and how they control the agents. Thus he distinguishes sharply between 'trust accorded to the performance of certain *tasks* and that accorded to *positions*' (Armstrong, 1987: 426, emphasis original). This distinction helps us to deal with the issue, much more prominent now than in 1987, as to whether the trust granted to shopfloor employees though 'empowerment' schemes is qualitatively the same as that given to managers. A Goldthorpean approach arguably does not permit an answer, whereas one which looks at positions and functions identifies the role of managers as agents of capital and thereby establishes the distinctive nature of the trust that they enjoy. As Armstrong (1989: 320, emphasis original) concludes,

> the agency approach views [management] as a *relationship* based either upon trust or upon performance monitoring and control, as substitutes for trust. Because trust is expensive, there arises a contradiction between its indispensability and employers' economic interest in substituting for it. From this contradiction, there arises a historical dynamic within capitalist organisation, whereby emergent managerial occupational groups attempt to aggregate trust to themselves.

Such an approach is surely a reasonable feature of class analysis. It has specific benefits, moreover, in addressing the idea of 'moral commitment'. Trust and long-term relationships do not necessarily entail a strongly internalized sense of acceptance of the values of the organization. We do not need to suppose that 'organization man' feels deep loyalty; indeed, the faceless nature of bureaucracy suggests that he will not. All that is required is an appropriate bargain.

The second question concerns national and other differences, for example in the selection and reward of managers. It is surely not out of the question to develop analyses of how the agency relationship operates in different contexts. For example, it has become received wisdom that in Anglo-Saxon countries managers are controlled through short-term individual incentives whereas in countries such as Germany and Japan, longer-term trust relationships develop (eg, Dore, 1989). The reasons for this can be found in the size and structure of firms, the nature of financial institutions and so on. The same approach could be extended to different sectors. One might, for example, argue that in the past managers in public sector organizations had more of a moral commitment and more of a diffuse service contract than did private sector managers, and go on to suggest that this difference is now being eroded. One can, in short, examine the dynamics of particular service relationships and assess how they are changing.

Managers: still the service class?

If we turn from general observations to evidence on occupations and look first at managerial grades, there is certainly evidence of an increased sense of job insecurity in the face of downsizing and delayering (Collinson and Collinson, 1997; Gratton *et al.*, 1999). But the question is, what does this signify? It does not mean that management is disappearing. Thus surveys continue to show a clear gradient of occupational advantage in terms of pay levels and other benefits between the top and the bottom of the hierarchy (O'Reilly and Rose, 1998). The well-known fact that the dispersion of pay has widened since 1979 would suggest that in some respects managers' position is improving. How can we equate this with the evidence of downsizing? Part of the answer may lie in fragmentation within management. Some people have gained if, for example, they have been able to participate in management buy-outs and thereby own shares in their firms while others, for example those made redundant, have lost. Such fragmentation may, moreover, be driven more by accident than any class-related logic: managers in some establishments may survive and prosper while their counterparts elsewhere lose their jobs in corporate re-organizations. There is no reason to expect any systematic process whereby distinct categories of managers lose their jobs while others do not.

There are those who argue that the nature of management is changing fundamentally. Heckscher's (1995) well-known American study argues not only that the loyalty characteristic of former bureaucratic careers is declining but also that this is trend is to be welcomed since old-style loyalty leads to inflexibility. The implication is that Goldthorpe's stress on moral commitment as a feature of the service class is increasingly outdated. However, two features of Heckscher's study suggest otherwise. First, its methodology is unconvincing for it is neither an extensive survey of managers nor an in-depth case study which relates views of careers to specific contexts. Instead, it draws on 'a set of loosely structured interviews with about 250 middle managers in 14 units – divisions, headquarters or plants – spread across 8 large industrial companies' (p. 9). It is thus specific in being based on manufacturing rather than on the economy as a whole but also general in having a broad definition of the middle manager and conflating different levels of organizations. Its many generalizations seem to lack any clear basis, either in statistical data on a defined population of managers or in specific contextualized case information. Second, its dismissal of loyalty is in fact less sweeping than first appears. In the four leading 'dynamic' cases, managers had abandoned loyalty in the sense of expecting to stay with the one firm throughout their careers and having a strong identification with the organization as an entity, but they were replacing it with a strong sense of commitment to specified goals, underpinned by 'unusually deep understanding' of their firm's business strategy (p. 122). This suggests not a collapse of trust but a redefinition of it, away from bureaucratic proceduralism and towards an engaged involvement in organizational goals. Indeed, trust is in some ways deepened if firms rely on managers' skills and enthusiasm rather than expecting them simply to follow the rules.

Managers also remain managers in terms of their functions in the division of labour. The key point of Armstrong's analysis discussed above is that the developments observed by writers such as Heckscher are not just the product of the behaviour of individual firms. They reflect some deeper processes within the organization of management in its agency relationship with capital. As Armstrong (1989) noted, the relationship is contradictory in that capital depends on trust but wishes to minimize its cost. Relationships between groups of managers and capitalists emerge around this contradiction. At particular historical points, they take particular turns, that of the 1990s being marked by pressures towards cost-cutting and closer monitoring of managers on the one hand and efforts to decentralise and to empower on the other. Four further studies illustrate the point in different ways.

An analysis of managerial careers in four British (and also four Japanese) firms in the late 1980s and early 1990s found that there were certainly concerns about career prospects, in the more traditionally bureaucratic firms in particular (Storey *et al.*, 1997). But, in line with the above comments, some managers welcomed the changes in train. In a bank, for example, traditional branch managers felt that they were losing autonomy while those in sales functions welcomed the new commercial emphasis on selling financial products. The latter group, moreover, were relaxed about the decline of traditional internal labour markets since they were confident that they could move to other firms. Yet both groups shared the perception of being managers. They would certainly have seen themselves as having a 'service' rather than a 'labour contract' relationship with their firm. They expected to exercise discretion on the firm's behalf and to take responsibility for their actions. A manager in another firm neatly captured the tensions of decentralization and control. He was responsible for a large manufacturing plant and welcomed the freedom to organize the plant (which included handling pay negotiations, formerly the cherished property of central management) that decentralization gave. But he also complained at the need to meet financial targets that were not only demanding but also liable to change at short notice (the latter feature a function of the changing nature of capitalist competition). And he regretted the loss of clear career planning that had existed under a centralized regime. It is also worth noting that across all eight firms in the sample 38% of the managers surveyed felt that they were evaluated 'closely' by higher management: an indication of the fact that trust does not exist without controls.[4]

The second study, significantly entitled *Managing in the Corporate Interest* (V. Smith, 1990), examined middle managers in a bank based in California. It describes processes of restructuring and argues that these generated a 'coercive autonomy' wherein managers were required to use more discretion and to take more responsibility while also being more closely monitored from above. (Keen, 1995, offers a similar analysis in the British public sector, which suggests that some of these trends may be general). The managers did not follow demands on them passively, and they did not pursue corporate policy to the letter. For example, rather than accept the policy that they should hide from their staff the goal of employment reductions, they revealed the true picture. Yet, Smith (1990: 151) stresses, such behaviour was not resistance to higher management but rather a shaping of how re-structuring was handled. The middle managers still pursued the firm's goals and displayed no common identity with their workers. This case also indicates notable variations between groups, with branch managers again feeling a loss of autonomy whereas others, in this case credit card centre managers, enjoying increased responsibility and rewards as their operations became more important in the bank's market position.

The third study is Watson's (1994) ethnography of managers in a UK manufacturing firm, 'ZTC'. Watson analyses a complex world in which managers were to some extent controlled by their superiors, notably through acceptance of a culture of long hours and the requirement to meet performance targets. Yet the managers also took pride in their ability to achieve results and to be 'in control'. By the last phrase, they meant that they could control their own circumstances, not that they were necessarily controlling others (Watson, 1994: 201, 143, 67, 85). This study brings out neatly the ambiguity of the managers' position. On the one hand, they resented performance targets and indeed sought ways to avoid them, and they also felt insecure and distanced from corporate decision-making. Surveys repeatedly find that re-structuring and take-overs are ever-present; decisions on such matters are taken well above the level of the managers in Watson's or the other studies discussed here.[5] Yet, on the other hand, these are still managers who still express strong feelings of 'them and us' in relation to shopfloor workers and who accept the logic of the market to which they are subject.

Finally, we have Hanlon's (1994) analysis of accountancy. This makes the point that in this sector high levels of labour mobility are accepted and natural.

Thus there is nothing inherent in such service class occupations which requires a formalized internal labour market. The point is obvious, but it tends to be neglected in analyses which describe the decline of 'organization man' as though all managers were in the past such men. Hanlon also makes some useful contrasts with the liberal professions: accountants differ from doctors, for example, because they do not control the relationship with their clients (p. 109). As for class position, Hanlon (pp. 192–206) picks up the idea of the trust relationship as lying at the heart of the service class's position. For Goldthorpe, he notes, trust depends on the delegation of authority and the possession of specialist knowledge. Yet this is not a technical issue, for some groups are more trusted than others as a result of social and political choices, with accountants being more in demand and thus more trusted in the UK than in countries such as Germany. The Weberian focus on the market 'can only suggest that one particular skill is in more or less demand than another' (p. 192) and cannot explain why this should be so.

This last point of Hanlon's parallels some familiar debates on labour markets. Early segmentation theory asked why some groups of workers enjoyed relative job security and career paths and found the answer in technical skills (Doeringer and Piore, 1971). Radical segmentation theorists argued that these benefits were more to do with the control strategies of employers than with technology alone (R. Edwards, 1979), and a further phase of analysis showed that it was not just employer choice which was important, for worker activity also played a role (Rubery, 1978). Thus hierarchies of jobs, with access to the best ones depending on seniority, in industries such as steel reflected the outcome of specific bargains between workers, unions, and employers. Occupational re-structuring is a process in which the occupations themselves play a part. A contemporary illustration is Legge's (1995) analysis of human resource management. Asking why it is that HRM has received such attention when most serious analysis has undermined its pretensions, Legge argues that the answer lies in the interests of various groups in using the concept. Such groups include academics and personnel managers seeking to sustain their own role but also line managers who, faced with the threats of down-sizing and delayering, find the fact that they now have the responsibility for managing their 'human resources' a source of power.

There are conditions under which managerial groups may feel alienated from their firms or may display a possibly surprising acceptance of their situation. Some research offers some pointers to which of the two responses emerges. First, a case study of Alcan's aluminium smelter at Lynemouth examined the effects of teamwork (Wright and Edwards, 1998). Shopfloor workers enjoyed more autonomy with the removal of a whole layer of supervision. Among managers, two responses were evident. Some departmental managers were initially highly sceptical about teamwork but were eventually won round to its benefits such as greater worker flexibility and a willingness to take on new tasks. The scepticism was evident in 1995 when the main study was carried out and much more muted in a small re-study in 1997.

These managers did not articulate the explicit rationalization for HRM which Legge would expect but they were willing to go along with HRM in the guise of teamwork and it certainly helped to sustain their own position (not so much class struggle without classes as acceptance of HRM without explicit use of the term). But a small group of technical and engineering staff expressed strong discontent, which grew over the two-year period. They felt that their own roles had been reduced as more responsibility was given to shopfloor teams. They also felt ignored by more senior managers and devalued by them (as with a series of pay settlements which gave the same cash amounts to all employees, thus narrowing differentials). This latter group experienced a strong sense of de-skilling, which plainly reflects its changing position in the division of labour. In circumstances such as this, delayering can lead to resentment. Yet even here there was no sense among this group of any unity with the shopfloor. On the contrary, and in line with Armstrong's (1983) findings from his study of supervisors, there was resentment at the concessions allegedly granted to the shopfloor: the issue was not sharing the position of shopfloor workers but seeking a return to a former situation in which the differences were clear and accepted.

A non-manufacturing example offers similar lessons. Lloyd and Newell (1998) studied sales reps of a pharmaceuticals company, who probably fall within the service class in view of their traditional job autonomy and expectation of careers. Changing competitive conditions were pushing the firm to control reps' behaviour by defining more closely whom they should visit and how often and by monitoring the results. There was a loss of autonomy among the reps, together with uncertainty about career progression.

A related unpublished study covers technical and sales staff in a large multinational. Pay systems were highly informal, with workers on the same grade receiving significantly different salaries and with promotion being based on individual deals rather than formal arrangements. The best way to win a pay rise, according to one senior sales manager, was to go to the company 'with a job offer [from another firm] in one hand and your resignation letter in the other'. Yet there was very little resentment at this. A combination of factors could have been at work. They included, in comparison to the Lloyd and Newell results, a reasonably high level of job security and a relatively indirect and unobtrusive monitoring of performance. In this case there were few direct targets for performance. Even the sales staff were not set monthly targets, and they distanced themselves from the 'reps' who had such targets: they saw themselves as working with customers to offer 'solutions' and not as people selling defined amounts of a product. They also stressed the strong team ethos among the sales force. This set of perceptions may, in turn, have reflected the technical nature of the task, in which there were a few large customers with whom the company had long-term relationships. There was thus acceptance of the needs of restructuring.

These contrasting situations show that it would be wrong to suppose that 'technical staff' share common life chances. The studies discussed above are also clear about the changing nature of the managerial career, with job security and career progression being less certain than in the past. In terms of the debate on the service class, the conclusion is that it is now even more difficult than it was in the past to draw a sharp distinction between the service and other classes. Trust and autonomy are matters of degree, and the extent to which a given group enjoys service class relationships will vary over time. This is not to deny the validity of the basic concept but to argue that its application needs to be sensitive to the changing dynamics within occupations as revealed in what Goldthorpe likes to describe as the relevant research monographs.

Manual workers: still struggling on

Manual workers may be considered more briefly. The many changes in the structure of the working class, such as its industrial distribution, propensity to unionise and proneness to strike, have been mentioned above. Yet such trends are surely no more than the latest in a series of developments in the shaping of the working class, and not a fundamental reversal of the underlying processes of class formation.

The debate on new developments in the workplace is confused, but some broad positions can be identified. First, there are those who argue that new managerial techniques have undermined traditional differences between manager and worker. The implication in terms of class is that differences have been dissolved, and replaced perhaps with an 'enterprise consciousness' in which managers and workers in one firm share the same goals, namely, to compete against other firms. A second position would agree with the first that overt opposition to management has been eroded, but explain this in terms of *force majeure* rather than willing consent. Here, class struggle is repressed rather than dissolved. Third are writers who argue that resistance remains in evidence, though they would differ in how far they see this as having any class basis. The tendency is to focus on small-scale adjustments in the labour process (see Hodson, 1995) which may be important in their own right but which may have little apparent class relevance. Others in this third group argue that traditional forms of workplace conflict in fact remain.

The problem is that evidence from individual case studies is used to make general statements. Each view could be right in relation to different workplaces. With the exception of the first, moreover, each is perfectly consistent with evidence from the past, when class was allegedly a more explicit feature of workplace relations. The individual activities of modern workers are not different in kind from those of employees who feature in the pages of workplace sociology as far back as Mathewson (1931) or indeed further. The first view is different because it suggests that distinctively new processes are at work. However, it evidently has a truncated view of history, for similar claims have been advanced at times of apparent class harmony, and it also pertains to, at most, the very small number of workplaces in which new management practices have actually taken root.

Such systematic evidence as is available – and it tends to be limited because much of the case evidence is qualitative in nature – suggests that the more portentous of arguments are wide of the mark. Relatively large-scale surveys of employee participation schemes (Marchington *et al.*, 1994) and total quality management (Rosenthal *et al.*, 1997; Edwards *et al.*, 1998) suggest three things. First, workers do tend to welcome the opportunity to participate in decisions on the details of working life. Second, this does not affect very much their wider attitudes towards management. Third, acceptance is contingent on a reasonably high level of job security and is often greatest where effective systems of employee representation are in place. As Smith and Thompson (1998) conclude, neither a de-skilling nor an up-skilling model captures the dynamics, which embrace the development of new skills and the re-definition of roles but also the control of workers' skills by management and the deployment of skills around new demands for customer service and quality. In many ways, responses to these initiatives illustrate Mann's (1970) argument that acceptance of managerial ideologies is pragmatic rather than deep-seated consent and Abercrombie *et al.*'s (1980) critique of theses of a ruling ideology which wins hearts and minds. None of this should be very surprising, and the fact that relatively routine and indeed even obvious ideas such as involving workers in decisions about quality have provoked extreme interpretations from proponents and critics alike says more about academic debate than it does about the real world.

A good illustration of these points is provided by Milkman's (1997) study of the GM plant at Linden, New Jersey. From its opening in 1937 until the early 1980s this was the archetypal Fordist workplace. There then followed a period of intense restructuring involving the elimination of many jobs and the re-organization of those that remained. Milkman makes three key points about the process. First, the period of Fordism, though it gave workers security and rising real wages, was not – in contrast to those who see it as an era of stability – a time of calm or consent. Workers disliked their jobs intensely, and, interviewed in the late 1990s, displayed no nostalgia for the period. Second, those who stayed in the plant did welcome the opportunity to have some say in workplace decisions. Taken together, these two points suggest that there was no sharp contrast between job control under Fordism and managerial autocracy under lean production. Third, the workers who left the plant did not, in contrast to the image of unskilled workers entering unemployment, end up on the labour market scrap heap. Many found jobs that were quite well-paying, albeit rarely as remunerative as those at GM, and, at least as important, intrinsically interesting. Milkman is careful to highlight the special conditions – including the workers' youth, a buoyant labour market and the substantial severance package offered by GM – generating such results, but also argues that they represent one important set of circumstances in the recomposition of work.

The implication in terms of class is that it is certainly true that the uniformity of experience of the mass of semi-skilled factory workers has been eroded. But it was never the case that such uniformity characterized all of the working class, for many did not enjoy conditions like those at Linden and even those who did were divided by skill, race and gender. The emerging working class contains more people like those who left Linden (that is, relatively independent and mobile) than did the old. But it is still a working class, and life is as much of an economic struggle as it was in the past, as illustrated by the need for most American working class families to have both adults in work if they are to sustain a satisfactory level of income. And this is the key point. Workers are still struggling through their lives, responding to what Marx called the dull compulsion of economic relations. The class structure is changing but it remains based on the fundamental principles of the generation of surplus value and the efforts of differing groupings to respond to this process.

Conclusions: no, two and many classes

The question of how many classes there are is on many ways one of the great non-questions. But it at least provides a convenient focus to draw some strands together. It is a familiar charge that Weberian social science leads to an infinity of different class positions, and we saw above that Giddens' explicit efforts to avoid this problem led him to identify three bases of class formation and then to argue that exploitation in the labour contract provided the basis of classes without apparently recognizing that this leads to two-class model. Carter (1995) has recently reviewed the links between labour process analysis and class theory and has criticised several labour process writers (myself included: Edwards, 1990b) for assuming by implication a two-class model. So is there an answer?

It turns on levels of analysis again. If like Giddens, and presumably also like Carter (for he wishes to pursue a Marxist approach and has offered some criticisms of the class-as-classification approach which parallel those attempted above: see Carter, 1997), we take exploitation as a core concept at the basic level of the class structure, and if we argue that there are exploiters and exploited, then we have to come clean and say that at this level we adopt a two-class model. That is, it is the set of social relationships around exploitation which is the bedrock of social classes and which explains why it is that conflict is inherent in class relationships.

These relationships take place at the level of class formation in specific economic and social contexts. The fact that there is exploitation does not say how many distinct classes may be recognized in the sense of meaningful social aggregates. In feudalism, for example, in addition to serfs and feudal lords it may make sense to identify merchants and independent urban craft workers. For the exercise to be consistent with the fundamental premise of levels of analysis, namely, that the more fundamental levels exert pressures on the levels closer to actual experience, it would also need to be shown how such positions arose as the feudal mode of production developed and how they were tied to the basic functioning of the system. For example, urban crafts emerged as the division of labour became more differentiated. Yet such crafts were still part of a feudal system. Though one could say that there was a distinction between those working directly for a feudal lord (the serfs) and those whose market capacity rested on craft skills, the meaning of these different capacities depended on the fundamentals of the system. Thus craft workers did not enjoy the benefits of a capitalist system in which they could set prices according to the 'laws' of supply and demand. Ideas of the just price and the just wage survived into the nineteenth century, and they did not give up without a struggle (Rule, 1986).

Likewise, as indicated above, in capitalism the rise of such occupations as accountants, engineers and supervisors can be related to the development of the mode of production. Large-scale industry, for example, called for co-ordination and monitoring. How this activity in fact emerged was not determined by this functional need and was shaped by the activities of the groups in question as well as by states and other influential actors.

This analysis would agree with Goldthorpean class analysis in several important respects. First, class remains a central feature of social life. Second, it makes sense to distinguish a service class from a working class and to argue that each retains a substantial internal coherence. Third, class analysis (Marshall, 1997) and workplace studies (Edwards, 1993) both generate progressive research programmes in the sense that empirical phenomena are better explained and conceptual understanding is enriched. A feature of this third point is that post-modern analyses are largely rejected. However, class analysis does not stop where Goldthorpe leaves it, for it is essential to understand, for example, whom the service class is serving. It may not be sufficient to define the class in terms of trust and the material concomitants such as promotion opportunities since some working class positions enjoy a degree of trust and even some job security while erstwhile service class positions have clearly lost some of their former benefits in terms of career progression. It may be fruitful to try to reassess the service class in terms of the functions which it performs. As argued above, its members need not display any particular moral commitment to the enterprise, and Goldthorpe cites little evidence that they do so. More central is the idea of delegated authority which without too much difficulty can be rendered in terms of using this authority to perform certain delegated functions of decision-making and control. Distinguishing between the functions of capital and those of labour is no more difficult than deciding whether an employee has a labour or a service contract.

At a more concrete level of analysis, the fact of being in the service class does not mean that an employee will feel no tensions or resentments in the role. Class analysis and workplace studies have differed in their emphases, with the former treating managers, for example, as part of a service class enjoying distinct benefits while the latter stress the discontents and tensions in the role. Any possible conflict between these emphases can be resolved if it is recognized that managers are as subject as anyone else to the uncertainties of a capitalist production process. They may suffer from restructuring, and their work may be more closely monitored. They will be expected to perform against specified targets. But they are also in a relationship in which they exercise delegated functions, and perhaps it is these which are critical in defining a service relationship. In short, the service class serves because it carries out some of the delegated functions of capital.

Around the (two-class) basics of exploitation, then, several class positions emerge at the level of class formation. It may be that, at the level of action, class consciousness is less evident than it was. The workers who left Linden stand as one example of a group whose ideas of class are likely to have changed substantially, as are their links to potential class actors such as trade unions. But whether or not future groups come to see their activities in class terms remains a very open question. Even if they do not, it will continue to make sense to ask why occupants of some positions in the division of labour enjoy better life chances than others and how struggles around the regulation of labour underlie the changing class structure.

Acknowledgements

This chapter draws on unpublished research which also involves Anthony Ferner, Ewart Keep and Martyn Wright. I am also grateful to participants at the ESRC seminar and to Peter Fairbrother for comments on an earlier draft.

Notes

1 The reference to Williams is to *Marxism and Literature*, p. 85.
2 The inflexibility of 'Fordist' systems has in fact been exaggerated. What is now seen as an inherent rigidity of the whole approach was in many respects simply a contingent outcome of Fordism. But it is true that a degree of inflexibility tended to grow and, crucially, that managers came to believe that rigidity was a problem and that they would now find salvation in flexibility.
3 As Zunz (1990: 106) argues, in America the office was being rationalized from the 1870s, with implications for the position of clerks and managers, whereas in Britain these groups continued to mix with the sons of gentlemen and to behave accordingly.
4 Note also that we found that the managers who were the most closely evaluated were the most, and not the least, likely to report satisfaction with such things as how they were evaluated, a result which proved to be robust when we controlled for sector and country effects. The implication is that present-day managers do not resent control systems, and may welcome the sense of discipline and purpose that they bring.
5 A good illustration is one firm, Lucas, which was included in the Storey *et al.* (1997) study. At the time of the fieldwork in the early 1990s, it appeared to the researchers that managers' career prospects in the firm depended on its ability to secure its goal of being an integrated global firm, with the likelihood of short-term pressures and take-over making this goal hard to attain. Subsequent events proved them right: throughout the 1990s various parts of the firm, which had been claimed to be integral to it, were sold off and it was eventually merged with, though in many respects taken over by, the American firm Varity, with the new management proceeding to restructure with a vengeance.

References

Abercrombie, N., Hill, S. and Turner, B.S., (1980), *The Dominant Ideology Thesis*. London: George Allen and Unwin.

Armstrong, P., (1983), 'Class Relationships at the Point of Production', *Sociology*, 17: 339–58.

Armstrong, P., (1984), 'Competition between Organizational Professionals and the Evolution of Management Control Strategies', in K. Thompson (ed.), *Work, Employment and Unemployment*. Milton Keynes: Open University Press.

Armstrong, P., (1987), 'Engineers, Managers and Trust', *Work, Employment and Society*, 1: 421–40.

Armstrong, P., (1989), 'Management, Labour Process and Agency', *Work, Employment and Society*, 3: 307–22.

Batstone, E., Boraston, I. and Frenkel, S., (1978), *The Social Organization of Strikes*, Oxford: Blackwell.

Brody, D., (1980), *Workers in Industrial America*, New York: Oxford University Press.

Burawoy, M., (1979), *Manufacturing Consent*, Chicago: University of Chicago Press.

Burawoy, M., (1985), *The Politics of Production*. London: Verso.

Cappelli, P., Bassi, L., Katz, H., Knoke, D., Osterman, P. and Useem, M., (1997), *Change at Work*, New York: Oxford University Press.

Carchedi, G., (1987), *Class Analysis and Social Research*, Oxford: Blackwell.

Carter, B., (1995), 'A Growing Divide: Marxist Class Analysis and the Labour Process', *Capital and Class*, 55: 33–72.

Carter, B., (1997), 'Class Analysis and Theoretical Convergence', *Labour Studies Working Paper 15*, Centre for Comparative Labour Studies, University of Warwick.

Casey, C., (1995), *Work, Self and Society after Industrialism*, London: Routledge.

Cohen, G.A., (1978), *Karl Marx's Theory of History*, Oxford: Clarendon.

Collinson, D. and Collinson, M., (1997), 'Delayering Managers', *Organization*, 4: 375–407.

Doeringer, P.B. and Piore, M.J., (1971), *Internal Labour Markets and Manpower Analysis*. Lexington, Mass.: Heath Lexington.

Dore, R., (1989), 'Where We Are Now', *Work, Employment and Society*, 3: 425–46.

Edwards, P.K., (1986), *Conflict at Work*, Oxford: Blackwell.

Edwards, P.K., (1990a), 'Class and Work', *Warwick Papers in Industrial Relations*, 32: Industrial Relations Research Unit, University of Warwick.

Edwards, P.K., (1990b), 'Understanding Conflict in the Labour Process', in Knights, D. and Willmott, H. (eds), *Labour Process Theory*. Basingstoke: Macmillan.

Edwards, P.K., (1993), 'Objective Sociological Knowledge', in Payne, G. and Cross, M. (eds), *Sociology in Action*. Basingstoke: Macmillan.

Edwards, P.K., (1995a), 'Strikes and Industrial Conflict', in Edwards, 1995b.

Edwards, P.K. (ed.), (1995b), *Industrial Relations*, Oxford: Blackwell.

Edwards, P.K., Collinson, M. and Rees, C., (1998), 'The Determinants of Employee Responses to Total Quality Management', *Organization Studies*, 19: 449–75.

Edwards, R., (1979), *Contested Terrain*, London: Heinemann.

Erikson, R., and Goldthorpe, J.H., (1993), *The Constant Flux*, Oxford: Clarendon.

European Foundation, (1997), *New Forms of Work Organisation*, Luxembourg: Office of Official Publications of the European Union.

Field, K., (1997), 'Redundancies in Great Britain', *Labour Market Trends*, April.

Fox, A., (1974), *Beyond Contract*, London: Faber and Faber.

Friedman, A.L., (1977), *Industry and Labour*, London: Macmillan.

Geary, J.F., (1995), 'Work Practices: the Structure of Work', in Edwards, 1995b.

Giddens, A., (1973), *The Class Structure of the Advanced Societies*, London: Hutchinson.

Giddens, A., (1981), *The Class Structure of the Advanced Societies*, 2nd edn. London: Hutchinson.

Goldthorpe, J.H., (1971), 'Theories of Industrial Society', *European Journal of Sociology*, 12: 263–88.

Goldthorpe, J.H., (1980), *Social Mobility and Class Structure in Modern Britain*, Oxford: Clarendon.

Goldthorpe, J.H., (1995), 'The Service Class Revisited', in Butler, T. and Savage, M. (eds), *Social Change and the Middle Classes*, London: UCL Press.

Goldthorpe, J.H. and Marshall, G., (1992), 'The Promising Future of Class Analysis', *Sociology*, 26: 381–400.

Gratton, L., Hope Jailey, V., Stiles, P. and Truss, C., (1999), *Strategic Human Resource Management*, Oxford: Oxford University Press.

Gubbay, J., (1997), 'A Marxist Critique of Weberian Class Analysis', *Sociology*, 31: 73–89.

Haiven, L., (1994), 'Workplace Discipline in International Comparative Perspective', in Bélanger, J., *et al.* (eds), *Workplace Industrial Relations and the Global Challenge*, Ithaca: ILR Press.

Halsey, A.H., Heath, A.F. and Ridge, J.M., (1980), *Origins and Destinations*, Oxford: Clarendon.

Handy, C., (1995), *The Empty Raincoat*, London: Arrow.

Hanlon, G., (1994), *The Commercialisation of Accountancy*, Basingstoke: Macmillan.

Heckscher, C., (1995), *White-collar Blues*, New York: Basic.

Hodson, R., (1995), 'Worker Resistance: An Underdeveloped Concept in the Sociology of Work', *Economic and Industrial Democracy*, 16: 79–110.

Hyman, R., (1987), 'Strategy or Structure?' *Work, Employment and Society*, 1: 25–56.

Katznelson, I., (1986), 'Working-class Formation', in Katznelson, I. and Zolberg, A.R. (eds), *Working-class Formation*, Princeton: Princeton University Press.

Keen, L., (1995), 'Organisational Decentralisation and Budgetary Devolution in Local Government', *Human Resource Management Journal*, 5 (2): 79–98.

Larson, M.S., (1980), 'Proletarianization and Educated Labor', *Theory and Society*, 9: 131–75.

Lee, D.J., (1996), 'Weak Class Theories or Strong Sociology?' in Lee and Turner, 1996.

Lee, D.J. and Turner, B.S. (eds), (1996), *Conflicts about Class*. London: Longman.

Legge, K., (1995), *Human Resource Management*, Basingstoke: Macmillan.

Littler, C.R. and Salaman, G., (1984), *Class at Work*, London: Batsford.

Lloyd, C. and Newell, H., (1998), 'Computerising the Salesforce; The Introduction of Technical Change in a Non-Union Workforce', *New Technology, Work and Employment*, 13: 104–15.

Mann, M., (1970), 'The Social Cohesion of Liberal Democracy', *American Sociological Review*, 35: 423–40.

Marchington, M., Wilkinson, A. and Goodman, J., (1994), 'Understanding the Meaning of Participation', *Human Relations*, 47: 867–94.

Marshall, G., (1997), *Repositioning Class*, London: Sage.

Mathewson, S., (1931), *Restriction of Output among Unorganized Workers*, (Republished 1969, Carbondale: Southern Illinois University Press).

Milkman, R., (1997), *Farewell to the Factory*, Berkeley: University of California Press.

Nichols, T. and Beynon, H., (1977), *Living with Capitalism*, London: Routledge and Kegan Paul.

O'Reilly, K. and Rose, D., (1998), 'Changing Employment Relations', *Work, Employment and Society*, 12: 713–34.

Rosenthal, P., Hill, S. and Peccei, R., (1997), 'Checking Out Service', *Work, Employment and Society*, 11: 481–503.

Rubery, J., (1978), 'Structured Labour Markets, Worker Organization and Low Pay', *Cambridge Journal of Economics*, 2: 17–36.

Rule, J., (1986), *The Labouring Classes in Early Industrial England 1750–1850*, London: Longman.

Savage, M., Barlow, J., Dickens, P. and Fielding, T., (1992), *Property, Bureaucracy and Culture*, London: Routledge.

Scarbrough, H., (1998), 'The Unmaking of Management?', *Human Relations*, 51: 691–716.

Schatz, R., (1983), *The Electrical Workers*, Urbana: University of Illinois Press.

Sewell, G. and Wilkinson, B., (1992), 'Someone to Watch Over Me', *Sociology*, 26: 271–90.

Smith, C. and Thompson, P., (1998), 'Re-evaluating the Labour Process Debate', *Economic and Industrial Democracy*, 19: 551–77.

Smith, J., Edwards, P. and Hall, M., (1999), *Redundancy Consultation*. Department of Trade and Industry Employment Relations Research Series 5. London: DTI.

Smith, V., (1990), *Managing in the Corporate Interest*, Berkeley: University of California Press.

Stark, D., (1980), 'Class Struggle and the Transformation of the Labor Process', *Theory and Society*, 9: 89–130.

Storey, J., Edwards, P. and Sisson, K., (1997), *Managers in the Making*, London: Sage.

Thompson, E.P., (1977), *Whigs and Hunters*, Harmondsworth: Penguin.

Thompson, E.P., (1978), 'Eighteenth Century English Society: Class Struggle without Classes?' *Social History*, 3: 133–65.

Watson, T.J., (1994), *In Search of Management*, London: Routledge.

Wright, E.O., (1985), *Classes*, London: Verso.

Wright, M. and Edwards, P., (1998), 'Does Team Working Work and if so Why?' *Economic and Industrial Democracy*, 19: 59–90.

Zunz, O., (1990), *Making America Corporate, 1870–1920*, Chicago: University of Chicago Press.

The gendered restructuring of the middle classes: employment and caring

Rosemary Crompton

Introduction

The occupational structure has long been used as a proxy for 'class' (Erikson and Goldthorpe, 1992; Wright, 1997), despite the fact that there are a number of difficulties associated with this convention. Although occupation may give a reasonable indication of 'life-chances', and a carefully-constructed scheme may also take into account relations of ownership as well as authority in paid work, there are nevertheless a number of important aspects usually deemed germane to 'class' that cannot be accommodated within occupational classifications. Perhaps most importantly, occupation gives no reliable guide to wealth holdings (Westergaard, 1995). There is also the problem of establishing a 'class' situation for those without employment, such as the long-term unemployed (who may never have had a permanent occupation), and those dependent on the earnings of others, such as housewives and other dependents. However, besides this latter problem, a major feminist criticism of occupational class schemes has been that, because of the persistence of sex discrimination within the labour market, together with patterns of occupational segregation, such schemes (a) produce very different outcomes when applied to male and female populations, and (b) the same occupation (ie, class situation) may be associated with different 'life chances' for men and women.[1]

As a consequence of these and other criticisms,[2] the position of the dominant 'employment-aggregate' practitioners in relation to gender has been clarified. It has become apparent that both Goldthorpe and Wright have a rather static approach to the occupational structure. Goldthorpe (1983) has been explicit that it is not the purpose of 'class analysis', as he sees it, to incorporate any account of class (ie, occupational) structuring – including any role that gender differentiation may have played in this structuring. He emphasizes that no particular theory has contributed to his class scheme which must be judged by its empirical adequacy – 'it is consequences, not antecedents, that matter'.[3] In contrast, Wright's location of jobs into particular classes is guided by Marxist class theory. However, this is couched at a highly abstract level and, as feminists have long remarked, the neglect of the domestic sphere means that Marxist theory *per se* gives an incomplete account of the societal (and class) position of women (Walby, 1986). In summary, therefore, neither Goldthorpe nor Wright pay systematic attention to the actual *processes* of occupational or labour market structuring, but rather focus on the *outcomes* of this structuring as measured by employment-derived class schemes. Thus these approaches explore the interaction between 'class' (as indicated by occupation) and gender (as indicated by sex), but do not include the gendered constitution of the 'class' (or occupational) structure within their remit.[4]

However, it has been argued that the occupational structure is not merely a system of 'slots' into which individuals are located, but rather is fluid and in a process of constant development (Crompton, 1989; 1996). However 'class' is defined, 'class analysis' cannot cut itself off from any analysis of the processes whereby 'classes' are generated (Scott and Morris, 1996). Indeed, feminists have argued that the processes of class formation and emergence in modern societies – the divisions of capital and labour which led to the development of the bourgeoisie, and mass proletariat – were intimately bound up with parallel processes of gender differentiation (eg, Bradley, 1989). They have described the processes whereby the sexual division of labour which culminated in that stage of modern capitalism that we may loosely describe as 'Fordist' was characterized by the 'male breadwinner' model of the division of labour, around which 'masculine' and 'feminine' gender blocs were crystallized. Thus the occupational structure emerging in many industrial societies in the 19th and early 20th centuries was grounded in a division of labour in which women took the primary responsibility for domestic work whilst male 'breadwinners' specialized in market work. Today this is changing in that married women have taken up market work, and this has had important consequences for class theory and analysis.

The recent changes in employment and the occupational structure are not, of course, solely gender-related, although women's employment is nevertheless often affected by them. For example, one of the most significant shifts in employment in recent decades has been from manufacturing industry to services, and service employment includes many jobs that by convention have been thought of as 'women's' – such as personal services and routine clerical work. As discussed in the previous chapter, new strategies of management have changed employment relations, making jobs less likely to be secure and generating increasing long-term unemployment. As more women have taken up paid employment, so the number of jobs associated with caring work has grown, as the unpaid work previously done by women is marketized. Much of this work is also carried out by women, and there are indications that a new servant class is in the process of development (Gregson and Lowe, 1994). The proportion of professional, administrative and managerial occupations has increased, but this has also been accompanied by an increase in social polarization, as the kinds of semi-skilled manual jobs that once paid a 'male breadwinner' wage have been eliminated. Another factor contributing to social and economic polarization has been the widening gap between 'two-earner' and 'no-earner' households, brought about by the combination of all of the factors discussed here (Rowntree, 1995). Changes in women's employment patterns have also had an impact on relationships within the family (Leiulsfrud and Woodward, 1987). In their turn, family arrangements impact on patterns of social reproduction – particularly social mobility – a point to which we will return in our concluding discussion.

To fully investigate the changes in the 'class structure' brought about by the increasing market work of women would require a series of different investigations. In this chapter, however, we will be focusing in particular on a number of questions relating to the increasing entry of women into managerial and professional occupations.

The growth of women in management and the professions

The process of the formation of traditional managerial and professional occupations signified the emergence of the modern, non-entrepreneurial, bourgeoisie. It was accompanied by the exclusion of women from these better-paid jobs, and from access to professional training and employment, together with their confinement to the 'domestic sphere' (Davidoff and Hall, 1987; Witz, 1992). Thus in relation to the professional and managerial middle classes, women have figured largely as either subaltern, 'semi-professional' employees (eg, nurses and other ancillary professions servicing the male-dominated medical profession), or as the wives of professional and managerial men, providing the domestic supports which made it possible for their husbands to carry out jobs in the 'public' sphere of paid employment (Crompton, 1986). Thus middle class employment has been male-dominated, particularly in its upper reaches.

Today, the situation is changing. As women have increased the level of their labour force participation, so they have also improved the level and extent of their academic and professional qualifications. Over the last ten years, women in all countries have been steadily increasing their representation in professional and managerial occupations. In the case of England, in 1998 women were 44% of all in employment, 32% of managers and administrators, and 40% of those in professional occupations. In their recent review, Thair and Risdon (1999: 113) conclude that:

> Women, particularly those with young children, have increased their labour market participation over the last decade. The increase has been concentrated among women with higher qualifications and in professional and managerial occupations ...

Cross-national comparisons suggest that it is possible to make some broad generalizations as to the patterning of women's entry into professional and managerial occupations. First, the increase of women in such occupations is, in general, greater than the increase in their representation in the labour force as a whole. For example, in France, whereas the overall increase in the proportion of women in the labour force between 1982 and 1990 was 2.5%, the increase in the proportion of women lawyers was 8%, doctors 8.6%, and financial managers 8.6% (Crompton, 1998: 159). Given that men's labour force participation rates are falling, this relative increase in women's higher-level employment is further enhanced. Second, the level of increase of women in professional and managerial occupations is not evenly distributed, but is moulded to existing patterns of gender segregation. Thus the level of the increase of women in some heavily feminized professions such as teaching is relatively low, suggesting that these occupations might be nearing female saturation. However, the increase in the proportion of women in other professions where they are very under-represented, such as engineering, is also low, suggesting the likelihood of the continuing under-representation of women in these occupations. Well above average rates of increase in the numbers and proportions of women, however, are to be found in 'people focused' management jobs such as public service, marketing, and finance (Indeed, an important element in the organizational transformation of banking has been the increased recruitment of women to managerial positions. See Halford *et al*., 1997). Above average rates of increase are also found in the classic professions of medicine and the law.

Thus the increase of women in higher-level occupations has been heavily concentrated in the service-type aspects of management and the professions – as Esping-Anderson (1993) has argued, the 'post-fordist' service economies are increasingly dominated by women's employment. Case study evidence (Devine, 1992; Evetts, 1994; Halford and Savage, 1995; Crompton and Le Feuvre, 1997) suggests that women tend to cluster in occupations in which it is possible to work flexibly and thus combine employment with family life. Within organizations women have tended to consolidate their positions through the exercise of individual skills, rather than organizational office-holding. These studies also demonstrate that women continue to be subject to masculine exclusionary practices in some better-paid and higher-level occupations. For example, within medicine, surgery is highly prestigious, highly paid – and male dominated (Crompton, Le Feuvre and Birkelund, 1999). These trends make it likely that the entry of women into professional and managerial occupations will have relatively less impact than might have been anticipated on the basis of their numerical increase alone, and that men will continue to dominate the higher levels of the occupational structure.

Should we, therefore, conclude that '*plus ça change, plus c'est la même chose?*' That is, that despite the apparently dramatic change represented by the entry of women into higher-level occupations, this has merely resulted in a re-drawing of conventional gender boundaries within the higher levels of the occupational structure, rather than any kind of fundamental transformation? As far as the broad outlines of the balance of occupational and labour market power between men and women is concerned, then it is true that men in aggregate continue to have the advantage over women in aggregate. Nevertheless, beyond this level of generalization, the changing division of labour between men and women is likely to have profound implications for the way in which 'work' as a whole is organized, which will affect both employing organizations as well as interpersonal and household relationships. In this chapter, we will be exploring these consequences only in relation to 'middle' or 'service' class employment, but the ramifications of these changes will have an impact at all levels of the class structure.

The consequences of the feminization of the middle classes

One possibility that has been extensively discussed by feminists is that the increasing penetration and representation of women in a 'public sphere' traditionally dominated by men will bring about a change in these 'masculine' institutions (Segal, 1987; Davies, 1996). In respect of occupational change, Le Feuvre (1999: 156) has described this possibility (amongst others) as a process of 'feminitude':[5]

> ... the influx of women into the male bastions of power and prestige offers the opportunity for the diffusion of feminine values (altruism, sensitivity, empathy, etc) within the public sphere of employment and (potentially) politics. In sufficient numbers, women transform the (inherently masculine) value system of high status occupations ...

However, contrary to this kind of suggestion, the position taken in this chapter is that 'gender' is not, as would be implied by 'feminitude', a set of fixed capacities or predispositions. Their historic responsibility for caring does make women as a whole more likely to be sensitive to the needs of others than men taken as a whole. However, it will be argued in this paper that the work of caring is gender-coded rather than 'gendered' as such, – that is, care is not an 'essential' component of either masculinity or femininity. Men may care, as well as women. More particularly, a cross-national comparative study of the medical profession, a profession in the process of rapid feminization (Crompton, Le Feuvre and Birkelund, 1999), suggests that women's entry into specialties reflects not merely women's attraction to gender-stereotypical 'caring' niches[6] but, of even more importance, specialties in which employment can be combined with family life (as will be discussed below). Thus it may be suggested that the impact of women in management and the professions is more likely to have an impact on the way in which employment is organized, rather than on any supposed intrinsically 'masculine' nature of the profession or occupation itself.

Professional work and employment flexibility

It has been noted above that within the middle class, women have tended to cluster in occupational niches that facilitate a combination of employment and caring. There is nothing particularly new in this phenomenon. For example, women have historically predominated in the teaching profession (particularly in areas such as primary school teaching), an occupation which is uniquely well-adapted to the employment-family combination.[7] The rapid rate of feminization in some professions, such as pharmacy, may also be explained to a considerable extent by the fact that part-time and flexible employment opportunities abound within this occupation (Crompton and Le Feuvre, 1994; 1996). It is not difficult to understand why women might be attracted by occupations that afford this kind of flexibility. In general, however, managerial occupations do not have these characteristics. Indeed, one of the key features of 'new wave' management which has been identified in recent commentaries has been the culture of 'competitive masculinity' (Halford *et al.*, 1997) which involves very long working hours.

Professional work is regulated by an external (occupational) body that sets standards and regulates performance. The professional qualification gives a 'licence to practice' which is not specific to any particular locality, organization, or employer. Thus in the 1960s and 70s, for example, the nurses and school teacher wives who were following their bank manager husbands through the necessary changes of locality required to make a career in branch banking would usually have found it possible to pick up part-time work when necessary. In contrast, although managerial qualifications abound, they do not constitute the 'licence to practice' of a professional qualification and do not, therefore, offer the same kind of employment flexibility.[8] Furthermore, as noted above, a managerial career has to be developed within a context in which both organizational knowledge, as well as the willingness to devote time to it, may be seen as major determinants of suitability for promotion.

Different kinds of middle class employment, therefore, may be better or worse suited to an employment/family combination career, and it is here being suggested that the broad distinction between 'professional' and 'managerial' work gives an indication as to whether 'carer-friendly' employment is likely to be available.

Doctors and bankers

These arguments are supported by evidence drawn from a recent cross-national study of doctors and bank managers – that is, a 'professional' as compared to a 'managerial' occupation. Biographical interviews were carried out with women doctors and bankers, in five different countries. The research has subsequently been extended to male doctors and bankers in Britain, France and Norway.[9] Our research strategy has been, as far as possible, to interview a set of male respondents corresponding to the characteristics of the women we interviewed (aged between 30 and 50, in employment).[10]

One of the most striking findings to emerge from interviews with women in the first stage of the research was the substantial difference in family-employment patterns between women in medicine and banking, despite the very considerable *national* differences in gender systems (or regimes) between the different countries (Crompton and Harris, 1997). In all countries, the women doctors had a relatively conventional domestic division of labour and were also more likely to have had more children (Table 1).[11] We have explained these differences with reference to the characteristic career structures of professional, as compared to managerial, occupations. Professional training in medicine is long; career routes in medicine are well known in advance and can therefore be planned for. We found that the majority of women doctors, even before they had had children, had tended to opt for a career and/or specialty that would enable them to combine employment and family life. These decisions had usually been made on the assumption that they would be the major carers of their children, and this was reflected in the gender division of caring work in their households. Thus the relative autonomy offered by a professional qualification had, paradoxically, been reflected in a tendency towards relatively conventional domestic arrangements amongst women doctors.

In contrast, managerial careers in banking have been achieved by *responding* to the very substantial upheavals, reorganizations, and re-reorganizations that have been a feature of banking around the world for the last fifteen years. Our respondents had not been able to plan, rather, they had had to react and accommodate to changes in the banking sector. Many women had not had children, and those that had had often found themselves constrained to 'force' their partners into assuming a larger share of domestic/caring work – or making a change to a 'family-friendly' partner.

However, the majority of the men interviewed, if they had children, lived in households in which there was also a wife who took the major responsibility for domestic labour and childcare. The men had also had more children than the women. Table 1 shows that although the occupational contrast still persists (in that male doctors are likely to have more children than male bankers), whereas the difference in the proportion of male and female doctors with two or more children was 18%, the difference in male and female bankers with two or more children was 31%.[12]

Table 1 Family size amongst female and male doctors and bankers in Britain, France and Norway (totals)

	Doctor		Banker	
	Women	Men	Women	Men
No, or only one, child	35	17	63	32
Two or more children	65	83	37	68
	100	100	100	100
Number	46	42	48	44

It would seem, therefore, that an organizational career is particularly incompatible with family life, and our qualitative data provided ample evidence of the difficulties of combining a managerial career with caring and motherhood:

> Throughout my career I've very deliberately never made an issue of children ... I know that the minute I announced that I was intending to have a family, that my career would take a nose dive, and I was absolutely right, it went down badly ... (Interviewer: Would you like another child?) ... the thought of trying to work with two children fills me with cold horror ... the logistics of trying to do it are very very hard ... and it physically wears you out (2/30 English banker, married, 37 one child).

A French banker, who described the impact of the announcement of pregnancy at work as a 'nuclear catastrophe', and who had recently had a miscarriage, was nevertheless still reluctant to have a second child:

> ... it's very difficult for me to manage a full-time job with all the constraints that a mother of a family has ... I'm very torn between the desire to have a second child – but then I say to myself: 'Chantal, the little liberty you still have will go if you have a second child. Because already with one child you've got a weight on your back – with a second, you're finished'. (5/21)

In contrast, interviews with the women doctors furnished ample evidence of the forward planning of employment and family careers:

> I decided to go for dermatology because this was a field one might enter without being totally eaten up with regard to the family. Dermatology is possible to combine with a family life. I did some investigations into this before I chose a specialty (3/10 Norwegian doctor, two children).

> I chose to specialize because I really couldn't see myself setting up in practice as an *omnipracticien*, not as a woman ... I thought that for a man that would be fine, but for a woman ... having to be on-call day and night ... at the time I didn't have any family responsibilities, but in anticipation of those to come I thought it would be better to specialize (5/05 France, radiologist, salaried, one child)[13]

These examples could be multiplied, drawing upon the interviews carried out in all three countries. Indeed, recent research drawing upon longitudinal data has conclusively demonstrated that '... There is an important distinction between managerial and professional occupations for women in terms of the ease of combining work and family life' (Elliott *et al.*, 1998). To the extent that *women* retain the primary responsibility for caring and domestic work, then this generalization will hold, and it is likely to do so. What, however, about *men* with caring responsibilities?

Although it is something of a truism to note that, while women may have increased their participation in market work, this has not been matched by a similar increase in men's caring work (Hochschild, 1997; Gershuny, 1994), there are nevertheless a number of trends that suggest that the extent of men's caring work will increase. The increase in divorce means that men who remain in regular contact with their children will assume some level of independent responsibility, however minimal. Smaller families, and an increase in the proportion of elderly people, will require continuing input from adult children – and adult males can no longer assume that this task will be met by non-working wives. In respect of the total quantity of caring work required in society, these trends will be to some extent countered by the decline in the birth rate. However, it has been suggested that the 'rarity value' of the smaller number of children born has meant an increase in the level of input from their parents (Beck and Beck-Gernsheim, 1995). As well as these demographic trends, nationally comparative statistical evidence suggests that stereotypical gender roles are slowly being eroded, and that men are taking on more domestic work and caring responsibilities (Scott *et al.*, 1996).

As already noted, most of the male doctors and bankers interviewed, if they had children, had wives who had taken the major responsibility for childcare. However, amongst the interviews there was a small number of 'involuntary' male carers, forced to assume domestic responsibility after death or divorce. It is of interest that all of the four men who had involuntarily taken on caring responsibilities (two doctors and two bankers, one each in Britain and Norway)[14] spontaneously mentioned that their careers had suffered as a result:

> 'I came to Birmingham intending to be a professor, but I haven't done as well as I'd hoped to (ie, is still a senior lecturer) – my personal problems and responsibilities have interfered with my research' (2/56 male British doctor, three children).

> I wish I'd started earlier ... turned down quite a few opportunities 'cos of my own domestic circumstances ... turned down jobs, it would have been disruptive for them (ie, his children) ... I feel I can get higher but it will be very difficult – certain constraints on me now ... (2/84 male British banker, two children).

> If you want to be in the rat-race you have to make a choice ... it is difficult (he turned down an interesting job offer) ... Now that I am a lone father I am more conscious about setting my own limits as to what time I can work and not work (3/77 male Norwegian banker, three children).

> I should have done things differently. I knew it ... to take a doctoral degree ... it's essential for a career ... I had started working on a dissertation,

> but I gave up, because I thought it would be too much, since I had the kids (3/53 male Norwegian doctor, two children).

These examples serve to make the rather simple but very important point that taking the primary responsibility for children is likely to have a substantial impact upon an employment career. By convention, women have assumed this responsibility, but if it falls upon a man, then the impact on his career is likely to be very similar. Thus it is important to recognize that caring is gender coded, rather than 'gendered' as such – that is, caring is not an intrinsic component of either 'masculinity' or 'femininity'. If men have to assume primary care responsibilities, then it is likely that their careers will be affected – even in countries, like Norway, that have instituted 'family-friendly' policies at the national level (Ellingsaeter, 1999).

Three of the male interviewees (one each in Britain, France and Norway) had voluntarily chosen to share childcare equally with their partners. All of these men explicitly placed their family lives before their career aspirations, and all three were doctors. It has previously been emphasized that women doctors were more gender conventional in respect of their division of domestic labour than women bankers (Crompton and Harris, 1997, 1999). It might seem paradoxical, therefore, that these examples of gender equal employment/family partnerships are all drawn from the medical profession. However, the paradox is easily explained. An occupation in which the relative autonomy of the practitioner allows for the strategic planning of a relatively conventional employment-family combination is also more likely to be an occupation in which *less* conventional employment-family combinations can be planned as well. The key feature here, it may be suggested, is individual occupational autonomy, which is more characteristic of professional, rather than managerial, occupations.

This capacity for autonomy was emphasized by the General Practitioner (2/52) who shared the care of his two children under five with his architect wife – they both worked two and a half days a week:

> Autonomy ... If I were in a hospital career structure then I would be working full-time – have to put an awful lot of effort in to structure a part-time career and a lot of justification: 'A man – wanting to go part-time'?! (2/52)

This case demonstrates how careful planning had been necessary in order to achieve shared care. Their first child had been born during his GP training, during which he had worked full-time. When he had finished training:

> Our plan had always been to share the childcare. ... and the best way was a straight split so when I started looking for (GP) partnerships I was only looking for part-time partnerships so the right one came up so I took that. So I work two and a half days and Amanda then changed her hours to work

> the other two and a half days a week so we don't have any nursery care now, it's great, it's excellent – ... that (practice) was the most attractive because it's a majority of women there, they were going to have a positive attitude towards part-time working – within that partnership there isn't going to be any pressure to just 'stay on for an extra hour'. In our partnership it's very much family is as important if not more important – in my view family's more important than work – and in my view if there is a balance there – if you have to go home to your family then you have to go home to your family and someone else will carry the can.

Similarly, the Norwegian GP commented that the fact that he worked only with women meant that there was a greater understanding of his family needs at his workplace.

It has been argued that the level of autonomy enjoyed by the professional is an occupational factor that facilitates the arrangement of shared care, and that this occupational characteristic cuts across national differences – as is illustrated by the differences between professional and managerial women summarized earlier. Nevertheless, a comparison of the British and French doctors suggests that national differences can still be important. The British doctor and his wife had both arranged to work part-time; in contrast, in the French case both partners worked full time:

> We have constructed an atypical life, because we see each other very little and our children see us separately ... We spend very few weekends together – I often look after the children by myself ... In my family life ... my wife and I are interchangeable, when the children were young we each did every other night, we each did every other weekend (5/64, married, two children).

Full-time working amongst mothers of children is well supported and has an established history in France, and even though this is only a single case, therefore, it neatly encapsulates national differences.

All three of the doctors who had voluntarily undertaken major childcare responsibilities had explicitly placed their family life before their employment careers, as summarized by the Norwegian doctor:

> I chose family medicine (general practice, *almenpraktiken*) because of the hours, in other specialties there is more shift work ... a job is just to earn money, ambitions are less important now. To be a specialist involves time and this affects the family (3/50, married, two children).

The major source of 'family-friendliness', which may be identified in respect of professional occupations, therefore, is the time sovereignty they offer. Besides the possibilities of self-employment, particular specialisms within professions may be chosen with a view to achieving control over working hours. It should be stressed that this does not always mean short hours working, but rather, the possibility of tailoring hours to meet caring responsibilities. It has by convention been women who have made these kinds of choices, but men, as well as women, might choose to place family responsibilities before the demands of employment – that is, there might be an increase in 'voluntary', as well as 'involuntary', caring amongst men. Thus, an increasing number of men, as well as women, may find themselves combining employment with some level of childcare (or other caring) responsibilities. As a consequence, there might be increasing pressure for family friendly employment arrangements from professional and managerial employees of *both* sexes.

Recent evidence relating to family friendly working arrangements, however, suggests that the issue is highly problematic. Hochschilds' (1997) work in the US not only documents the collapse of 'family friendly' employment arrangements in a 'leading edge' company, but also the subsequent intensification of work demands on employees. Halford *et al.* (1997) have shown how the redefinition of 'career' following organizational restructuring was one which was at odds with domestic responsibilities, in that very long hours were demanded, and Lewis and Lewis (1996) have described how time pressures have increased the difficulties in securing organizational legitimacy for entitlement to 'family' related benefits. However, as a return to the 'male breadwinner' model is not very likely, then the proportion of employee-carers in the labour force – female and male – is likely to increase. It has earlier been emphasized that caring is gender coded, rather than gendered as such, and *men* with caring responsibilities can find themselves under considerable pressures, as in the case of this British banker:

> ... although my manager said to me 'take as much time as you like' (when his daughter was born with health problems and his wife was ill), I was given the message ... how busy the office was – and I was expected to be back at work ... at the end of the day the profit margin is the most important ... Unless you get your life sorted out you're not going anywhere, you'll just end up being downgraded and possibly they'll want to get rid of you (2/76, two children).

In combination with the pressures brought about through increased job insecurity, therefore, the contradictions between employment and caring would seem to be getting worse, not better. The pressures of modern employment in combination with the erosion of the male breadwinner model have generated what some have described as a 'parenting deficit'. This has set up pressures for change and increasingly, therefore, it is being recognized that caring is not simply a 'woman's problem'. Bradley's study of gender and power in the workplace identifies the potential, with the entry of women into employment and trade union activity, for a 'redefining of class interests' to reflect the experiences of women. As she notes ' ... the provision of childcare for employees may be seen as a class and not just a gender issue' (1998: 188). Thus changes in class interests and objectives may follow upon the restructuring of gender relations and the gender division of labour, and vice versa.

Discussion and conclusions

The division of labour in employment and the family which emerged with the development of bourgeois capitalism in the West (the 'male breadwinner' model) was widely associated with an extensive and relatively rigid gender coding. Employment was considered to be a masculine sphere, and caring, carried out in the domestic sphere, was considered feminine. The occupational structure associated with this division of labour between the sexes was dominated by male jobs. It was on the basis of these structures, together with the existing state of sociological knowledge of the nature of the occupations in question, that sociological class schemes were devised in the 1970s.[15] These schemes generated very different 'class structures' for men and women taken as individuals.

However, although the labour market may once have justifiably been described as a 'male' territory (Reay, 1998: 259), this characterization increasingly makes less and less sense. In many countries, the proportion of women in the labour force is nearly equal to that of men. Occupational segregation persists, but is in decline, especially vertical segregation. In this chapter, we have argued for the need systematically to address the consequences for class analysis of the changes brought about by this shift in the processes of labour market structuring. In so doing, we find ourselves returning to some of the important issues relating to the gender division of labour in both paid employment and the domestic sphere that were first raised by second-wave feminists and which were not, arguably, completely resolved at the time (see for example the essays in Allen and Barker, 1976).

More men are moving into caring occupations, and more men find themselves with care responsibilities. There exists a substantial literature on 'managing employment and family life', much of it directed at women. Until recently, a feature of much of this discussion was that it was assumed that families have to be fitted around employment, rather than the other way round. Thus the emphasis has been on arranging for care whilst the carers work (workplace crèches and other help with childcare), as well as arranging for career breaks, flexible working hours, etc. Recent discussions, however, have increasingly begun to recognize that the combination of caring and paid work is likely to require even more fundamental changes in conceptions of 'work' and careers (Lewis and Lewis, 1996). There is here, of course, a paradox in that just as the relative incompatibility of employment and caring is increasingly being recognized as a problem, so developments in approaches to the management of employees are demanding even more greater levels of commitment, and time, from employees (Hochschild, 1997).

It should be remembered that making a job family-unfriendly has also been an historic strategy for keeping women out of it. For example, the requirement to be geographically mobile, which was once a prerequisite for promotion in many financial institutions, was one of the first indirect exclusionary practices to be successfully challenged by the EOC. In their studies of banking and local authorities Halford *et al.* (1997) find that direct gender exclusionary practices are no longer evident, but suggest that within such bureaucracies a new distinction has emerged between 'encumbered' and 'unencumbered' workers – that is, those with and without caring responsibilities (in organizational terms, this is an accurate, albeit somewhat negative, characterization). Discriminatory practices aimed at women or other groups can be removed by legislation. The work of caring, however, cannot be similarly eliminated. It was once the case that the distinction between those with and without caring responsibilities could be assumed to be a gender difference. However, in this chapter it has been argued that caring has been gender *coded* as female, rather than being an intrinsic aspect of the feminine, and that men can care, as well as women.

We began this chapter with a brief review of feminist criticisms of employment-derived class schemes. Another feminist criticism of 'class analysis' more generally was that the contribution of women to social reproduction, and thus, albeit indirectly, to production itself had been ignored by class theorists. Or to put the same point in a slightly different fashion, that the structure of paid employment left out of account women's contribution to production. One response to this kind of criticism has been to emphasize that class is about *class* rather than anything else – ie the exclusive focus upon productive activity is justifiable – and it is therefore misleading to identify as 'missing' dimensions of social differentiation that have never been incorporated into the concept (Mills, 1995). Whilst these kinds of arguments certainly cannot be dismissed entirely, it is nevertheless the case, as Devine (1998) has argued (in a different although parallel context) that this approach is an extremely narrow one. She argues that Goldthorpe's recent theoretical formulation of the processes sustaining patterns of social mobility, for example, focuses entirely upon economic resources and excludes the significance of cultural and social resources. Devine advocates as an alternative an asset-based approach, drawing upon the framework used in Savage *et al.*'s (1992) investigation of the middle classes.

Savage *et al.* have argued that the middle classes are characterized by three different kinds of resource, property assets, organizational assets, and cultural assets. Organizational assets, or 'property in positions', are characteristic of managerial groupings, whereas cultural assets (ie, education and training) are characteristic of professionals. These variations in assets, Savage *et al.* argue, constitute important differences within the 'service class'. Goldthorpe (1995) rejects these arguments, suggesting that differences in professional and managerial 'situses' have little or no impact on issues of concern to 'class analysis' – such as social mobility.

Savage *et al.* have shown that professionals are more successful in transmitting their occupational position to their children – particularly their daughters – than are other middle-class groups (1992: 149). They also argue that whereas '... sons of professionals are ... able to follow their father's footsteps into professional employment with reasonable regularity, manager's sons are less likely to follow their fathers into managerial work' (1992: 139). In this chapter, it has been shown that there is a systematic difference between 'professional' and 'managerial' occupations, in that for both men and women, 'professional' jobs offer greater possibilities for meshing employment with caring responsibilities than do bureaucratic managerial jobs. Professionals have more children than managers, and the evidence of our interviews indicates that the relative structures and pressures of the two different types of occupation has contributed to this difference. Professionals who give priority to family life are likely to choose a specialty or niche that enables them to put their priorities into practice.[16] In short, it would appear that there might be important *cultural* differences between professionals and managers – in values, aspirations and expectations – in respect of family organization, and which have contributed to the variations in the patterns of social mobility observed by Savage *et al.* This kind of argument (*contra* Mills, 1995 cited above) emphasizes the essential *interdependence* of social and material production activity, as stressed by the first generation of 'second-wave' feminists.

It has not been the intention of this chapter to suggest that feminist criticisms have invalidated employment-aggregate class analysis. Rather, it has been argued that the feminist critique has played a significant role in clarifying the employment-aggregate approach to class analysis, and revealing its limitations. Subsequently, Wright (1997: 239ff) in particular has recognized that gender and class interact and reciprocally affect each other. However, the recognition of and research into the interaction of class and gender, for which Wright correctly argues, requires us to focus on the meso level of occupational, organizational, household and family structuring, that is, on the *processes* of class and labour market formation, and not just on the interaction of nominally defined employment and sexual categories alone.

As more employees find themselves with caring responsibilities, therefore, we may anticipate that the caring dimension will assume increasingly more importance as an axis of labour market differentiation. A wider issue, which is extremely important, is raised by the question of whether the extreme 'family *un*friendly' characteristics of some occupations might result in demands to transform employment relations and conditions – particularly those associated with excessive and/or unsocial hours. If this did prove to be the case, it would be an example of a major transformation brought about by the tensions and conflicts arising out of the relationships of caring, rather than those of class.

In conclusion: from the eighteenth century onwards, the division of labour between men and women has left its peculiar stamp on class societies. The erosion of the conventional gender division of labour as represented by the male breadwinner model implies that gender relations as such will be less firmly imprinted on occupational structure than they have been (although we are obviously still a long way from this situation). Thus occupational class schemes might be becoming less susceptible to some of the kinds of criticisms articulated by feminists from the 70s onwards. More importantly, however, the debates over gender and class have brought into prominence significant sources of tension and conflict in the organization of market capitalism that have long been masked by the predominant gender division of labour, a recognition of which is long overdue. The resolution of this conflict – through, for example, a shift towards the extensive availability of 'family-friendly' employment – would change both employment relations and the occupational structure. This would raise further difficulties for the application of sociological class schemes.

Acknowledgements

The author would like to thank Dr. Fiona Devine for her helpful comments on an earlier version of this paper.

Notes

1 The best-known example here would be clerical work, which for much of the twentieth century was a dead-end occupation for women, but a pathway to management for men (Crompton and Jones, 1984).
2 Most notably Pahl's (1989) argument that employment aggregate 'class analysis' failed to make the linkages between structure and action.
3 It has in fact been suggested that a theoretical account is given via the concept of 'employment relations'. See Marshall (1997).
4 One important difference between Goldthorpe and Wright, however, is that for Goldthorpe, the family is the unit of class analysis, whereas for Wright, it is the individual.
5 It should be noted that Le Feuvre herself does not endorse this view.
6 Such as, for example, pediatrics, or geriatrics.
7 It should be noted that teaching was also one of the few higher-status occupations that was not actually closed to women.
8 However, an MBA from an internationally-rated business school *is* likely to enhance individual marketability to such an extent as to constitute a *de facto* 'licence'.
9 The project is supported by the ESRC, (R00022283), the Norwegian Research Council, and Conseil Régional Midi-Pyrenees. This research may be criticised as 'unrepresentative' by those who favour large data sets. However, it should be stressed that, although some summary figures are given, no attempt is being made here to ape the methods of large-scale quantitative analysis. Comparative case study work, of which this is an example, rests upon theoretical (as opposed to statistical) thinking, together with the careful selection of cases (Mitchell, 1983). Thus I am confident that these findings would be confirmed by aggregate level data. Indeed, Elliott *et al.* (1998), using longitudinal data (NCDS) have recently confirmed this difference between managerial and professional occupations, which was first established as a result of previous case study research (Crompton and Sanderson, 1990).

10 All of the interviewees were either fully qualified doctors (ie had completed their post-qualification registration), or were on managerial (or *cadre*) grades within retail banking. Although we have not achieved exact equivalence in all cases, considerable efforts have been made to achieve as close a match between interviews in different countries as possible.

11 Other research has also shown that women in managerial jobs are likely to have fewer children. In Norway, for example, it has been shown that women in administrative/managerial work have fewer children than women in other occupations (Strand *et al.*, 1996), and this has been attributed to the difficulties of combining managerial work with a linear career. In Britain, census data shows that women in managerial occupations are less likely to live in households with children than are professional women (Crompton, 1996).

12 This research is being carried out in collaboration with Gunn Birkelund in Norway and Nicky Le Feuvre in France. Whilst the difference between female bankers and doctors was statistically different, the difference between male bankers and doctors was not.

13 The structure of the medical profession in France is rather different from the English case. Specialists working from their own *cabinets* have a greater control over their hours, and sole practice amongst *omnipracticien* (GPs), which is common, involves very long hours. See Crompton, Le Feuvre and Birkelund, 1999.

14 There were no involuntary male carers in France.

15 Goldthorpe, 1987: 40–3. Wright's original class scheme was not an occupational classification, and indeed, generated substantially more 'female' proletarians than male. However, over the years the approaches of Wright and Goldthorpe have converged, see Crompton, 1998.

16 National data also indicates that in Norway, there is a significant difference in birth rates between women in professional and managerial occupations. See Strand *et al.*, 1996.

References

Allen, S. and Barker, D.L. (eds), (1976), *Dependence and Exploitation in Work and Marriage*, London: Longman.

Beck, U. and Beck-Gernsheim, E., (1995), *The Normal Chaos of Love*, Cambridge: Polity.

Bradley, H., (1989), *Men's work, women's work*, Cambridge: Polity.

Bradley, H., (1998), *Gender and Power in the Workplace*, Houndmills Basingstoke: Macmillan.

Butler, T. and Savage, M. (eds), (1995), *Social Change and the Middle Classes*, London: UCL Press.

Crompton, R., (1986), 'Women and the "service class"' in Crompton, R. and Mann, M. (eds), *Gender and Stratification*, Cambridge: Polity.

Crompton, R., (1989), 'Class Theory and Gender', *British Journal of Sociology*, 4 (40): 565–87.

Crompton, R., (1993, 1998), *Class and Stratification*, Cambridge: Polity.

Crompton, R., (1996), 'Gender and Class Analysis', in Lee, D.J. and Turner, B.S. (eds), *Conflicts about Class*, Essex: Longman.

Crompton, R. (ed.), (1999), *Restructuring Gender Relations and Employment*, Oxford: OUP.

Crompton, R. and Harris, F., (1997), 'Women's employment and gender attitudes: a comparative analysis of Britain, Norway and the Czech Republic', *Acta Sociologica*, 40: 183–202.

Crompton, R. and Harris, F., (1999), 'Employment, Careers and Families, the significance of "Choice" and "Constraint" in women's lives', in Crompton (ed.) *op cit*.

Crompton, R. and Jones, G., (1984), *White-Collar Proletariat: Deskilling and Gender in the Clerical Labour Process*, London: Macmillan.

Crompton, R. and Le Feuvre, N., (1997), 'Choisir une carriere, faire carriere: les femmes medicins en France et en Grande-Bretagne', *Cahiers du GEDDIST*, Paris: editions L'Harmattan.

Crompton, R. and Sanderson, K., (1990), *Gendered Jobs and Social Change*, London: Unwin Hyman.

Crompton, R., Le Feuvre, N. and Birkelund, G., (1999), 'The gendered restructuring of the medical profession', in Crompton (ed.) *op cit*.

Crompton, R. and Le Feuvre, N., (1992), 'Gender and bureaucracy: women in finance in Britain

and France', in Savage, M. and Witz, A. (ed.), *Sociological Review Monograph*, Oxford: Blackwell.
Crompton, R. and Le Feuvre, N., (1996), 'Paid Employment and the Changing System of Gender Relations: A Cross-national Comparison', *Sociology*, 30 (3): 427–45.
Davidoff, L. and Hall, C., (1987), *Family Fortunes*, London: Hutchinson.
Davies, C., (1996), 'The sociology of the professions and the profession of gender', *Sociology*, 30 (4): 661–678.
Devine, F., (1992), 'Gender segregation in the engineering and science professions', *Work Employment and Society*, 6: 557–75.
Devine, F., (1998), 'Class analysis and the stability of class relations', *Sociology*, 32 (1): 23–42.
Ellingsaeter, A-M., (1999), 'Dual breadwinners between state and market', in Crompton (ed.), *Restructuring Gender Relations and Employment*, Oxford: OUP.
Elliott, J., Dale, A. and Egerton, M., (1998), 'The influence of qualifications on women's work histories, employment status and occupational attainment at age 33', Cathie Marsh Centre for Census and Survey Research, Manchester.
Erikson, R. and Goldthorpe, J.H., (1992), *The Constant Flux*, Oxford: Clarendon Press.
Esping-Andersen, G. (ed.), (1993), *Changing Classes: Stratification and Mobility in Post-Industrial Societies*, London: Sage.
Evetts, J., (1994), 'Women and career in engineering', *Work Employment and Society*, 8: 101–112.
Gershuny, J., Godwin, M. and Jones, S., (1994), 'The Domestic Labour Revolution: a Process of Lagged Adaptation', in Anderson, M., Bechhofer, F. and Gershuny, J. (eds), *The Social and Political Economy of the Household*, Oxford: OUP.
Goldthorpe, J.H., (1980; 1987), *Social Mobility and Class Structure in Modern Britain*, Oxford: Clarendon Press.
Goldthorpe, J.H., (1983), 'Women and Class Analysis: in Defence of the Conventional View', *Sociology*, 17 (4): 465–78.
Goldthorpe, J.H., (1996), 'The Service Class Revisited', in Butler and Savage (eds), *Social Change and the Middle Classes*, London: UCL Press.
Gregson, N. and Lowe, M., (1994), *Servicing the middle classes*, London: Routledge.
Halford, S., Savage, M. and Witz, A., (1997), *Gender, Careers and Organisations*, London: Macmillan.
Halford, S. and Savage, M., (1995), 'Restructuring Organisations, Changing People', *Work, Employment and Society*, 9 (1): 97–122.
Hochschild, A., (1997), *The Time Bind.*
Leiulsfrud, H. and Woodward, A., (1987), 'Women at Class Crossroads', *Sociology*, 21 (3): 393–412.
Lewis, S. and Lewis, J., (1996), *The work-family challenge*, London: Sage.
Mills, C., (1995), 'Managerial and professional work-histories', in Butler and Savage *op cit.*
Mitchell, J.C., (1983), 'Case and Situation Analysis', *Sociological Review*, 31.
Pahl, R.E., (1989), 'Is the Emperor Naked?', *International Journal of Urban and Regional Research*, 13 (4): 711–20.
Reay, D., (1998), 'Rethinking Social Class', *Sociology*, 32 (2): 259–275.
Rowntree Foundation, (1995), *Inquiry into Income and Wealth*, York: Rowntree.
Savage, M., Barlow, J., Dickens, A. and Fielding, T., (1992), *Property, Bureaucracy, and Culture*, London: Routledge.
Scott, J. and Morris, L., (1996), 'The Attenuation of Class Analysis', *British Journal of Sociology*.
Scott, J., Alwin, D.F. and Braun, M., (1996), 'Generational Changes in Gender-Role Attitudes: Britain in a Cross-National Perspective', *Sociology*, 30 (3): 471–492.
Segal, L., (1987), *Is the future female?*, London: Virago.
Strand, K., Wergeland, E. and Bjerkedal, T., (1996), 'Fertility patterns according to occupational grouping in Norway, 1989', *Scandinavian Journal of Social Medicine*, 24 (1): 50–54.
Thair, T. and Risdon, A., (1999), 'Women in the Labour Market', *Labour Market Trends*, March: 103–114.

Walby, S., (1986), *Patriarchy at Work*, Cambridge: Polity Press.
Westergaard, J., (1995), *Who Gets What?*, Cambridge: Polity.
Witz, A., (1992), *Professions and Patriarchy*, London: Routledge.
Wright, E.O., (1997), *Class Counts*, Cambridge: Cambridge University Press.

Conclusion: renewing class analysis

Fiona Devine and Mike Savage

Introduction

In this conclusion we consider how the chapters in this volume might renew the class analysis tradition sketched out in the introductory chapter by Crompton and Scott. As part of this aim, we also reflect more broadly on the state of stratification theory and research in the light of current debates. Let us start by noting that although the chapters of this book are diverse in content and theoretical orientation, there are some arresting points that clearly indicate certain trajectories in class analysis and stratification research. The major point that emerges is the need to reconsider the relationship between economic inequalities – by which we mean material inequities arising out of market processes – and social inequalities and specifically cultural differences springing from consumption and lifestyles. We want to argue that an understanding of the mutual constitution of the economic and the social is the key to understanding the structuring of class and stratification.

This chapter is organized as follows. In the first section, we begin with some general comments on the relationship between economic and social inequality and consider how some sociologists in the field of class analysis have neglected economic restructuring and the implications for material inequalities in the 1980s and 1990s. In the second section, we consider the varied ways in which the authors of the chapters consider economic processes in the last twenty years and how they look at the implications of these processes for material inequalities. We thus retread similar ground to Crompton and Scott but we focus less on the chapters themselves and more on how they contribute to a rethinking of class analysis. In the third section, we examine the recent debate on culture and class and it is here that we explore how the two discussions on economic and social inequalities might be brought together. We argue that recognition of the fact that economic and social practices are embedded in each other rather than separate spheres of life might be a way of renewing the study of class and stratification in a more holistic fashion than has characterized the sub-discipline of late.

Economics and class analysis

We see the most significant point of convergence in this volume in the way that most authors are concerned with the intersection between sociological theories of stratification and the 'economic', broadly defined. This is a striking departure. For much of the 1980s and 1990s sociologists of class and stratification tended to neglect the 'economic'. Those practising class analysis within the 'employment aggregate' approach (Crompton, 1998) distanced themselves from income based definitions or measures of class, preferring to conceptualize class in terms of people's location within employment relationships. One consequence of this trend within British sociology is that class analysis has not addressed the growing income and wealth inequality that has dominated research in American sociology in the last ten or more years (eg, Levy, 1995). Instead, a more general trend in Britain has been a growth of interest in questions of culture and identity rather than economic inequality. Indeed, insofar as it is possible to detect an interest in the 'sociology of money', its orientation is to the culture of finance, rather than its relationship to economic inequality (eg, Dodd, 1995; Giddens, 1991).

The tenor that runs through the chapters in this volume is rather similar. They all suggest, in very different ways, that economic issues are far too important to be neglected by sociologists and thereby left to economists. Sociologists need to develop a critical economic theory of class and stratification that relates trends in contemporary political economy to the reworking of the relations of class, gender and ethnicity. None of the authors of the papers in this collection (with the exception of Crompton) have squarely addressed the once dominant Nuffield tradition of class analysis before and only some of them (Sørensen, Gershuny, Ingham and Edwards) refer to it here. Be that as it may, the contributors seek a renewal of the core concerns of the sociology of class and stratification by considering the sociological implications of new processes of economic restructuring and the generation of material inequalities. Inevitably, this orientation requires an engagement with the concerns of economists and political economists.

This marks a significant departure from recent class analysis. The Nuffield tradition of class analysis has rarely had much direct interest in economics (bar the recent interest in rational choice theory (Goldthorpe, 1996)). Thus, one of its signal failures in recent years has been its inability to offer any explanation of new processes of economic inequality (see also Beynon and Glavanis, 1999). As a consequence, there has been little sustained examination of how new kinds of social divisions can be related to processes of class formation. In an era of growing economic inequality within most capitalist nations, and between capitalist nation states (eg, Castells, 1996; 1997a, 1997b), sociologists of class and stratification have rarely had much of consequence to say about the processes driving new forms of social inequality. The general tone, most evident within the work of Goldthorpe (1987; Goldthorpe and Marshall 1992) is to deny contemporary social change or to downplay the extent of change (see Devine, 1998 on this point in relation to social mobility). Thus, the most significant engagement with debates about new forms of inequality comes in the form of critiques of any new arguments in the area (the sociological critique of the underclass debate comes to mind as an obvious example: see Gallie, 1988; Marshall *et al.*, 1996).

The reasons for the failure of class analysis in this respect, we would argue, are several. Within the Weberian tradition (and perhaps against the spirit of Weber's own close interest in the intersection between the economic and the social), the focus has been on the relationship between 'economic' and 'social' orders, rather than in the specific operation of the 'economic' itself. This has led to an interest in how economic inequalities leads to class formation, through what Giddens (1973) refers to as class 'structuration'. This 'class formation problematic' is not directly concerned with analysing economic processes themselves – these are almost taken as given – but in whether and how they lead to the formation of distinct social classes. This perspective can be found in the writings of Goldthorpe (1987; Erikson and Goldthorpe, 1992) as well as Wright (1985, 1996), though these writers have somewhat different reasons for upholding this view. It would appear that Goldthorpe recognizes the social and political constitution of economic inequalities, but because he thinks that the precise nature of this constitution is historically specific he simply doubts that sociologists can say much of interest about them (see Goldthorpe, 1991, 1995).

Wright defines the mechanisms of class inequality deductively from game theory (1985) or rent theory (1996) and thereby focuses his attention on showing the ways that such deductively defined classes become socially manifest. As Crompton (1998) has emphasized, both these approaches have ignored the role of gender (and ethnicity) in the creation of class structures. Furthermore, whilst the class formation approach can produce historically sensitive work, in an era where class formation appears to be rather weak, it leads to an explanation of what does not exist rather than what does. As Scott's (1996s) analysis of the contemporary working class shows, there is today rather little evidence that classes exist as any kind of collective force. If this is so, both Goldthorpe and Wright are on rather shaky ground in defending class analysis (Holmwood and Stewart, 1991; Savage, 2000).

The lack of concern with the economic in class analysis goes further than this, however. What is also striking is that even within the 'employment aggregate' approach to class analysis (Crompton 1998), class has been defined through employment relationships separately from the market processes that are embedded within them. Marxist work has always been critical of the idea, present in some versions of the Weberian definition, that sees class inequality as derived from market relations. In the 1970s, for example, Crompton and Gubbay (1977) argued that relations of production and not just market relations should be considered in explanations about the structuring of class and stratification. Recent neo-Weberian writing has become increasingly concerned to distance itself from linking class positions to the market[1]. In seeking to protect the integrity of his class schema, for example, Goldthope (Erikson and Goldthorpe, 1992) has moved away from linking class positionsto the market by dropping the notions of market situation and work situation from his conception of class. The result has been to leave the idea of the market to others, even in a period when there has been a dramatic expansion of the use of market mechanisms in providing services and goods.

This is a very different perspective, for instance, from that found in the sociology of welfare (Esping-Andersen, 1990), or consumption (Warde, 1992), where attention has been addressed to examining the intersection between market mechanisms (in all their varieties) and the 'social'. A further problem with the trajectory that class analysis has taken, therefore, is that by abstracting class and inequality from market processes it has not made sufficient attempt to provide sociological analyses of market mechanisms and related economic processes. This is where the papers in this volume point in a rather different direction. They consider how market processes inter-relate with class processes, and offer possible ways of developing reflections on the social embedding of markets (see as another intervention in this venture though from a different tradition of sociology, Callon, 1998). Having made these preliminary points, this is a good moment to reflect on the different ways in which our contributors wish to situate their contributions and to reflect on how their chapters impact on the new agenda for stratification research.

Economic inequalities and classes

All of the contributors to this volume attach primary importance to the study of economic and market processes as a way of understanding persistent inequalities in wealth, income, consumption and lifestyles. In doing so, they reject one of the central tenets of the Nuffield class tradition which was dominant in the 1980s: namely, that the economic order should be taken as given and sociologists should only concern themselves with the social consequences of it. In contrast, the authors here – especially Sørensen and Edwards – emphasize that sociologists must concern themselves with economic relations which are grounded in market processes if they are to say anything about the generative mechanisms by which consequences are produced. In this respect, their endeavours can be seen as similar to those of other American sociologists such as Tilly (1998) who are concerned to theorize rather than describe the mechanisms of class relations. Moreover, as Crompton's contribution shows, the study of class relations can be 'opened up' by making connections between, for example, the domestic division of labour, the patterning of employment rewards and class formation (see also Glucksmann, 1995).

Inevitably, explanations of economic inequalities lead sociologists to engage with the work of economists and economic theory as can be seen in the first part of this book. A consideration of rent theory, for example, is central to Sørensen's contribution. He is not alone in this project (Erik Wright, 1996, has also sought recently to define class assets in terms of rents), but offers a particularly thoughtful and worked through account of how this approach might work in practice. Strikingly, Sørensen, like Wright, seeks to renew the

Marxist tradition of class analysis rather than the Weberian tradition, because he sees the Marxist tradition as having more explanatory power given its concern with mechanisms and processes, rather than correlation and description. By liberating the concept of rent from a specific concern with land or fixed assets and by examining in Marxist fashion how rents can be attributed to labour as an asset, Sørensen develops a sophisticated and thoughtful perspective on understanding the mechanisms that might generate inequality.

A number of attractive features of Sørensen's arguments can be delineated. Although neo-Marxist in its inspiration, it is clearly not dogmatic and makes no teleological claims about any inherent tendencies in class processes. It can be argued that Sørensen offers a much richer way of considering the tension between capital and labour than simple references to class antagonism may allow. He shows how forms of class compromise as well as class conflict can be generated by rent mechanisms. The haggling over the composite rents inherent in the labour contract may lead onto broader structural conflicts between capital and labour. Attempts to create and undermine career ladders and internal labour markets can be related to this tension. By making this move, Sørensen is able to position class theory so that recent trends in the erosion of organizational careers and the rise of new kinds of sub-contracting arrangements, for example, can be given a central place within its purview.

An index of personal resources is employed by Gershuny as a means of offering an alternative explanation of inequality to that provided within class theory. He draws on the idea of human capital, widespread in labour economics, which refers to the way that investment in an employees' skills can lead to economic rewards. Gershuny interestingly relates the theory of human capital to Bourdieu's arguments to show how skills and dispositions are accumulated by individuals over their life and thus, not unlike Tilly (1998) again, lead to cumulative processes of advantage and disadvantage over the life-course. Gershuny argues that a measure of a person's resources gives a better prediction of a person's economic position than does their simple class position, and that his measure of resources gives a stronger correlation with economic position over time. In this venture, he adopts a mode of analysis that is not dissimilar to labour economists who have examined the determinants of income levels using regression techniques, though he is considerably more aware of the social relationships embedded in the measures that he uses.

One response to Gershuny's paper (which is anticipated by Gershuny himself) might simply be to question whether his results are particularly surprising. Goldthorpe does not claim that his class schema is supposed to be indexed by measures of income. Rather he defines his class schema in terms of its ability to measure diverse facets of the employment relationships (see Evans, 1992, for a trenchant defense of the validity of Goldthorpe's class schema along these lines). Therefore, he can hardly be criticised when Gershuny's measure of resources, specifically designed to correlate with economic position, outperforms it. Indeed, it could be argued that what is remarkable is that

Goldthorpe's class scheme performs nearly as well as Gershuny's. Nonetheless, Gershuny's paper poses important issues. With the growing sophistication of analysis made possible by the development of complex data sets such as the British Household Panel Study, it can be argued that the concept of class can be unpacked into more specific and discrete measures of numerous determinants of life chances. Such developments also facilitate an appreciation of the complexities of temporal trajectory (Sørensen, 1986; Savage *et al.*, 1992). Perhaps the idea of class is made redundant when more complex, biographical data is used?

'Matthew effects' are central to Ingham's reflections around the intersection of economics and sociology. He argues that both Weber and Marx have an inadequate understanding of money, and tend to see it as a 'neutral veil' of capitalist social relationships rather than an autonomous mechanism for the creation of economic inequalities. In contrast, Ingham argues that money is a mechanism in its own right that produces economic inequality, and has nothing to do with class processes as conventionally defined within class analysis. Ingham analyses the 'Matthew effects' which operate around the production and supply of money, and which tend to allow the economically advantaged (regardless of their occupational class position) to be able systematically to generate more income than the economically disadvantaged.

Of course, class analysts are perfectly free to say that Ingham's analysis has no relevance for them, and that inequalities arising out of purely financial processes should not be confused with class inequalities. If they take this step they must, however, recognize that the scope of class analysis as a tool to understand economic inequality is thereby limited. Ingham also shows that one's relationship to money is also socially significant in leading to kinds of social mobilization (for instance around LETS schemes) and therefore that money processes can be seen as socially relevant. He also demonstrates that it is not the amount of money that is important but the relational qualities of having relatively much or little which is of decisive importance in generating Matthew effects. In all these ways he champions a sociological perspective on money rather than a purely 'economic' one and challenges more conventional class analysis to consider how it would handle the processes he identifies.

Indeed, the 'Matthew effect' comes out clearly in the papers grouped in the second part of the book. Pahl, for example, develops Ingham's discussion of 'financial citizenship' in her consideration of consumption as a way of differentiating social groups'. She examines new forms of money, its implications for patterns of consumption within households and the implications for social polarization. Pahl's central argument is that new forms of money are creating a set of filters that enhance or constrain the access which individuals and households have to the market. She looks, in particular, at the circumstances of the credit-card poor and the consequences for the excluded who are forced to remain in the cash economy. The rich focus group discussions highlight the penalties of remaining in the cash economy – from paying more interest to being excluded from discounts – so that the group who can least afford it end by paying more. Thus, despite the fact that it is easier to operate in the cash economy, those on low incomes are being further disadvantaged by the rise of new forms of money. The cumulative effects of advantage and disadvantage and how they contribute to the processes of social polarization are clear.

The concept of social polarization is not unproblematic for it implies there are two groups of people who are moving further apart and it ignores the many groups who lie in between the extremes of consumer rich and consumer poor (see Westergaard, 1992, on this point with respect to the underclass debate). At the same time, it might be a useful way of capturing the widening gulf between extremes and highlight the very different economic and social worlds in which such households exist. That is to say, there are work-and consumer-rich households that exercise power and choice and work-and consumer-poor households who are constrained and penalized for their predicament. These aspects of power and inequality, we want to argue, are central to research on structured inequality for they highlight the processes by which class inequalities are reproduced over time and space.

The spread of polarization across the advanced societies of the capitalist West is vividly described in Wacquant's paper. Interestingly, Wacquant argues that the process of polarization 'from below' is not some sort of residue from the past but a 'harbinger of the future'. This point reinforces the one made above: namely, that polarization is an issue for a future class analysis too. He identifies four structural logics that fuel the new urban marginality – social, economic, political and spatial dynamics. Wacquant's account of the different logics contributing to the process of polarization is convincing in almost all respects. While we would entirely agree that there are economic, political and spatial processes at work, his analysis of social dynamics refers, in fact, to economic trends in occupational dualization and says nothing of changing patterns of family formation and family practices. Now, public discourse about the family in America is certainly one from which most scholars are keen to distance themselves. Nevertheless, it is possible – as Castells (1996; 1997a 1997b) has done – to integrate changing family forms into an account of how social inequalities are transforming in the current era.

Wacquant acknowledges – correctly in our view – that the spectre of transatlantic convergence whereby European ghettos are becoming more like American ghettos should be treated with considerable caution. (That said, Britain has a remarkable capacity to be more like the US than its European counterparts, not least in relation to the penal state). While similarities can be easily identified, there are important differences especially in relation to the political response to economic and social change. The US has been at the forefront of the process of the retrenchment and disarticulation of its already meagre welfare state while European societies – especially the Netherlands and Scandinavian countries – have been far slower to curtail public assistance. The problem for policy makers and academic commentators, however, is that any attempts fundamentally to reconstruct the welfare state must admit that the US has virtually full employment while the European Union is still beset by massive levels of unemployment.

The lived experience of polarization is evident in MacDonald and Marsh's detailed account of the impact of economic restructuring on the lives of young working-class men and women in a local labour market in the Northeast of England. Work opportunities, they argue, have been dramatically 'recast' as permanent employment has been replaced by cyclical transitions in and out of employment, training initiatives, voluntary work, informal activities and unemployment. Like others (Gershuny and Marsh, 1993; Morris, 1994), they emphasize that members of the working class are not permanently excluded from the labour market as overly simplistic underclass theories led us to expect. The processes by which young people move in and out of employment and work are more complex than this. New forms of economic inequality pose more difficult questions about the economic position of members of the working class or what might be more appropriately referred to as the working classes.

There are those, after all, who continue to experience unemployment in cities and towns where the service sector is still unable to soak up all the job losses from manufacturing and who are excluded in a myriad of ways. Then there is the growth of the working poor: namely those people who have found employment albeit in lowly-paid insecure jobs in the service sector. Katherine Newman's (1999) recent ethnographic research on the working poor in inner-city Harlem offers some interesting insights into this group. She suggests that poor work may be trap rather than a bridge to permanent employment and that opportunities for advancement are limited. Finally, there are still members of the working class in relatively secure employment who continue to enjoy opportunities for advancement and are in the position to secure their children's mobility. To date, however, we have little explanation of all these economic processes and their implication for class and stratification.

These, then, are some of the economic processes and consequences that are shaping and reshaping the working class but they are not confined to them. Economic structuration and new forms of inequality are also affecting the middle classes as Edwards and Crompton ably demonstrate. Edwards, for example, considers debates on workplace relations since the mid 1980s and how the discussion of human resources management and other new management techniques – with the emphasis on better communication, increased involvement and commitment and individual empowerment – has seen the demise of a class perspective. He takes issue with this neglect in arguing that an analysis of how and why employment relations are changing (or not as the case may be) is central to understanding the reproduction of class and stratification. While these debates usually fall outside the interest of a narrowly defined class analysis, they are crucial for understanding new forms of economic inequalities and cannot, therefore, be ignored.

Edwards is suspicious of workplace studies that proclaim the decline of class in the workplace. Such commentators, Edwards argues, confuse 'particular features of class with its general nature'. Managers, for example, may be experiencing restricted career opportunities as the bureaucratic career ladder changes but this is not to say the service class to which they belong has disappeared. The distinct service relationship, based on the mixture of trust and the monitoring of performance, is still crucial for understanding the service class. The nature of management has changed in the 1990s and trust has been redefined 'away from bureaucratic proceduralism and towards an engaged involvement in organizational goals'. The consequences of economic changes for classes cannot be easily understood without reference to the causes of change: ie, why some occupations have grown or others declined, why they are associated with certain terms and conditions of employment and so forth. Moreover, the causes of economic change cannot be understood without references to the processes of how change has occurred.

The growth of professional and managerial occupations has been accompanied, recently at least, with the growth of women in these middle-class jobs although occupational segregation by sex and sex discrimination in the labour market generate very different life chances for men and women in the same position. Thus, gender differentiation, as Crompton argues, is key to an understanding of the processes of economic restructuring and the social consequences of it. Drawing on comparative research, she notes that women have made inroads into the medical profession and are able to construct carer-friendly medical careers. In contrast, less progress has been made in banking management because of the masculine culture that prevails in management. Women professionals are more likely to have a family than women managers who find that an organizational career is not compatible with family life. These processes affect women because they usually retain the primary responsibility for caring and domestic work but it also affects men who have caring responsibilities. This points to the fact that 'caring has been gender coded as female, rather than being an intrinsic aspect of the feminine'.

A key feature of the professions, of course, is autonomy (and associated trust noted by Edwards) which facilitate family-friendly employment conditions not just for women but also for men. At the same time (and in a similar vein to Edwards), Crompton acknowledges that just as women have made inroads into the professions, they are not the jobs they once were, especially, it could be argued, in the public sector. After all, professionals are more often than not employed by organizations that have been subject to the harsh competitiveness of the wider political economy of the 1980s and 1990s (Friedson, 1995; Devine *et al.* forthcoming). Crompton's research, therefore, suggests that further work could be undertaken on how the professions are changing and the implications of such changes for combining employment and caring responsibilities as American researchers such as Hochschild (1997) have considered. How these pressure points will affect professional and managerial occupations and the life chances of men and women in the service class has yet to be worked out. All of the contributors, therefore, address the most recent debates about economic structuration and the implications for class and stratification more generally.

Renewing class analysis

In this final section of our conclusion we wish to return to some of the current concerns of class analysis. For in some respects the chapters in this volume, with their interest in the 'economic', seem to push in a very different direction to other recent attempts to renew class analysis. Several writers have seen the main failure of recent class analysis to lie not in its lack of concern with the 'economic', but in its difficulties in explaining the relationship between class and culture. To take only a few examples, theorists, especially David Lockwood (1981, 1992), have emphasized the difficulty of finding a non-instrumentalist mechanism which relates class position to cultural outlook (see also Hindess, 1987). Also, it has been argued that new forms of cultural pluralism and cultural fragmentation (sometimes linked to post-modern culture, or to the rise of reflective modernization) mark the end of any direct association between class and culture (Featherstone, 1987; Bauman, 1982; du Gay, 1996; Giddens, 1990; Beck, 1992; Lash and Urry, 1994).

The main intellectual inspiration for exploring the intersection between class and culture in recent years has been Pierre Bourdieu (especially 1984), who has claimed that new kinds of consumer culture can be related to the development of a 'new petty bourgeoisie'. Bourdieu's work has been important in demonstrating that the power of cultural privilege is such that it problematizes any straightforward link between class and culture (see Skeggs, 1997, for a demonstration of this argument). However, there is still a tendency in Bourdieu's work to 'reduce' cultural forms to specific material bases and to adopt an instrumentalist orientation to culture. Despite his own intentions, a somewhat crude and simplistic economic determinism still underpins his account of the relationship between class and culture. This problem is not unique to Bourdieu of course. The dominant approach within class analysis rests on a version of the Structure – Consciousness – Action model (Lockwood, 1981; Crompton, 1998), in which class positions may (in specific situations) generate forms of class consciousness which may, in turn, lead to forms of class action. Lockwood's consideration of the SCA model is considerably more subtle than the more familiar Marxist 'base and superstructure' metaphor. Nevertheless, the problem of economic structural determinism still besets class analysis (Pahl, 1989 and 1993) and is not confined to those of Marxian disposition.

The sociological implications of Bourdieu's ideas, therefore, are rather similar to the dominant approach within class analysis in leading to a tendency to regard class structure and class cultures as occupying different 'parts' of society. This way of thinking, in turn, generates an interest in examining how the mediation between the 'economic' and the 'cultural' takes place. This leads us back to the idea of the 'class formation' paradigm, in which the focus is on exploring the linkage between separately constituted economic relations and class relations. A rather different way of inter-relating the two spheres is suggested from the papers here, in which culture and class are inextricably bound together in specific material practices. Rather than seeking to isolate the two so that the interaction between separate spheres can be determined, we might instead focus on how cultural processes are embedded within specific kinds of socio-economic practices.[2] The studies in this volume indicate particular kinds of 'cuts' into the interaction between culture and social practice in diverse social settings. Edwards, for instance, shows how modes of cultural perception are related to the lived experience of the shop floor (in a way that can be linked to the shop floor ethnography tradition, see for instance Beynon, 1975). Similarly Ingham shows, in his reflections on LETS, how certain kinds of financial practices can be related to specific kinds of social action in particular contexts. It is not especially useful to isolate the economic from the cultural but to show their embeddedness within specific kinds of social contexts.

The chapters in this book suggest that exploring the embeddedness of the economic in the cultural and *vice versa* may be a useful way forward. Issues of culture, identity and subjectivity, for example, loom large in Du Gay's (1996) analysis of changing work-based identities in retailing. He argues that organizational change and especially the associated rhetoric and politics of reform is leading to changes in workplace identities as employees are given seemingly more autonomy and responsibility than in the past. Du Gay is keen to remind us, however, that this cult of the individual as some sort of entrepreneur is far from liberating for individual employees. The consequences of reform, whereby organizational life has been re-imaged in consumer culture, is that the boundaries between production and consumption are no longer so clear cut. Culture and subjectivity are also central to Wajcman's (1998) study of women and men managers employed in major global companies. Women have made significant inroads into junior and middle management positions. However, a masculine organizational culture which defines management in terms of a 'male standard and positions women out of place' (Wajcman, 1998: 2) pervades the workplace and ultimately excludes women from senior management positions. Organizational culture, therefore is central to understanding the ways in which power and authority remain highly gendered in the workplace. Both studies highlight the economic and the cultural are implicated in the production of class and other inequalities.

Another example, from a different field of research, concerns the interesting connections between the economic and the cultural that have been raised in the debate about the development of the 'cultural omnivore'. Here the emphasis is on the difficulty in detecting a simple association between a particular class habitus and certain kinds of cultural dispositions in ways that are consistent with Lockwood's SCA model. Sociologists have recently argued that people who in the past may have had cultural dispositions that led them to engage exclusively in one kind of class taste appear more likely to sample different tastes. In the field of music, people do not just like jazz, or classical music, or dance music, but are becoming 'cultural omnivores' who move between these genres in specific kinds of social contexts (Petersen and Kern, 1996; Longhurst and Savage, 1996; Warde, Olson and Martens, 1999). One gloss on this is to suggest that it marks the end of clear class tastes, and is indicative of the rise of an individualized, post-modern, consumerist cultural forms. That is to say, there is no relationship between class and culture.

However, as writers such as Erickson (1996) have suggested, another explanation might relate these cultural forms to changing kinds of social relationship. As increasing numbers of workers are engaged in communicative types of work relationships in which the performance of their work involves communication with diverse others (customers, colleagues, etc). Thus, it becomes more important to be able to conjure up topics for brief discussion that will allow communication to be facilitated. Erickson points to the role of 'sports talk' in this context, whereby most people are able to rehearse brief accounts of the performance of 'their' sports team as a means of establishing a minimal degree of rapport necessary for communication. Specific kinds of cultural competencies and dispositions can be related to particular contextual settings. It is not the case that given economic relations lead to particular kinds of cultural dispositions, but rather that certain modes of cultural deportment may be crucial to the smooth working of 'economic' relationships.

What, then, are the implications of this way of interrelating class and culture? Initially, what we are suggesting here may sound rather nondescript, as an advocacy of simple empiricism. It may even sound somewhat familiar. Certainly, there are some similarities with anthropological concerns to link culture and everyday life. Traces can be found, for instance, in EP Thompson's formulations about the need to relate class formation to lived experience. That said, Thompson remained committed to a focus on organized formal politics as a privileged arena in which class formation ultimately impacted on historical development. We would view the project rather differently, however. It marks a distancing from an attempt to establish how class position impacts on class awareness, even in the modest way proposed by Lockwood (1966) or Williams (1973). An example of the different approach is to recognize the difference between the account of the cultural omnivore in the previous paragraph to the account of post-modern culture in Savage *et al.* (1992) which attempts, albeit in a nuanced form, to find a distinct social base for particular cultural dispositions.

The argument is that there is no privileged field of social relations where culture is 'found'. What establishes the relationship between class and culture (ie, what establishes the classed nature of cultural dispositions) is not the existence of class consciousness, or the coherence or uniformity of a distinct set of cultural dispositions. Rather, the relationship is to found in the way in which cultural outlooks are implicated in modes of exclusion and/or domination. For instance, in the case of the cultural omnivore, the ability to move between cultural fields – to be able to talk about Manchester United's performance one minute followed by Damien Hirst's latest art the next – is itself dependent on the acquisition of cultural confidence. This is, in turn, made possible by the acquisition of cultural capital (see generally Bryson, 1996, on how graduates are better able to appreciate different musical genres). We can see here the weaving together of the cultural and economic into a complex linked structure.

Conclusion

We are of the view that the chapters in this collection point to some new directions that a renewed class analysis might take. A focus on how, in various settings of social life, processes of inequality are produced and reproduced routinely and how this involves both economic and cultural practices, is clearly needed. The practice of everyday life, as de Certeau (1984) notes, is all-important. It is in this respect that we recommend that the economic should be brought back into class analysis, although not the economic in a narrow sense but as a set of practices that are imbued with cultural meanings and experiences. Indeed, the concept of class is crucial for understanding the mutual constitution of the economic and the social. Recent debates in class analysis and other sub-disciplines have highlighted how some sociologists focus their attention on the material inequities of class while others are preoccupied with cultural differences between classes. We believe these separate debates demonstrate the extent to which the concept of class usefully embraces both the economic and the social.

These points lead us back to our opening remarks about how sociologists of class and stratification have left the 'economic' to the economists in the 1980s and 1990s. Economists often define economic practices in a narrowly instrumental way and, arguably, some sociologists in class analysis have fallen into the same trap (see, for example, Scott (1996) and Devine's (1998) critique of rational choice theory). We venture to suggest that the 'economic' needs to be defined more widely by embedding it in social and cultural practices. Just as places cannot be separated from the people who fill them (Stewart *et al.*, 1980), so economic practices cannot be separated from social practices and the context in which they occur (see also Halford, Savage and Witz, 1996). The advantage of this approach is that the issue of economic determinism – which has cast a long shadow over class analysis in the last fifty years – is rendered unproblematic and the renewal of a more holistic approach to the study of class and stratification can begin.

Notes

1 The most striking example of this is the way that the definition of the Nuffield class schema has shifted from its reference to market situation as being one of the defining features of class location to employment relations. Compare Goldthorpe (1987) with Erikson and Goldthorpe (1992).

2 This has similarities with the realist approach to class analysis (see Savage *et al.*, 1992 and the review in Crompton 1998).

3 It can be argued that this is to draw on Marx's argument that relate the culture of capitalist societies not to specific class bases but to the power of commodity production in general to generate modes of commodity fetishism. (See Postone, 1993).

References

Bauman, Z., (1982), *Memories of Class*, London: Routledge..

Beck, U., (1992), *Risk Society: Towards a New Modernity*, London: Sage Publications.

Beynon, H. and Glavanis, P., (1999), *Patterns of Social Inequality*, London: Longman.

Bourdieu, P., (1984), *Distinction*, London: Routledge.

Bryson, B., (1996), '"Anything but Heavy Metal": Symbolic Exclusion and Musical Dislikes', *American Sociological Review*, 1: 844–899.

Callon, (1998), *The Laws of the Markets*, Oxford: Blackwells (Sociological Review Monograph).

Castells, M., (1997a), *The Power of Identity*, Oxford: Blackwells.

Castells, M., (1997b), *The Information Age*, Oxford: Blackwells.

Castells, M., (1996), *The Rise of the Network Society*, Oxford: Blackwells.

Crompton, R., (1998), *Class and Stratification*, (Second Edition), Cambridge: Polity.

Crompton, R. and Gubbay, J., (1977), *Economy and Class Structure*, London: MacMillan.

De Certeau, M., (1984), *The Practice of Everyday Life*, Berkeley: University of California Press.

Devine, F., (1998), 'Class Analysis and the Stability of Class Relations', *Sociology*, 2: 23–42.

Devine, F. *et al.*, (forthcoming) 'Economic restructuring and the professions: a case study of Manchester's business and financial sector'.

Du Gay, P., (1996), *Consumption and Identity at Work*, London: Sage.

Dodd, N., (1995), *The Sociology of Money*, Cambridge: Polity.

Erickson, B.H., (1996), 'Culture, Class and Connections', *American Journal of Sociology*, 102: 217–51.

Erikson, R. and Goldthorpe, J.H., (1992), *The Constant Flux*, Oxford: Clarendon Press.

Esping-Andersen, G., (1990), *The Three Worlds of Welfare Capitalism*, Cambridge: Polity.

Evans, G., (1992), 'Testing the Validity of the Goldthorpe Class Schema', *European Sociological Review*, 8: 211–32.

Featherstone, M., (1987), 'Lifestyles and Consumer Culture', *Theory, Culture and Society*, 4: 329–60.

Friedson, E., (1995), *Professionalism Reborn*, Cambridge: Polity.

Gallie, D., (1988), 'Employment, Unemployment, and Social Stratification', in D. Gallie (ed.), *Employment in Britain*, Oxford: Basil Blackwell.

Gershuny, J. and Marsh, C., (1983), 'Unemployment in work histories', in D. Gallie *et al.* (eds) *Social Change and the Experience of Unemployment*, Oxford: Oxford University Press.

Giddens, A., (1991), *Modernity and Self-identity in the Late Modern Age*, Cambridge: Polity.

Giddens, A., (1990), *The Consequences of Modernity*, Cambridge: Polity.

Giddens, A., (1973), *The Class Structure of Advanced Societies*, London: Hutchinson.

Glucksmann, M., (1995), 'Why Work? Gender and the "Total Social Organisation of Labour"', *Gender, Work and Organisation*, 2 (2) 63–75.

Goldthorpe, J.H., (1996), 'Class Analysis and the Reorientation of Class Theory: The Case of Persisting Differentials in Educational Attainment', *British Journal of Sociology*, 47: 481–506.

Goldthorpe, J. H., (1995), 'The service class revisited', in T. Butler and M. Savage (eds.) *Social Change and the Middle Classes*, London: UCL Press.

Goldthorpe, J. H., (1991), 'The Uses of History to Sociology', *British Journal of Sociology*, 42: 211–231.

Goldthorpe, J. H. and Marshall, G., (1992), 'The Promising Future of Class Analysis', *Sociology*, 26: 381–400.

Goldthorpe, J. H., (1987), *Social Mobility and Class Structure in Modern Britain*, (Second Edition) Oxford: Clarendon Press.

Gubbay, J., (1997), 'A Marxist Critique of Weberian Class Analysis', *Sociology*, 31: 73–89.

Halford, S., Savage, M., Witz, A., (1997), *Gender, Careers and Organisations*, Basingtsoke: MacMillan.

Hindess, B., (1987), *Politics and Class Analysis*, Oxford: Basil Blackwell.

Hochschild, J., (1997), *The Time Bind*, New York: Metropolitan Books.

Holmwood, J. and Stewart, A., (1991), *Explanation and Social Theory*, Basingstoke: MacMillan.

Lash, S. and Urry, J., (1994), *Economies of Signs and Space*, London: Sage.

Levy, F., (1987), *Dollars and Dreams: the changing American income distribution*, New York: Norton.

Lockwood, D., (1992), *Solidarity and Schism*, Oxford: Clarendon Press.

Lockwood, D., (1988), 'The Weakest Link in the Chain: Some Comments on the Marxist Theory of Action', in D. Rose (ed.) *Social Stratification and Economic Change*, London: Hutchinson.

Lockwood, D., (1966), 'Sources of Variation in Working-class Images of Society', *Sociological Review*, 14: 249–67.

Longhurst, B. and Savage, M., (1996), 'Social Class, Consumption and the Influence of Bourdieu: Some Critical Issues', in Edgell, S., Hetherington, K. and Warde, A., (1996), *Consumption Matters*, Oxford: Blackwells, 274–301.

Marshall, G. *et al.*, (1996), 'Social Class and the Underclass in Britain and the USA', *British Journal of Sociology*, 47: 22 44.

Morris, L., (1994), *Dangerous Classes*, London: UCL Press.

Newman, K., (1999), *No Shame in My Game*, New York: Knofp.

Pahl, R., (1993), 'Does Class Analysis Without Class Theory have a Future: A Reply to Goldthorpe and Marshall', *Sociology*, 27: 253–8.

Pahl, R., (1989), 'Is the Emperor Naked: Some Questions on the Adequacy of Sociological Theory in Urban and Regional Research', *International Journal of Urban and Regional Research*, 12: 247–67.

Pakulski, J. and Waters, M., (1996), *The Death of Class*, London: Sage.

Petersen and Kern, (1996), 'Changing Highbrow Taste: From Snob to Omnivore', *American Sociological Review*, 61: 900–907.

Postone, M., (1993), *Time, Labor and Social Domination: a reinterpretation of Marx's critical theory*, Cambridge: Cambridge University Press.

Savage, M., (forthcoming), *Class Analysis and Social Transformation*, Buckingham: Open University Press.

Savage, M., (1992), 'Women's Expertise, Men's Authority' in M. Savage and A. Witz (ed.) *Gender and Bureaucracy*, Oxford: Blackwell.

Savage, M. *et al.*, (1992), *Property, Bureaucracy and Culture*, London: Routledge.

Scott, J., (1996a), *Stratification and Power*, Cambridge: Polity.

Scott, J., (1996b), 'Comment on Goldthorpe', *British Journal of Sociology*, 47: 507–12.

Skeggs, B., (1997), *Formations of Class and Gender*, London: Sage.

Sorensen, A.B., (1986), 'Theory and Methodology in Social Stratification on Social Mobility and Socio-economic Inequality', *Acta Sociologica*, 34: 71–87.

Stewart, A. *et al.*, (1980), *Social Stratification and Occupations*, London: Macmillan.

Thompson, E.P., (1968), *The Making of the English Working Class*, Harmondsworth: Penguin.

Tilly, C., (1998), *Durable Inequalities*, Berkeley, California: University of California Press.

Wajcman, J., (1998), *Managing Like a Man: Women and Men in Corporate Management*, Cambridge: Polity.

Warde, A., (1992), 'Notes on the Relationship Between Production and Consumption', in R. Burrows and C. Marsh, *Consumption and Class: divisions and change*, Basingstoke: MacMillan, 15–31.

Warde, A., Olsen, W. and Martens, L., (1999), 'Consumption and the Problem of Variety: Cultural Omnivorousness, Social Distinction and Dining Out', *Sociology*, 31, 1: 105–128.

Westergaard, J., (1992), 'About and Beyond the "underclass": Some Notes on Influences of Social Climate on British Sociology Today', *Sociology*, 26: 575–87.
Williams, R., (1973), *The Country and the City*, London: Paladin.
Wright, E.O., (1996), *Class Counts*, Cambridge: Cambridge University Press.
Wright, E.O., (1985), *Classes*, London: Verso.

Notes on contributors

Rosemary Crompton is Professor of Sociology at City University, London. She has previously taught at the universities of East Anglia, Kent and Leicester. She is currently directing an ESRC-sponsored project that is examining the employment and family biographies of doctors and bank managers in Britain, France and Norway. Her most recent books are: *Women and Work in Modern Britain*, OUP, 1997, *Class and Stratification* (second edition), Polity, 1998, and *Restructuring Gender Relations andEmployment: the decline of the 'male breadwinner'*, OUP, 1999.

Fiona Devine is Reader in Sociology at the University of Manchester. She is the author of *Affluent Workers Revisited* (1992), *Social Class in America and Britain* (1997) and (with Sue Heath) *Sociological Research Methods in Context* (1999). She is currently writing a book on social mobility drawing on qualitative research in the US and the UK.

Jonathan Gershuny is the Director of the Institute of Social and Economic Research at Essex University, and a Professor in its Sociology Department.

Geoffrey Ingham is Director of Studies and Political Sciences and Fellow at Christ's College, Cambridge. His publications include *Capitalism Divided* and he is currently completing *A Sociological Treatise on Money*.

Robert MacDonald is Reader in Sociology at the University of Teesside and has researched and written about young people and about changing cultures of work. His most recent book is an edited collection entitled *Youth, the 'Underclass' and Social Exclusion* (1997, Routledge).

Jane Marsh is currently employed as a researcher on a project investigating young people and social exclusion in Teesside, as part of the ESRC's *Young People, Citizenship and Social Change* programme. Her previous research interests are in the area of social exclusion and young, single motherhood.

Jan Pahl is Professor of Social Policy at the University of Kent at Canterbury and Head of the Department of Social and Public Policy and Social Work. She has a longstanding interest in the control and allocation of money within the household. Her publications in this field include *Money and Marriage* (Macmillan, 1989) and *Invisible Money: Family Finances in the Electronic Economy* (Policy Press, 1999).

Mike Savage is Professor of Sociology and Head of the Department of Sociology at Manchester University. His recent books include *Gender, Career and Organisation* (with Susan Halford and Anne Witz) and *Social Change and the Middle Classes* (edited with Tim Butler).

John Scott is Professor of Sociology at the University of Essex and Adjunct Professor at the University of Bergen. He is the author of *Corporate Business and Capitalist Classes* and *Stratification and Power*.

Aage B. Sørensen is Professor of Sociology and Chair of Harvard's Doctoral Programme in Organizational Behaviour. His research interests are in the areas of social stratification and in the sociology of education. He has published numerous articles in scholarly journals and chapters in anthologies. His most recent article, 'Towards a sounder basis for class analysis' appears in the *American Journal of Sociology* (2000).

Loïc Wacquant is a researcher at the Centre de Sociologie Européenne du Collège de France and an Associate Professor at the University of California-Berkeley. A MacArthur Prize Fellow, he is the author of *An Invitation to Reflexive Sociology* (with Pierre Bourdieu) and of *Les Prisons de la Misère*. Aside from the role of penal institutions in the government of misery in advanced societies, his interests include comparative urban inequality and marginality, racial domination, bodily crafts, and social theory.

Index